THE
SACRED ART
OF
SOUL MAKING

ALSO BY JOSEPH NAFT

Non-Fiction

Weekly Inner Work

Fiction

Restoring Our Soul

Agents of Peace

THE
SACRED ART
OF
SOUL MAKING

Balance and Depth in Spiritual Practice

JOSEPH NAFT

I.F. Publishing

I.F. PUBLISHING COMPANY
Baltimore, Maryland USA
info@ifpub.com

ISBN: 0-9786109-0-3

Cover Art:
William Morris 18th century Thistle Weave pattern by Yitz Woolf

Printed in the United States of America on acid-free paper

CONTENTS

CHAPTER TWO

BODY • 51

CHAPTER THREE

HEART • 75

CHAPTER FOUR

MIND • 135

CHAPTER FIVE

I AM • 153

CHAPTER SIX

BEYOND OURSELVES • 229

CODA

SEVEN PILLARS OF SPIRITUAL PRACTICE • 263

Acknowledgments

This book presents my own experience-based understanding of how a human being can intentionally move toward realization of the deepest Truth and unconditional Love. I am fortunate in having worked with many spiritual teachers, for whose help I am deeply grateful. Principal among these is John G. Bennett, with whom I studied in 1974 during the last period of his life. The flavor of Bennett's approach to spirituality informs many parts of this book, with formal references where the influence is most direct. Other inspiring teachers to whom I am personally indebted come from Buddhist, Sufi, Christian, Jewish, Hindu, and other traditions. The taste of their spirit also nourishes these pages. Eventually, though, we all learn from the one Divine Teacher.

I have participated in or led over a dozen groups, wherein my fellow travelers on the path have always challenged and inspired me. To these many friends, thank you.

Finally I thank my wonderful wife, Andrea, who has supported this writing throughout.

THE
SACRED ART
OF
SOUL MAKING

CHAPTER ONE

ORIENTATION

Introduction

To deepen our level of being, to open to the spiritual reality, to discover compassion for all of life, to align ourselves in service to the Source of meaning, we must do more, much more than believe, think, dream, hope, or wish for such transformation. With every fiber of our heart, every moment of our day, with every action in our nascent soul, we cleave to the silent call of that monumental Greatness that creates and sustains us all. Though we may adhere to the highest ethical standards and shoulder our responsibilities to family and society, morality alone, even morality coupled with belief, will not carry us to the infinite ocean. Though healing our psychological wounds and immaturities does help, health of mind and heart alone cannot fulfill our true destiny.

We need more. We need a soul. We need to follow that profound, bittersweet longing at the core of our being. We need wholehearted engagement in effective practices of an authentic spirituality. The more heartily we give ourselves over to such practice, the more possible our transformation becomes. With practice we move toward the eternal, without practice our time passes as we slowly wither. With practice our inner life thrives in harmony, without practice chaos reigns. This is our choice of life — or death. Can we rise to this choice? Can we even recognize the constant presence of the choice? Once made, can we reaffirm it moment by moment?

Deep within each of us dwells the source of peace, purpose, and love. Yet we live in the chaotic dissonance of the superficial layers of our hearts and minds. A sea of the most precious spiritual energies surrounds us, inside and out, yet our thirst remains unquenched, our souls malnourished and unformed.

Although our aim lies beyond time, time itself remains far too valuable to waste. Birth thrusts us into this world with a partial, incomplete soul. The unique shard of Divinity entrusted to each of us needs a proper vehicle to manifest through. That vehicle, that bridge from the higher realm to this world is the soul. A few of us may develop a soul during our time on this Earth. The overwhelming majority, however, dies without having tendered to God the full measure of strength and love that the Divine may accept from us, and without having brought into this world the love, wisdom, and energies we could transmit from the higher.

The wise among our ancestors discovered and created literally thousands of spiritual practices, which serve the purpose of developing soul, of true transformation, of serving the Earth. We can continue the rituals and communal prayer of our own religious tradition, building on that childhood-based, essential connection. But the typical engagement in religion never rises to the level of spiritual transformation and soul formation. Only sincere, prolonged spiritual practice enables a person to embody and manifest the core values of any of the great religions.

We might ask: in addition to our religion, which spiritual practices should we pursue? Here, our own taste, our own intuition must guide us. Though we share much, that kernel of Divinity makes us each unique. That is why our personal flair and insight so crucially underpin the whole process. If a particular path sounds promising, we can try it. If it fills our need, we will know it and follow it. Commitment will develop. We may join with a practice community. Over the years, what is suitable for us will change and our developing intuition will prompt us accordingly. Yet we dare not flit lightly between paths, never following one far enough to deepen our understanding. Nevertheless, as our heart and soul grow, new practices may reveal their value to us. Our recognition of right and wrong matures into discerning what advances soul and what retards it.

In the past century many Westerners have adopted Eastern spiritual practices and found in them an unmatched degree of efficacy and subtlety. Put simply, Buddhist and Yoga practices enjoy their popularity because they work. Yet as Westerners raised as Christians or Jews progress in their Eastern practices, they often find themselves drawn back toward their own religious roots and the search for the Divinity. They rediscover their need for a personal relationship with the Divine, for the practice of prayer, openness to conscience, and the understanding of will found in the monotheistic religions. Conversely, followers of Christianity and Judaism receive crucial spiritual help from the depth of understanding of meditation and similar practices found in Buddhist, Hindu, and Taoist traditions. We look for a fully balanced approach that engages the best of both East and West. In the great life work of spiritual transformation, we need both the love of God and the depth of meditation. They complement and reinforce each other.

Spiritual work is not simply a private matter, even when much of our practice is personal and private. Communal prayer and other collective practices surprise us with their power. The shared intention and vibrant atmosphere of the congregation, the sangha, the minyan, and the halka, wondrously multiply our personal efforts on the way of transformation and spiritual service. The long-term evolution of human beings and human society, the eventual eradication of the disease of violence perpetrated by humans, the common discovery, recognition and understanding of the true purpose of life — all of this and more depend on rightly conducted spiritual practice. Imagine what this Earth would be like if everywhere we went, all our relationships embodied fundamental, mutual, and open trust and kindness, even with complete strangers. The purposes, however, go beyond our human interests. Spiritual practices benefit not only our community and us, but also, with sufficient depth, benefit the Supreme. Can it be that God needs us as much as we need God? Perhaps such questions offer clues to the purpose of our creation.

In these pages you will find some of the more substantial spiritual practices that have stood the test of time. Drawing on Christian, Sufi, Buddhist, Hindu, Kabbalah and other traditions, this book presents a balanced approach to inner work addressing the wholeness of our humanity and spirituality. Chapter 1 offers elements of a map of our inner landscape to help orient your path and support your understanding of the practices. Chapters 2 through 6 offer the basic spiritual practices and concepts of a complete and effective way of transformation. A companion volume entitled *Weekly Inner Work* provides an extensive, non-linear series of methods to focus your practice for a week at a time on particular aspects of the path.

These formulations have proven their efficacy in long work

with groups of spiritual seekers. If you pursue them diligently and with heart, these practices will help you in your quest to transform your being, to serve your highest destiny, to take your spiritual practice further, both in depth toward the higher worlds and in breadth into more of life.

Basics: Heart, Energy, and Will

We weave the tapestry of our path with threads of heart, energy, and will. The way starts and ends with heart. The first stirrings of the spirit guide our heart toward the path. Without this call we would never begin. Along the way, the closer we approach the Source of all, the more our heart opens. Our commitment and determination to practice grow, coupled with newfound reservoirs of kindness, compassion, and love. But our heart's range extends from the most self-centered desires to the most sublime and hidden depths. Whenever we wish to assess our progress on the path, we need look no further than the state of our heart.

The inner substance of the path, the field of our practice, consists of energies. Energies drive our inner life and form the various levels of our soul, yet we typically remain unaware of them. An astonishingly wide range of inner and spiritual energies nourish and condition our life and our practice, from the automatic energy that enables us to function in a pre-programmed way with minimal awareness, all the way up to the transcendent energy of the Divine. One of the great adventures of the spiritual path consists of gradually discovering the profound subtleties of the energies within us.

Any endeavor first requires contact with the necessary materials. A major challenge of the energies, the substances that form our inner world, lies in their disparate natures and our inability to see or recognize them. We work most effectively with those energies that we can actually perceive. Step-by-step, the path refines our perceptions, so that we can recognize more of the energies and learn to use them.

As our contact with energies grows, we notice variations in the amount of particular energies present. We start to see that some of our inner and outer activities waste our energies. In response, we pursue efforts to plug the holes in our bucket, to conserve our energies for more important uses, such as deepening our awareness or building our soul. Unnecessary muscular tensions, for example, needlessly waste our energy. Relaxation of those tensions conserves the energy.

Awareness of an energy and actions to conserve it show us that more energy enables more inner work, enriching our inner life. Understanding this, we fervently seek to increase the quantity of energy available and to concentrate it within ourselves. We learn and practice methods like energy breathing to draw in energy directly from outside ourselves, augmenting the energy our bodies ordinarily produce.

The extra energy, however, disperses from us just as readily. To assimilate those energies into our growing soul, we practice methods to allow the energies to settle in us, to merge with our own substance. One such method of energy absorption is deep relaxation. The new energies assimilated gradually accumulate in the reservoir of our being.

A pool of a particular energy provides a base which helps us attract the next higher quality of energy. Our work with the lower energy prepares our perceptions for the further refinements required for contact with the higher energy. Our endeavor to deepen the quality of energy that we can perceive starts another cycle of energy work, but at a new level.

These cycles of practice bring a variety of energies to our being. Certain interactions among the different levels of energies produce new energies in a process of transformation. Most meditation practices lead to such energy transformations.

But this emphasis on energies raises a whole series of questions: what holds these energies together, what draws them in, what brings them to assimilation, what enables their transformation, what contains them, and what tools work in the medium of energies? The one answer to all these questions is will, the core of who we really are. The timeless realms of energy and will closely interact at all the levels. The whole work on energies hinges on will, on choice, intention, and attention. But will, in turn, needs energies to make its acts effective. Will can operate with any of the energies, but works quite differently depending on the level of energy available to it. The direct understanding of will as that central factor in us which intends, chooses, decides, attends, and acts, proves crucial to our inner work.[1]

Will is essential to spiritual transformation. Like energies, will belongs to a realm outside of time and space. So our limited perceptions condition the process of working with will. However, with will the problem deepens even further. Energies can be perceived, whereas will can never be seen or perceived. Will is always the one who sees, the one who perceives, the one who does. This most subjective element in us cannot readily turn back to perceive itself. In a profound sense, we are our will.

But despite its absolute subjectivity, we can experience will as who we are. We can be our will. Thus, contact with will comes through being it, whether an affirming will, as in directed attention, or an open, accepting will, as in non-directed meditation. We can be will in action in the choices we make, in everything we do. Will participates in all our experiences as the one in us

7

who is having the experience, who is making our choices or non-choices. All spiritual practices from every tradition concern will as their key but sometimes hidden factor. The more we intentionally work with aspects of will, the more our recognition and contact with it grows.

Early on we notice the fragmented state of our will. A multitude of conflicting urges, desires, dreams, fears, and habits coexist uneasily in us. We rarely act from the whole of ourselves. Our inner life suffers from chaotic disarray. This state of affairs results from the fact that our activities run in a pre-programmed mode with the automatic energy. We operate on autopilot, reacting in a conditioned manner to the situations and events of our life. Our inner automatism, our conditioning and programming dominate us. All this constrains our will into working almost exclusively through the automatic energy with its inherent fragmentation.

Through our spiritual practice, we initiate a process of defragmenting our will. As we gain access to higher levels of energies, the isolated pieces of our will start coalescing into greater wholeness, less fragmentation. We become more fully ourselves, more unique.

Despite this reconstruction, we soon discover that nearly all that drives us arises solely from our self-centered agendas and attachments. We call this false center of the universe ego, the great usurper. Our growing dismay with this thief in our midst starts a process of deconstruction and purification. With the help of the higher energies, we gradually release the multifarious grip of self-centeredness. We become more open to the magnificent world of which we individually form a small but significant part – a significance precisely due to our special potential for will to act consciously through us.

As the purification of our will, intentions, and motivations proceeds on the periphery, the egoistic core at our center stands immune, slipping through unscathed. The day comes, however, when the only way forward is for us, for our ego to give way, to surrender, to empty ourselves utterly. Through the stages of this surrender, the Divine Will finds a home in us, as our will rejoins It, opening the door for Love.

In this process of liberating our will, we seek a strong, affirming will in ourselves, and a tenderhearted will open toward the Divine. Our strong, affirming will in this lower realm then transforms into a substantial instrument for the higher. Liberation, whether partial or full, enables the person to serve more deeply, more effectively.

Every spiritual tradition, every spiritual practice, and every person on a spiritual path plays a role in the universal processes of the transformation of energies and the liberation of will. In contemplating the context of our life journey, we may catch a glimpse the awe-inspiring evolution and spiritualization of life on the Earth. The evolutionary process confronts and challenges the ever-increasing entropy of the universe. That challenge manifests in our own inner work as the disordering influence of much of life, making spiritual practice like swimming upstream against the currents of time that draw us into our lower potentials, our pre-programmed, reactive modes of living. Our nascent soul constitutes the inner frontier in which the upstream and downstream forces interact. Pursuing the path to liberate our will and open to the Divine, we participate, on our own small scale, in the prodigious process whereby the Divine Will extends into the material universe, including our human community. All this touches our hearts intimately because the greatest force for spiritualization, the highest form of order is Love.

The Structure of the Soul

What is soul, this mysterious something that forms our true essence? Many speak of the soul, but rarely does anyone attempt to say what it is. And so soul remains a vague but profound question mark at the center of our life. Dare we wait until we die to explore our soul, in the hope that death will offer a ray of clarity? Despite the confusion, we feel that our soul is who we really are, undeniably important even if always hidden.

To begin to make sense of this, we can look to the major spiritual traditions for guidance on questions of the soul. All religions propound notions of soul, of levels of soul, and of corresponding levels of experience. Soul serves as the bridge between Heaven and Earth, and is thus central to all spirituality. Christianity, Islam, Taoism, Hinduism, Judaism, and the ancient Greeks view the soul as a composite, incorporating various levels or parts. The lower level exhibits similarities to our physical body. Higher levels are progressively more refined, with the highest approaching God. Christianity speaks of the carnal, natural, and spirit bodies. Islamic Sufis call the parts nafs, ruh, and sirr. The Hindu soul has etheric, astral, and causal bodies, while Judaic Kabbalah teaches of the nefesh, ruach, and neshamah.

Buddhism, on the contrary, denies the concept of an eternal, individualized soul. However, Buddhism does include some soul-like ideas, such as the collection of aggregates, or skandas, which bear a person's karma into future lives. Tibetan Buddhism teaches that the most advanced practitioners can attain the Rainbow Body, which enables the person to exist in a body beyond the physical body.

A detailed comparison of all these systems of the soul is

better left for an academic thesis. Here we focus on distilling those aspects of soul that may be held as common to some or all of the great religions and spiritual paths.

We begin by noting that the various levels of soul interpenetrate and influence each other. The fully evolved human comprises an organic whole, with all aspects integrated. So we must start with the physical body and all its marvelous subsystems, which interact with the foundational part of the soul.

Our thoughts, emotions, and physical sensations, while driven to a large degree by our physical body, contain the substance of our foundation soul, the sensitive energy, which we discuss in detail later. We learn from the traditions[2] that this energy, ordinarily an amorphous cloud, can be accumulated and organized until it forms the first body of our soul. This sensitive energy body is said to be similar in shape to the physical body but composed of a more-refined substance. Although not born with this foundation soul complete, we can create it through spiritual practice. Sufi, Taoist, Hindu, Judaic and other teachings relate this level of soul to the breath, and in particular to the life force within the air that becomes available to us through conscious breathing. The sensitive energy body keeps us grounded in the present moment in our physical body. So whenever we work to be present in our body or breath, we are, in effect, working to create our foundation soul.

The middle or inner soul forms from consciousness, an energy qualitatively different from the sensitive energy. Practices that support the development of the inner soul include presence, non-clinging, kindness, meditation and prayer. This soul of consciousness gives us a place in a higher world which we experience as stillness or silence. Beyond space and time, the inner soul does not have a particular shape like the foundation soul. Consciousness opens us to the timeless, the always present now. The traditions teach that when our practice reaches the stage in which we always dwell in consciousness, then this inner vehicle of soul reaches completion.

The inner soul depends on the foundation soul, for the sensitive energy body provides a container for consciousness. Otherwise consciousness, pure awareness, comes and goes with no stability. Practices of conscious presence in the now, lead primarily to frustration unless thoroughly grounded in physical sensation.

Christian,[3] Judaic and other traditions tell us that we receive the highest part of our soul, our spirit, as a gift at birth. This, our unique individuality and freedom, emanates from the Divine will. However, we soon lose contact with that innermost part of ourselves. To bridge the gap to our ordinary awareness and to enable its action in this world, our spirit needs the vehicles of the foundation and middle parts of the soul. Through dedicated spiritual practice to form and purify those lower parts, our spirit can return in service to the Divine as a particle of the Great Purpose. We move toward our spirit through prayer, deep meditation, equanimity and, at the ultimate stage of the path, through surrendering our will to the Divine will. The perfected will is the "I Am" of the individual wholly and freely given to serving God and neighbor.

At the earlier stages of soul development, we experience our spirit through the medium of conscience,[4] prompting us toward responsibility, toward right action, toward love, and toward constant inner work. We can serve the whole by inner and outer responsibility on our own scale. The Great Purpose, Who is responsible for the whole cosmos, remains inscrutable. But conscience translates It to our local situation. To hear conscience with clarity, we must be inwardly free. Egoism, self-centeredness, attachments and identifications garble the voice of conscience. Our spirit thus depends on the inner soul of consciousness to provide a base for the return to freedom from the tyranny of the small self.

The art and science of soul formation, along with the service enabled thereby, encompass the whole broad realm of spiritual practice. If it is true that our soul is unformed and incomplete, then it becomes an overarching imperative that we should do everything in our power to pursue the spiritual path, the way of inner completion, love, and service.

A Path of Fits and Starts

The spiritual path winds like a road toward a stately mountain, a road not well maintained or marked. It is riddled with potholes, detours, red lights, traffic jams, wrecks, and all the rest. The region lacks car dealers, so you are stuck with the car you have, with its monthly payments and its maintenance. If you stop to ask directions, you find conflicting answers. If you take an extended break, your car automatically shifts into reverse and you slip backwards. The fog lies so thick, that you often cannot even see the road.

Nevertheless, you drive, drive blind if need be, push when you run out of gas, shovel snow from the tires, remember landmarks in case you unintentionally circle back, look for better maps and reliable travel directions, deal forthrightly with a mechanical breakdown or wreck and start afresh, and always watch the horizon for the first light of dawn. And you never, ever give up when the road grows hard — or easy. Sometimes you drive past a beautiful vista, but you don't let that sidetrack you. Occasionally the sight is so compelling that you believe you have reached your destination, but you keep driving nonetheless.

Somewhere, a road winds steadily up the mountain. But that unfamiliar route is rarely used by anyone. We stick with the roads we know, forgetting that they do not lead to new territory. We settle for the false security of our habitual ways of living in our inner lowlands, unwilling to stretch ourselves into the unknown. The truly creative spiritual act builds our path out of the material of our life, discovering ways to dissolve or surrender our every obstacle.

The path is long — a lifetime. Our intelligence, strength, and passion fuel the way. Unrelenting commitment proves essential, but grows as we approach the high country. Our overriding obligation is to keep to the path, not to stop. The longer the stop, the deeper our regret afterwards when we, inevitably, embark yet again. Although the high country is not in time and space, our body and our path are. Every moment counts — or doesn't and is lost. Inevitability, however, befriends us. We discover what we must do, and our resistance to it dissolves.

Dimensions of Balance in Spiritual Practice

The many facets of our humanity call for balance. In growing up, we need a balanced education and a balance of discipline and love. For physical health we need a balanced diet as well as a balance between activity and repose. For mental health we need a balance between work, leisure, and family. So too, we need a holistic approach toward our inner work for spiritual development.

As complex beings with complex demands placed upon us, for most of us no single method of spiritual practice will prove adequate. An understanding of the variety of methods and their place in the spiritual path serves us well in discovering and filling the gaps in our inner work. Through actual practice we grow familiar with the relationships among the methods and their effect on our being. We acquire a taste for how to balance our inner life. Toward this, we now examine four dimensions of balance in spiritual practice: context, mode, vehicle, and style. Though handed down from ancient times, these were powerfully posed by G.I. Gurdjieff in the twentieth century. An understanding of these dimensions helps guide our steps in the unknown territory of the spirit.

Context

The first dimension of balance concerns the three possible contexts of practice: ourselves, our family and society, and the Ultimate. If we direct our spiritual life only toward ourselves, we risk growing self-absorbed and losing sight of the greater purpose. If our practice centers solely on serving others, we risk losing ourselves, losing the energy and peace of mind we need to serve well. If our practice focuses exclusively on the Divine, we risk losing our footing on this wonderful Earth, losing our ability to relate well. All three together, however, forge a remarkably potent combination. In our spiritual droughts, when we lose contact with one, another will provide a way to reinvigorate the first. Working in all three contexts, we discover a sense of completeness and integrity.

Mode

The second dimension of balance addresses the active, open, and harmonic modes of practice. The great traditions inform us that reality has a threefold nature. The ancient Indian Vedas, for example, instruct us about the three basic elements, the three gunas: rajas, tamas, and sattva. Christianity offers the image of the Holy Trinity of the Father, the Son, and the Holy Ghost. The Kabbalistic Tree of Life arranges its ten sephirot in three columns and with triadic connections. All these reflect the fact that threefoldness enters the whole of reality, including our inner work, through will.

The active mode of will displays an affirming, directed, outward flowing, effortful quality. The open mode embraces an allowing, accepting, receiving, inward flowing, non-directed, surrendering quality. This second mode can also manifest as passivity, inertia, laziness, and resistance. The harmonic mode brings a creative freedom, a catalyst enabling the other two modes to cooperate in a quite natural, balanced, unforced way. We see this harmonic mode in sports when an athlete is "in the zone," in effortlessly perfect action. In the spiritual path, we seek to be open to the higher while active toward the more external, in a harmonious, wise, loving, and productive way of life, with will flowing through us from the higher to the lower.

Balance is essential among these three modes, especially as they characterize our spiritual practices. If we always pursue an active practice, we shall have little peace and stillness, and our activity will be confined to the lower rungs of Jacob's ladder. If openness constitutes our sole choice in modes of practice, we will not gain the strength required to create a viable vessel for our soul. If we only seek harmony, we will fail because that bird cannot fly without the two wings of active and open practices. Working with all three modes, their interaction enlivens us, inspiring and enabling us to reach new and unexpected depths in our spiritual life.

Vehicle

The third dimension of balance operates among the four vehicles of our body, heart, mind, and spirit or I. Here, vehicle means the mechanism through which will acts in us. Our body has the ability to move, to act, and to maintain itself in the material world. In our heart vehicle we have the full range of emotions, which broker our contact with worlds outside and in. In our mind, we have the ability to think, visualize, plan, imagine, daydream, remember, and understand. Most of us tend toward unbalance in terms of these three vehicles. We might live primarily in our thoughts, or in our feelings, or in our physical abilities and appetites. Balanced spiritual work includes developing our neglected vehicles.

Our spirit typically remains hidden. Thus, our practice aims, in part, at reconnecting our daily life with our true spirit, our own "I am," which alone has the power to unify our body, heart, and mind.

Style

When we think of spiritual practice, we usually think of a formal style of practice: meditation, ritual or communal prayer, chanting, and the like. Such formal practices, repeated at regular intervals, constitute the foundation of the spiritual path. These practices collect and transform energies, exercise our will, and let us delve deeper than would be possible in more ordinary circumstances.

But a completely different genre of spiritual practices stands equal in importance to the formal style: continuous practice sustained throughout our ordinary day. Instead of getting up from meditation or prayer and leaving our spiritual work behind until the next day, we continue to practice awareness of bodily sensation, presence or prayer as much as possible all day long, even as we go about our normal daily activities. The practice that we continue while engaged in our day may not be as deep or as strong as formal practice, but it does enjoy the distinct advantage of having more time available for it. The cumulative effect of continuous practice can be even greater than that of formal practice. If you sustain and renew your inner work at frequent intervals, by the end of the day you may find yourself in a deeply centered and spiritually refined state. Furthermore, change of being means change of our usual state. The more continuously we practice, the more we raise our usual state, and the closer we come to permanent change of being.

Formal and continuous practice support and complement each other. Meditation and prayer can provide the surplus, high quality energy we need to practice more continuously. Work at presence throughout the day strengthens and purifies our will, consolidates our gains from formal practice, and deepens our meditation and prayer.

But formal and continuous do not exhaust the categories of practice. If we look at the continuum from inner to outer, we see that formal practice belongs primarily to the inner whereas continuous practice falls between inner and outer. In the fully outer realm of external manifestations of spirituality we enter the way of right action in the world, the way of responsibility and kindness, creativity and service. These constitute a third major form of spirituality, of equal standing to formal and continuous practice, supporting and complementing both. Our ability to be kind, responsible, or creative grows as our being and will transform. Formal and continuous practice together lead to that transformation. The potential of our own right action in the world, however, gives us a strong reason to pursue formal and continuous spiritual practice. If we wish to serve well, we need to develop our being and purify our will. The way of right action puts the results of our inner work to good use.

Between the styles of formal, continuous and manifested practice, we seek an appropriate balance, attuned to our own propensities and possibilities.

The Ecology of the Sacred

Imagine for a moment that each of us is entrusted at birth with a hope diamond in the rough, a precious and sacred particle of the Divine Will. Through us, the Will of the Creator can enter the material world. We bear the seed, we are the seed, the growing tip of the Universal Will. In a vast and incomprehensible process, the Unconditioned Will gradually spiritualizes the material universe, drawing it more directly into Its service. We may recognize this difficult and uncertain process in ourselves, if we endeavor to cooperate with this Great Work of the spirit. We cut and polish our diamond will, returning it to the service of the Divine Will from which it originates. As with any diamond, our initial roughness is not inherent, but results from our growth within the material world.

Probing this picture we ask a rather complex question: What does service to the Divine Will consist of? In partial response we envision an immense ecology of energies. Within the Earth's living ecosystem we witness the exchange, transformation, and recycling of the energies of heat, light, and molecular bonds in the food chain. Similarly, the sacred, universal ecosystem harmonizes the exchange and transformation of the energies of sensation, consciousness, and the rest, within the great chain of being. Human beings naturally use, convert, and store energies. The capacity for this can vary tremendously from one person to the next, depending on the state of their soul. Through spiritual practices we directly and powerfully transform energies, raising the quality and quantity of energies at work in us. Serving the Universal Will means, in part, not only conducting our lives creatively in accordance with conscience and kindness, but also transforming energies well.

This Earth depends on us for the higher energies. Through spiritual practice we reach up to transmit those energies, serving our planet, serving life, serving our own soul. People called to this sacred duty in the midst of ordinary life, find unsurpassed meaning and purpose.

Inner Energies

Scientists of the twentieth century discovered that the entire visible universe consists of matter-energy. All matter, including our bodies and our planet, may convert to energy and vice versa. All forces arise through the interaction of matter-energies. No surprise, then, that the matter-energies within us determine the quality of our inner life. Just as we cannot see electromagnetic or gravitational energy, but only the results of their action, so too we cannot measure or objectify inner energies. But we can experience their action directly. For this we need an acquired taste, a comprehension of what to look for, and a gradual refinement of our perceptions. The understanding of energies brings crucial support to our spiritual path, because energies provide the fuel, the light for all our experiences.

Each energy defines a particular mode of being, a particular kind of world. The energy with which we operate at any given moment determines the kind of experience we have, the kind of world we live in. The study of the spiritual worlds and their associated sacred energies is an ancient endeavor, with roots in Christian, Buddhist, Hindu, Sufi, Taoist, Kabbalistic and other sources. J.G. Bennett gives a particularly clear and modern account in his book *Deeper Man.*[5] His concepts and terminology form the basis of this presentation of energies.

The inner energies constitute a hierarchy. Actions undertaken with a higher energy can organize and subsume a lower energy. Lower energies can form a field in which higher energies may be contained, created, and transformed. Remarkably, we are able to transform a wide range of energies within our bodies and souls. At the simplest level, we transform food and oxygen to create the energy that powers our bodily actions. But this human ability to transform energies runs right up the scale toward the most sacred and likely stands as a major reason for the existence of life. Spiritual practices include methods for recognizing, containing, creating, and transforming progressively higher and finer energies. At first we study the energies to recognize their presence and action. Later we must shoulder the burden of learning not to waste our energies unnecessarily or misuse them. Finally, we contact, create, and transform energies directly, gradually refining our ability to do so.

As we advance on the path, the higher energies grow even more important to us, because only through their action on us can we find real transformation. And by becoming an instrument for the descent of the higher energies into this world, we serve not only our own soul, but also our fellow travelers through this life.

Energies characterize the stages of spiritual development. The pure-hearted occupy a spiritual station of a higher energy than the rest of us. When we are more deeply present, we live in a richer, more substantial, and more truly satisfying world than we experience with a perennially scattered attention.

We now briefly describe each step in the scale of energies beginning with the energy of our physical life.

Vital Energy

I once saw a just-captured, rather fearsome leopard pacing its cage in a Mexican jungle. Exuding strength and vitality, this dignified predator was no zoo animal. Stunningly beautiful and powerful, the leopard radiated a palpable, rippling energy. Some people, such as athletes in top condition, also exhibit an abundance of vital energy, the energy of physical life. When the glow of vital energy abounds, our bodies wax vigorous and ready for action. When the level of vital energy drops, our bodies grow tired or ill. Proper rest, food, exercise, and energy breathing feed our vitality and contribute to good health. Emotional stress, unnecessary muscular tension, excessive talking and other wasteful activities sap our vitality.

In our spiritual life, vitality matters because a depleted or distressed vitality may limit the quality of our contact with the higher energies. Conversely, contact with the higher energies often produces a remarkable cascade of vitality. Proper care of our body creates the vitality that supports our very life and sets the stage for our spiritual work. But the diminished vitality of aging and illness may inhibit our inner work. So while we have the vital strength, we work.

Automatic Energy

Have you ever gotten into the shower, shampooed your hair by habit, and a moment later stood there in the shower wondering whether you had shampooed yet? Have you ever looked for your glasses, only to find them on top of your head? My favorite example: sitting at dinner, frantically looking all around for my fork, until I finally discovered it in the least expected place — in my hand. To see the automatic energy in action like this is a sobering event. Whatever we do under the automatic energy, we only partially experience and only vaguely remember. Nevertheless, the automatic energy has its uses.

Awkwardness reigns when we first learn a complex new task, such as driving a car. Its unfamiliarity forces us to think about where the gas pedal is, where the brake pedal is, which foot to use, where the rearview mirrors are, what the traffic signs and signals mean, when we have the right-of-way, and so on. Thinking how to drive makes us clumsy and inefficient, as we use the mind to do the body's work. Eventually, we learn to drive with ease when it all becomes automated; the appropriate responses emerging without needing to think of them. Our body drives the car while our mind freely engages in conversation, listens to the radio, plans our day, dictates a letter, or considers higher level driving strategies like how to bail out of a traffic jam. The driving itself happens automatically.

The automatic energy can work in the body, in the mind, and in the heart. We learn to play a musical instrument, play a sport, brush our teeth, walk, type on a keyboard, speak and read a language, know the product of 7 times 8, recognize a face, recall a name, all with the help of the automatic energy. For such purposes, the automatic energy finds its appropriate place: directing repetitive or simple processes, thereby freeing up the higher energies for tasks befitting them.

The nearly continuous stream of random, loosely connected, aimless thoughts and images that flows through our minds usually carries us with it and prevents us from being fully present in the moment. This persistent current of automatic thought all too often captures our attention, drawing us into passivity in a dreamlike world, disorganizing and usurping the higher energies of sensation, consciousness, and creativity.

Another problem with the automatic energy occurs when it acts in ways that deplete us. Our habitual and unnecessary muscular tensions burn energy we could better use elsewhere. Our bad habits drain us: smoking, excessive drinking, overeating — all due, at least in part, to misuse of the automatic energy, letting it control rather than serve.

Automatic emotional reactions to life situations, such as anger, rage, fear, jealousy, lust, greed, timidity, and sadness, may be appropriate and even useful for a brief period. But when we allow our automatic energy to run with them, unseen by consciousness, our thoughts and feelings dwell on the reactive emotions. We wallow in them to the point where they take a central role in our inner life, controlling us. All manner of social and psychological troubles result.

The automatic energy, while useful and even necessary, does not bring us into real contact with life. To our unrecognized misfortune, we live almost exclusively under the domination of the automatic energy, enthralled by our habits and conditioning, forever repeating similar patterns of behavior, inner and outer. Our lives pass us by without our participation. Centered in the automatic energy, we are, in effect, asleep. We relish anything that temporarily alleviates the dullness. We even go for strong reactive emotions or thrill seeking, substituting them for a freer, more satisfying, non-automatized way of living. The proven remedy is to embark on a path of spiritual practice leading to greater wakefulness and greater awareness in the midst of normal life.

Sensitive Energy

The basic energy fueling inner work and the material of the lower body of the soul is the sensitive energy, which brings vibrant color and vivid impressions to our life. This energy is the substance of what we ordinarily consider to be self-awareness, connecting us to our perceptions, to the present moment. Within the sensitive energy we find our medium for actual contact with the particulars of life, for noticing the large and the small. We can breathe. We can taste our food. Though not yet fully awake, we are not as asleep as when the automatic energy dominates our being. Choice, initiative, and independence from merely reacting to events, all become possible. Life is enriched and natural, no longer habitual.

The possibilities enabled by the sensitive energy are immensely important to the quality of our inner life. Lasting benefits accrue when we explore and understand its role in our emotions, in our thoughts, and in our physical perceptions. We can learn specific spiritual practices to manage, collect, contain, and transform it into higher energies.

In the body, the sensitive energy enhances our kinesthetic and proprioceptive impressions: we sense directly that we actually have a hand or a leg. Under the automatic energy we move without contact with our body; unless we stub a toe, we walk with no awareness of our feet, like our half-awareness of the front tires when we drive. The sensitive energy, however,

25

provides an organic awareness of our body in movement and at rest, bridging the chasm between mind and body. In later sections we suggest methods for learning to be in touch with the sensitive energy in the body, to experience and even direct its flow. When we refer to the Energy Body, we mean the sensitive energy filling our physical body. Intentionally sensing the body affords a powerful grounding in the present, a most useful method on the spiritual path.

In the mind, the sensitive energy enables us to be aware of thoughts as thoughts. With the automatic energy, thoughts pass through our mind and we pass along with them, carried unawares by our thought stream. With the sensitive energy, we know our thoughts, we know their meaning, and can solve problems by intentional thinking.

In the emotions, the sensitive energy brings awareness of the spectrum of feelings passing through our heart. With the automatic energy, our emotions have us, we lose ourselves in them. With the sensitive energy we feel our emotions as emotions, without being completely immersed or entrapped by them.

As the highest energy under our direct control, the sensitive energy forms the immediate, tangible substance of our spiritual work. Through practice, we can collect and organize it into a robust whole, the basis of the lower part of our soul, a firm foundation and container for the higher energies, a platform from which to live a less-dreamlike, more natural and organically joyful life.

The world of the sensitive energy corresponds to the worlds known as Asiyah (Action) in Kabbalah and Ajsam (Bodies) in the Sufi cosmology.

Conscious Energy

Though the reality they point to is fundamental to our possibilities, we use the terms "conscious" and "consciousness" rather loosely. Usually we mean them to indicate a simple sensory awareness. So when we say "I am conscious," or "I am conscious of" something, we actually refer to the working of the sensitive energy, the substance of our awareness of our bodies, thoughts, emotions, and sensory perceptions. Here we adopt a quite different meaning for the term consciousness: the spacious, empty, infinite, cognitive field that forms the ever-present background of all awareness. In this sense, the full experience of consciousness is rare and fleeting in our lives. But to taste true consciousness, you need only place your attention through the gap between thoughts, into the space behind your thoughts.

Reworking an analogy due to Bennett,[6] if we compare the sensitive energy to the images on a movie screen, the conscious energy forms the screen itself. Consciousness enables us to be aware of our sensitive awareness. The still pool of consciousness underlies, permeates, and surrounds our ordinary awareness, in the relationship of context to content. This stillness of pure consciousness corresponds to sitting in the darkened movie theater with no images on the screen, nor sounds from the audio system. Like the screen during the movie, the subtle blank slate of consciousness remains profoundly difficult to recognize, because of its inherent emptiness. Chronically immersed in and concealed by our sensitivity, consciousness usually remains indistinct and lost to us. The movie so captivates us that we lose ourselves. Transported by the images, we forget the theater, the screen, and ourselves.

Sensitivity brings awareness of parts: an arm, a leg, a

thought, a sound, the person in front of us. Consciousness brings awareness of ourselves and our surroundings — as a whole. Lacking boundaries, more than personal, consciousness permeates everything. We cannot have it, but we may participate in it. Yet consciousness also provides a distinctive sense of being ourselves.

Attention is a form of will and acts through the conscious energy. Since attention can direct our senses and our sensitive energies, it must come from beyond the sensitive, i.e., the conscious energy and the will.

The pivotal importance of the conscious energy in our spiritual work cannot be overstated. Consciousness both connects us with will and forms the frontier of the truly spiritual realms. Spiritual practices, such as mindfulness, work to raise consciousness out of sensitivity and give us access to it. Awareness of bodily sensations organizes the sensitivity into a less chaotic and more stable vehicle in which consciousness may assume its rightful place.

The conscious energy resides in an eternal, timeless dimension, deathless and unchanging, not subject to the conditions of space and time. Coming into the vast stillness of consciousness is like entering a large cathedral, temple, or mosque. The expansive ceiling and cavernous space open to a new kind of freedom and a substantive peace. That great hall of peace is always here, just beneath our ordinary perceptions, where consciousness invites our participation in the world beyond me and mine. Though our contact with consciousness certainly varies, it constitutes the all-pervasive bedrock of our inner world.

At the same time, many of today's major writers and commentators on spiritual subjects overrate consciousness, confusing the ultimate expansion of consciousness with God. Consciousness is indeed unbounded and infinite. The various names applied to experiences of the true nature of consciousness include presence, non-dual awareness, consciousness and, in its more expansive form, cosmic consciousness. Spiritual seekers can mistake the boundlessness and peace of consciousness for nirvana or for the ultimate nature of God. While God may manifest at the level of the conscious energy, God also resides beyond this and all other forms of consciousness. Indeed, consciousness is merely the ground on which God walks. We may more aptly consider God to be associated with Will, with the action of Love and the Divine Purpose than with any of the energies such as consciousness.

Who uses the energies? At the level of our limited world, sensitivity and below, we do. At the level of the universe, God does. The Divine is no more identical with consciousness than we are with the electricity we use to power our gadgets. Yet we must work to understand and to live in consciousness because of its critical role in forming our being and because it brings us closer to will, to "I am."

The world of the conscious energy corresponds to the worlds known as Yetzirah (Formation) in Kabbalah and Arvah (Spirits) in the Sufi cosmology.

Creative Energy

Beyond and veiled by consciousness, behind the spacious stillness within, lies the realm of the creative energy, an ocean of bliss and light, the Primordial Sacred Sun, the hem of the garment that God wears. To become directly aware of the creative energy we must steer our perception outside consciousness itself. Although we might enter the creative world through an act of grace, our reach typically falls far short of that world.

Nevertheless, the creative reaches us. So instead of attempting to describe the world of the creative itself, we will look at how it manifests in our life.

The creative makes new connections and opens doors of opportunity. This energy can bring order out of the chaos of the higher energies. The creative domain encompasses synchronicity and karma, sowing and reaping the results of our actions, creating and selecting possibilities. It ushers events into our lives, events meant for us. The power of sex and the perception of beauty derive from this energy.

Only in emptiness can something new be created: the white canvas, the blank sheet of paper, the formless lump of clay. The creative energy introduces us to our essential emptiness, a prerequisite for entering the true depths of the sacred. The reverse also holds: to contact the creative energy we must empty ourselves, through an inner act of surrender. This act of emptying oneself of oneself opens a channel to the creative realm of the spirit, opening our heart to joy, generosity, and peace. The event releases an influx of the lower energies that we experience directly and unambiguously. Vitality, for example, pours down when the creative energy touches us, completely changing the state of our body. Superhuman feats of strength in dire circumstances are powered by the creative energy.

By its name, we would expect the creative energy to be intimately associated with the arts and sciences, and indeed it is. In any of the arts, the artist knows the crucial role of surrender, surrendering to the work, to its needs, to its possibilities. Discipline and training in the methods of the art prepare the artist to be a vehicle of art. Cultivating spontaneity helps open the channel to the creative. The artist empties herself, allowing her acts to be guided by the creative power, often accompanied by ecstasy. This is perhaps most obvious in music. The great musician gives himself over to the music in an ecstatic embrace, becoming an instrument of the music.

Similarly, in the spiritual path, we must empty ourselves to become instruments of the Divine Will. In this emptying, in our malleable nothingness, the creative energy creates our being. It is said that the perfected human, the great saint, the bodhisattva, achieves the station of being centered in the creative energy, able to transmit the higher energy of universal love. Thus, the creative energy serves as the abode of the heavenly host, the devas, the creative wisdom, responding directly to the Divine Will. This is the place of the demiurge, the elohim, agents of the intelligent force that continuously creates and sustains this great universe.

The world of the creative energy corresponds to the worlds known as Beriyah (Creation) in Kabbalah and Imkyan in the Sufi cosmology.

Love and Compassion

The sacred energy of love and compassion, the Great Heart of the World, embraces us all, without condition, unifying all of life, unifying the whole creation within the warm spirit of kindness, appreciation and concern. With good fortune, we may meet people in whom this unfettered love shines strongly, allowing all around to bask in its light. The great saints and bodhisattvas, utterly emptied of themselves, transmit such love and compassion. In some instances of communal worship, the substance of this boundless ocean of love may envelop the whole assembly. It may enter a true marriage and may inform the bonds between parents and children. Whenever we look into another person's eyes and recognize the sameness, that that person and I are the same, not really separate, this is love.

Despite appearances to the contrary, Divine love and compassion suffuse every corner of the world, even our own. Divine love stands before the awesome contradictions in our lives: our God-given freedom that offers the promise of profound joy as well as the suffering attendant on living. The Divine heart of compassion celebrates the beauty of the freedom within each person, a celebration made bittersweet by the price of freedom: inevitable suffering.

When we hear of or see another person's misfortune, and we feel the pang of their suffering, and are moved to extend the help that lies within our power, this is compassion. For this we need strength, because suffering lies all around us. The daily news' litany of catastrophes and evil deeds, large and small, could devastate us, were we awake to the whole of it and lacked the strength to bear it. But awakening through spiritual practice brings its own strength. And the suffering we see is more than balanced by the joy that flows to us along with love, protecting the compassionate from being overwhelmed by the force of suffering.

Universal love lies far beyond its pale imitation in the lower energies, where emotional attachment turns from "love" to hate, jealousy, or despair. Nevertheless, the world is so constructed that it remains within our possibilities to participate in love knowingly. But that can only happen to the degree we empty ourselves of ourselves.

Self-referential motives, self-centeredness, attachment, expectation of something in return, grasping, setting of conditions, partial-heartedness — none of these have any place in love and, in practice, completely block the action of love. Placing ourselves first and at the center forecloses the possibility of love. Yet moments do come even to us, perhaps with our children or our pets or with the unexpected stranger, when we are briefly free of egocentric attachment and the true heart of objective love opens within us. In unguarded moments, our natural response to people is friendship, one of the faces of love. To be able to love is a goal lofty and worthy enough to sustain our long journey along the path, drawing us ever forward.

Our common mother, the Earth, also loves, loves each one of us and all life in her biosphere. Like a self-centered and petulant child, we only too rarely return this love. And like a child, we so take for granted the love of our mother Earth, that we do not even recognize it. Yet her love is there for us individually, in nature and in the city, if we can but open to it. One simple expression of it manifests as the beauty with which nature adorns herself. And there are other more direct expressions we may perceive, including a reservoir of spiritual energies within the Earth that we can draw upon. But as a species, we need to mature and not expect the Earth to continue indefinitely absorbing every insult and injury we pile upon her. We push these limits at the Earth's, and our own, peril. The Earth gives and gives and gives, perhaps more than she can afford. But because our material strength now exceeds our collective wisdom, the Earth needs us to find a place in our hearts for her. By our inner work, by opening to higher energies, by purifying our will and intentions, we help cleanse our collective will, raise our collective level of being, and give back to the Earth and to human society. And we do this for love.

Love manifests in many forms, but always serves to unify. Love's unmistakable hallmark dissolves our veils of isolation and separation, allowing us to become more fully ourselves within the sweet scent of merging. Out of love we are born, and into love we depart. In between, we seek love and love seeks us.

The world of universal love, a world beyond all forms, even beyond the world of light, corresponds to the worlds known as Atzilut (Emanation) in Kabbalah and Lahut in the Sufi cosmology.

Transcendent Energy

The names abound: God, the Most High, the Unconditioned, the Divine, the Unfathomable, Allah, Nirvana, Brahman, Adonai, the Real, the Deathless, the Omnipresent, the One, the Unique, the Tao, the Absolute, Ein Sof, the Void. Not only does everything arise from the transcendent Source, but It also exerts the one powerful attraction on us all. Every other attraction merely misappropriates and distorts the primal draw of the Source. We call the abode of the Source the Transcendent Energy, the holy mountain.

With a wild, chaotic, and powerful freedom, this ultimate energy acts as the direct vehicle of the Divine Purpose, the Will of the World, the Creator and Sustainer of the Universe. Beyond space, beyond time, the Transcendent intimately touches everything within space and time, working through Its intermediaries of universal love and the creative energy, endowing life with freedom and the possibility of return.

By creating a coherent soul built of the energies of sensitivity, consciousness, and the creative, emptied of attachments and personal desires, with a profound yearning to serve the Greatness, a human being can have real hope of contact with the Transcendent Energy and the Divine Will. The deconditioning of our mind-heart opens the door to the Unconditioned, and utter surrender is the act of walking through.

State and Station

Progress on the path brings new and unusual experiences: some confusing, some exhilarating, most unexpected, but nearly all deeply satisfying. These markers along the way confirm the rightness of our efforts. But the undeniable attraction of spiritual experiences may lead us, counter-productively, into pursuing them as an end in themselves. However, it is not our purpose in the path to chase after new and fleeting experiences, as if the spiritual world were an amusement park. Rather we embark on a steady quest for permanent changes in our level of being, a quest to be able to serve more deeply. We need not play the spiritual tourist in a sacred land, snapping photos to help us brag about our journeys. Instead we seek to become residents of that land. Sublime spiritual experiences, in themselves, do not necessarily indicate changes in our level of being.

The Sufis offer a clear description of these issues with their two terms: *state* and *station*. States are temporary experiences, which come and go. Regardless of how high a state we might enter, we return to the same station when the state departs. Our station describes our level of being, our stable inner home, characterizing our usual modes of living and perceiving, defining the limitations of our daily life. We may even experience states corresponding to a very high station, but unless our being changes, we soon fall back to states more typical of our true station.

We can describe states and stations in terms of their characteristic energies. For example, we usually operate on the automatic energy. Thus, our station, our starting point in the spiritual journey is the automatic energy and the particular patterns and habits it drives in us. Sometimes an intense experi-

35

ence may shake us out of our autopilot mode: perhaps a beautiful sunrise touches us. At that moment, we temporarily live in the next higher energy, the sensitive, more aware of ourselves and our surroundings. Life vividly blossoms and fills us. A short time later finds us mired once again in our habitual patterns, associative thoughts and daydreams. Then we remember the state we entered during the sunrise, how wonderful we felt. We tell ourselves and our friends about how much progress we have made on the spiritual path and offer the sunrise experience as proof. We even begin to daydream about our progress, about how much we have learned and changed.

The problem is we have not changed. We still live primarily in the automatic energy. And instead of diligently pursuing the practices that could help us awaken by creating our stable home in the sensitive energy, we daydream about former glories. Passing experiences, passing states do not signify a change in our station, in our level of being. Bearing in mind this distinction, pointed out so powerfully by St. John of the Cross, helps us persist in our practice and prevents us from being sidetracked by high states. Wonderful experiences will come. We do not try to hold onto them, nor do we reject them. In fact, mulling over or boasting about them, even to ourselves, saps their benefit to us. We just let them come and go, without attachment, while we keep up our practice.

All this is not meant to imply that the experience of higher states constitutes a problem in itself. The problem only occurs if we grow attached to or identified with the state. But these higher than normal states can indicate progress toward permanent change of station. The new experience encourages us to continue the inner work. The excitement and enthusiasm in their wake enable us to practice more than before. This new level of practice may even repeatedly propel us into the new state. Alas,

36

the excitement inevitably wanes, our practice diminishes, the new state stops visiting us, and we slip back to where we were before.

Then we face the challenge of strengthening our inner work without the immediate gratification of the higher states we have tasted. This situation calls us to a steadfast, sober, and mature practice, bolstered by the faith awakened by our earlier experiences. Persistence pays, though. Perhaps after several cycles of this whole process and some years of practice, the higher state gradually becomes more normal for us, we enter it as our new and natural domain, and some of our old attachments no longer control us. Then we accelerate our practice again and we reach a tipping point. In retrospect, we discover that our station, our being has changed and we have a new freedom.

And then we practice more.

Stages of the Path

All major ways agree in depicting their final ineffable goal as union with, perfect service to, or liberation into the Ultimate. But we cannot see the Unconditioned, so we need another kind of beacon to guide our immediate steps. Fortunately, the vast body of spiritual teachings offers numerous maps and descriptions of the milestones along the path. These often-detailed accounts of the stages leading toward the Ultimate hold deep importance for us, as signposts marking the path. One view, common to the great ways, sees the path in terms of degrees of letting go and recognizing emptiness, purifying and awakening the heart.

The first significant letting go occurs when we discover that nothing in the material world, including people, can offer us true fulfillment. As one of many possible scenarios leading to that realization, imagine that your entire ambition, your whole desire, focuses on acquiring X, or achieving X. You work hard, fortune smiles on you, and after many trials X comes your way. Then follows a shattering realization: even though you now have X, you remain the same person with the same problems as before. X does not bring the lasting happiness you anticipated. You also realize that X is temporary. Then you see, with bitter disappointment, that if X could not offer you enduring joy, nothing will.

In Sufi terms this represents the first *fana*, or spiritual death: seeing and accepting the emptiness of the material world. In the Buddha's teaching, you have seen the impermanence (anicca) of material phenomena and their inability to bring true satisfaction (dukkha). You would not be reading this page if you had not already, to some extent, entered this first fana. Otherwise you would still be wholly and exclusively immersed in material pursuits, with all your hopes and dreams centered on externals.

Gradually you recognize the possibility of other avenues toward fulfillment and your search beyond materiality begins in earnest. Not rejecting the material world, you continue performing your duties to your family, your career, your society, your own body. Only now an added dimension enters. You seek enlightenment, purification, and spiritual development. Your heart and mind become your field of endeavor. You learn to meditate or pray. Perhaps you undergo psychotherapy to balance your emotional nature. You think "I am really growing now." Your practice brings positive results in terms spiritual experiences. But then your whole scenario falters and cracks appear. All your efforts to reform your mind and emotions bring only partial success.

Instead and unexpectedly, your practice strengthens that part of you that can see objectively. You notice that your mind seems to think its endless thoughts and daydreams without your participation or choice. You see your emotions reacting to the events of your life in the same old habitual ways. Slowly you come to realize and accept that there is no "I" in all of this. Your mind, your emotions, your personality live a life of their own, pre-programmed to their conditioned, experience-trained patterns. Your personality proves empty: there is no "you" in it. You see clearly that your thoughts are not you, you emotions are not you, your knowledge, skills, and desires are not you, and your sensory perceptions are not you. You arrive at what the Sufis term the second fana: letting go of your personality as your reality. In Buddhist terms (anatta), you have reached the first stage of seeing your own lack of an independent self.

Yet the belief in yourself as an independent something persists, only more subtly. You believe: "I am the knower, the one who sees all this." "I am consciousness, beyond all thought and sensory perception." "I am separate from others." By this point, though, your practice flows strong and deep, and reveals moments that belie your separateness. At times you see that your notion of yourself remains ephemeral and empty, that by letting it go, surrendering your separateness, you taste an immeasurable Greatness. Your own reality, your own true "I am" becomes the vehicle through which that Greatness acts.

Despite your distractions, your forgetfulness, the Unfathomable Heart of the World persistently draws you toward Itself, beyond consciousness. And you see that the absolute, unalterable condition of entry is to relinquish all vestiges of your imaginary separateness, thoroughly letting go of your self-centered world view and abandoning your illusory ego. Through a process of purification and surrender you move toward the flower of perfection, the third and fourth fanas, toward Nirvana, the Unconditioned and unconditional Love, toward Union with the Divine, in accord with the Tao.

As the Buddhist master Achaan Chah put it: "If you let go a little, you will have a little peace. If you let go a lot, you will have a lot of peace. If you let go completely, you will know complete peace and freedom."

Viewing the path in terms of stages is only one view, however, the sequential, time-oriented one. In truth, the path is also nonlinear and timeless. The linear view of the path involves a goal-orientation, variously presented as liberation, enlightenment, the Kingdom of Heaven, or union with God. In the timeless view we lift the veils to discover our fully-formed being and the purity of our will, which is already free, as our inmost spark that never was separated from the One. Because of that we practice as an act of service. Our inner work of transforming energies, of kindness and prayer, creates something new and needed for the spiritual economy of the world. All the aspects of the path combine and support each other in an evolving sense of the breadth, depth, and nobility of our true role and possibilities.

The Spiritual Group

The truism that no person is an island applies in the spiritual world even more than it does in the material. From the most ancient times, people have gathered in groups and communities to engage in spiritual practices addressing the Source of life, the Ineffable hidden beyond our senses. Monasteries and other spiritual communities bring seekers together to live in a protected and conducive environment. In lay or non-monastic environments, the work of the congregation, the sangha, the minyan, and the halka offer spiritual brotherhood and sisterhood within the context of life in the greater community.

Why has this always been the case? Primarily because the spiritual community or group multiplies, empowers, and reinforces the efforts of the individual. Meditation, prayer and other practices, when pursued in a group or community, qualitatively and quantitatively magnify what each person can offer and experience. The coalescence of the group into a shared will and shared consciousness in communal practice creates a greater spiritual whole that enhances individual possibilities. The vehicle of the spiritual group or community carries all its individual participants to far greater spiritual depths than they could typically reach on their own. The group serves as a container for energies and as a reminder of the sacred. Each person in the group or community helps all the others by their very presence and by their orientation toward the Divine, toward love.

In business and other life endeavors, people form alliances and partnerships to create much more than they possibly could by themselves. In the spiritual endeavor, the same holds. We can join forces, share our hearts' search for the spirit, and help each other climb the mountain of transformation.

Nevertheless, spiritual groups and communities often succumb to pitfalls. Some principles to consider in the work of a spiritual group or community include the following.

1. Equality in Relation to the Divine

In the most basic sense, we are all beggars and beginners in the spiritual path. In the face of Divinity, we are all equal, equally children of the Will of the World. This bedrock principle must pervade the work of any spiritual group. Elders, teachers and those with more experience of the path, if their inner work has been rightly conducted, will, through their genuine humility and respect for others, exhibit an implicit assumption of equality in all their relationships, including with people in the spiritual group or community. We all serve the same Source.

2. Shared Vision

For a group to function well, the members must agree on the path and methods to be studied and followed. Without some commonality of technique and direction, the group will (or should) be short-lived.

3. Peer Group Versus Having a Leader

The question of leadership in a spiritual group raises complex and difficult issues. If there is to be a leader, it must be someone with consistently deeper experience in the path than the rest of the group; otherwise the leaderless peer group offers a more appropriate form. Kindness and non-attachment form two more qualities required in a group leader. Without these, history teaches us that spiritual leaders tend to grow abusive, emotionally, sexually, and financially, or they demand loyalty to themselves and their particular path rather than loyalty to the Divine and to the great community of all life. The leader must inspire trust in his or her goodwill, and confidence in his or her wisdom and knowledge of the path. Condescension, a patronizing attitude, an air of being special, abuse of power, arrogance, and insults do not characterize an effective spiritual leader, regardless of the pious justifications and excuses offered for such behavior. The essence of the role of the spiritual mentor is to share his or her passion for the path and to instill confidence in the possibility of realization.

The leaderless peer group can operate by consensus. If the group spends time speaking about experiences and efforts in the path, then what each person shares must be treated with respect. If the members of the group analyze, criticize, offer advice, or make suggestions in response to another member, they risk poisoning the atmosphere of the group. For honesty and sincerity to prevail, an environment of trust and respect must be developed and protected. Peer group members should limit what they share to relating their own experiences and efforts, and not stray into playing the spiritual mentor. No one can do the spiritual work of another. Guidance, to be effective, must be asked for, not offered gratuitously. In a peer group, guidance can come from hearing the efforts, successes, and failures of the other members of the group.

Both forms, the peer group and the led group, have their place and can greatly accelerate the inner work of the members of the group. In the earlier stages of the path, having a leader offers important benefits. In the first years, we need to be taught the methods by someone who understands them. We need to be nudged back onto the path when we stray. We need to recognize the limits of our own understanding and be willing to ask for and receive guidance. This promotes humility and insulates us from that bane of spiritual work: arrogance. We also need confirmation of our understanding, so our confidence and self-reliance can grow. However, a led group requires a leader with the characteristics described above. Lacking such a person, the peer group can be an excellent alternative.

4. Frequency of Gathering

Living in a genuine spiritual community that works and practices together confers the blessings of a powerful, traditional way toward the spirit. Few of us, though, exhibit a willingness to become monks or nuns. Furthermore, living full-time in a spiritual community does not constitute the best approach for everyone. It depends on one's temperament and style.

Retreats convey the advantages of life in a spiritual community on a temporary basis. Periodic retreats, in which we focus entirely on the work of presence, deepening awareness, and opening our heart, can prove enormously beneficial in reinvigorating our inner work.

In our normal life situation, a weekly group meeting, attended regularly, offers an external reminder, a source of energy, and a shared commitment, enabling us to maintain our practice in the face of life's many distractions and pressures. In certain respects, this creates the ideal circumstance. We need great determination to continuously return to our practice in the midst of family, job, community, and other responsibilities. Life becomes our training ground. If our spiritual practice can flower within the challenge of normal life, our practice will grow strong indeed, our hearts open, and our lives transformed.

Practice in the special environment of a retreat or a spiritual community can usher us into deep experiences, tastes of the true spirit. Yet when we return to our normal life, those experiences gradually fade, while thankfully leaving a residue of purification and commitment. Practice in everyday life, however, can bring lasting transformation. Daily progress may not be as dramatic and rapid as during a retreat, but can be more permanent. Gradually, the path and our life merge, so that our life is our path, carrying us toward the opening of our hearts and the Great Source of All.

5. The Structure of the Group Meeting: Practice and Sharing

The spiritual group, to be effective, devotes time to both shared practice and shared discussion. A group which does not meditate, pray, or engage in some other collective spiritual practice misses the remarkable opportunity. Discussion alone, even of the most profound, heartfelt and weighty topics, rarely touches our soul. Discussion alone does not serve the transformation of energies and the purification of will in the way that shared practice can.

Group practice alone, however, may not illumine certain valuable details of the path. For this, the group needs shared discussion. The discussion, though, must not be solely theoretical: it should focus on the details of practice, how one actually practices, what obstacles one encounters, what helps, what experiments one tries, what new insights come, and so forth. If each person in the group describes such living details of their own spiritual efforts, every person in the group benefits thereby. Everyone can relate what the speaker articulates to their own life and path. A theoretical discussion of ideas rarely has such an impact.

Like every individual, each spiritual group or community is unique, and will have its own style, its own lifecycle. But all genuinely spiritual groups and communities support the transformation of their members and enable them to serve in a deeper way than would be possible on their own. If we are fortunate enough to participate in a spiritual group that suits our needs and our taste, well and good. If not, perhaps we can find one other person to share our practice with, forming a group of two. Otherwise, we do our best to pursue our spiritual practice on our own: for this also is possible and necessary. No one else can free us; no one else can do our inner work for us. But we can help each other.

Teachers and Paths: True or False?

The greatness of human civilization in the spiritual realm derives from its gradual and hard-earned accumulation of philosophical understanding, practical knowledge, and effective technique, all with layer upon layer of subtlety. We owe an enormous debt of gratitude to those have gone before in wisdom and in love, to those who teach us directly and personally, and to those who teach us through their books and other media. The advent of commercial airlines and instant communications has blessed us with a wealth of genuine paths, teachers, and groups. Indeed, the twentieth century brought an unprecedented transfer and adaptation of profound spiritual teachings across the planet.

Yet modern societies face a market profusion of superficial, consumer-oriented, pseudo-spiritual, profit-motivated, newly invented paths of so-called transformation. Our personal perceptions and intuitions can tell us whether a particular organization, teaching, or teacher is authentic or shallow, competent or deluded, or trading on marketed fame, superficial charisma, or meaningless credentials. However, until our perceptions grow subtle enough to shepherd us through such thickets, a few simple guidelines may help us avoid the worst of the lot. The primary point: nobody is perfect, regardless of how many followers they may have, or how pure, kind, and wise they appear to be. They may indeed be pure, kind, and wise, but perfect — no. Any spiritual teacher can be mistaken in his or her teaching methods or other actions. Teachers can, at times, be susceptible to misguided or even base motives.

If the path charges excessive fees, be concerned about greed. Spirituality and greed negate each other. An exorbitant demand for money as a test of the aspirant's sincerity serves to cover the avarice of the teacher or organization. Similarly, if a path promises rapid or easy progress, be concerned. Spirituality is a life's work.

If the leaders engage in abusive behavior, emotionally, physically, or sexually, be concerned. Excellent excuses can be made for this. Sexual adventures may be claimed to be a way for the student to draw closer to the guru and thereby closer to enlightenment or God. This is absurd. Emotional abuses may be couched in terms of "awakening" the student through insults or similar means. This may indeed work, but only temporarily at best. A pattern of insults from the teacher or group tends to make the student dependent on this external source for awakening. We need to find our inner source of awakening. Thus, an external dependence on emotional "shock" treatment works against our liberation. Emotional abuse also retards our progress by strengthening our egoism and driving us into defensiveness, self-pity, self-hatred, submissiveness, resentment, or anger.

If the path divides people into "us" and "them," be concerned. We are all, in our core, children of the same God. Furthermore, many genuine paths exist. None can truly claim to be the best, as different approaches work best for different people. The "us" and "them" mentality also fosters a group ego, which itself hinders our progress.

If the teacher or group offers to make your life decisions for

47

you, be concerned. A true path leads us to become more fully ourselves, to find our unique individuality. No one can give this to us, as we are born with it and must uncover it for ourselves. A teacher who tells us whom to marry, what job to take, where to live, or merely advises us on these and other such choices, takes away a piece of our will, takes away our opportunities to learn from our own mistakes, and mixes levels inappropriately. The teacher should let the student make his or her own life choices, guided by the student's own conscience.

If the path promises salvation or enlightenment as a result of merely adopting some belief system, be concerned. A mental or emotional belief only touches a small part of us. To be transformative, our spirituality must reach the whole of our being.

If the path promises to show us the way toward material wealth, it may be perfectly genuine in a business sense, but it is not about spirituality. The true abundance that will secure our heart's release lies in the spiritual, not the material. We need not, however, go to the other extreme and seek material poverty. We simply need to be responsible about providing for ourselves and our families, without an overarching attachment to money and goods.

So far, we have discussed the most flagrant problems, but more subtle ones also exist. Does a teaching demand loyalty? This question raises complex issues. We must enter a teaching deeply enough for it to act on our innermost core. That may indeed require us to devote ourselves exclusively to the one teaching. But while this novitiate may last for some years, it is a temporary phase. Afterwards, the teaching must permit us the freedom to search elsewhere if we need to. Loyalty, during the period of its necessity, should be to the teaching, not to the teacher.

Does the teaching focus exclusively on the psychological?

Dealing with our personal psychology can be an important part of our path, but on its own, psychology only reaches to the lower rungs of the great ladder. Such psychological "paths" may be hard to recognize, because they often use spiritual terminology. One may help us lower our stress, be happier, and communicate better, but is it truly transformative? Does it lead toward presence, toward deepening of our being and will, toward freedom from clinging, toward a natural kindness and joy? A similar indictment applies to paths that focus on physical health. We certainly need a healthy body, but that alone will not complete our soul.

Is the teacher and teaching part of a long lineage, which has refined its approach over the centuries? Or is it a new invention or a new revelation? If it is new, we should naturally be more skeptical. We need to ascertain that it is complete, effective, and connected to the spiritual depths.

Is the teaching appropriate for you? Does it fit? Does it address your idiosyncrasies? An example case is a path that has only a small set of practices. Perhaps that practice doesn't suit you and is not effective for you. It may be quite effective for others, but not for you. This is not to say that we should expect quick results from any path. But our taste and intuition can tell us whether a path corresponds to our own unique pattern.

Real teachers, though rare, do exist. Contact with them, while not necessary, can be enormously beneficial to our inner search. Two primary models exist for the relationship with a real teacher. In the guru model, the student devotes him- or herself to the guru. Through surrender to the guru, who serves as a temporary intermediary, the student finds the way to the Sacred Reality. In the instructor model, the teacher points the student directly toward the Reality without any intermediary.

Which style we prefer is a matter of taste. Both have advantages and disadvantages. A guru had better be a really high being, because the student becomes spiritually dependent on the guru. Furthermore, though the requirement of unquestioning obedience does work against egoism, it also hinders the growth of individuality. While our missteps deepen our understanding and our lack of progress can awaken our determination, an instructor can leave us to make too many mistakes and waste too much time.

But proximity to a real teacher does give a taste for truth, an understanding of love, and confidence in the higher reality. Unfortunately, teachers on that level are all too rare, although those who claim to be there are more common. Lacking a being meter, how can we judge this? We have to rely on our intuition of how substantial a person the teacher is, how much being they have. Certainly we can be fooled by appearances and outward trappings, by the number of followers, or by the style of communication. But we learn to trust our own perceptions and make our judgments accordingly. Even without a teacher of great being, we can effectively learn the methods of spiritual practice from more ordinary leaders and instructors.

Just as no person is perfect, no path is perfect. If we hold up too many requirements and unreasonable standards in judging a path, we may never embark. So we choose the best of what's available and dive in.

CHAPTER TWO

───────────────────

BODY

First, a cautionary note. A number of the practices presented in these pages can be undertaken during the ordinary activities of daily life. This is, in fact, what they are intended for. However, those that require control of attention and awareness, such as working with bodily sensations, breath awareness, presence, and so on, should not be used in potentially dangerous situations like driving a car, until we have a great deal of experience with the practice and have enough attention to both drive safely and engage the practice at the same time. When it comes to safety-critical situations, common sense must rule. We need our bodies as healthy as possible to pursue our path. Of course, the obvious complement to this cautionary note about not jeopardizing our bodily safety is that we also need our soul as healthy, as strong, and as refined as possible. For that, we pursue our spiritual practice with all vigor. Let us begin...

The Energy Body

This physical body serves not only as our means for participating in the world, but also as the primary channel for our contact with the present moment. Our thoughts and emotions tend to hop around in space and time, anticipating future events and remembering the past. However, our body remains tied to the present, affording a ready-made base for us in the here and now.

But first we might ask why this should matter to us. Why all the emphasis on being in the present? If the spiritual worlds encompass more than space and time, why should we be so concerned about keeping our awareness in the here and now? The simple answer: the only access to happiness, fulfillment, love, responsibility, and the deeper levels of spirituality lies in the here and now. The stronger our presence, the stronger that access can be. And the foundation of presence consists of a direct, full, intentional and continuing awareness of bodily sensations occurring now. But what do we mean by a direct awareness of bodily sensations?

You might try this quick experiment. Place your hands on your knees, palms down. Put all of your attention into your right hand. To help in this, make a fist with your right hand, keeping your attention in the hand. Be directly aware of the sensations in the hand, not just by thinking about the hand. Experience the unmediated right-hand-in-a-fist sensations. After your attention has fully settled into the right hand, slowly release the fist and put the hand back on the right knee, palm down. Continuing to focus your attention in the right hand, notice the sensations there. Notice your actual, simple, direct perceptions, your immediate proprioceptive experience of the hand.

Now notice the difference between your experience of your right hand and your left hand. Your right hand probably feels more alive than your left. All the attention you brought to your right hand has raised your level of awareness of the sensations there, bringing more sensitive energy into the right hand. And at this moment you very likely have much more sensation in your right hand than in your left. This is a physical experience, not a mental one. Your thinking need not intervene and can easily interfere with the experience of sensation.

Of course, you can reverse this by moving your attention to your left hand and holding your attention there until the sensitive energy begins to collect more strongly in the left hand. Indeed, you can raise the level of sensitive energy in any part or even the whole of your body simply through direct attention, without resorting to tricks like making a fist. The more relaxed your muscles are, the more sensitive energy will flow into and within your body.

Another method of coming into contact with bodily sensations is scanning. Imagine a flat plane parallel to the ground. Starting at the top of the head, we slowly move this plane down through the body, becoming aware of the sensations of that slice of the body through which the plane is passing, like an MRI or CT scan. A different approach has us notice the points at which our body is touching the world, e.g., the bottom of our feet when standing, the posterior when sitting, etc. In another set of techniques, we focus awareness on our postures, gestures, movements, facial expressions, and the sound of our voice.

The entire multitude of practices of contact with bodily sensations rests on a few basic principles. The awareness should be direct, without the mediation of thoughts or images, just a simple, organic perception of the sensations. Using a relaxed attention to the body, our muscles free of unnecessary tensions, we aim toward more frequent, lasting, and stronger contact with the energy of sensation. We begin with hands and feet, arms and legs, and, without focusing on particular inner organs (so as not to interfere with their instinctive operation), we gradually incorporate the whole of our body within the field of sensation and awareness.

This practice of intentional contact with bodily sensation, or sensing, provides us with an invaluable grounding in the present and a basis for our spiritual life. With bodily sensation as our anchor, we can be more distinctly aware of other sides of ourselves, such as the alluring passage of thought and the pull of emotion. Awareness of bodily sensation helps us to feel at home in our bodies, befriend our bodies, and open to the joy of life. Throughout a lifetime of spiritual practice, sensing can remain a fundamental component and guidepost of our way.

As the concentration of sensitive energy within us develops, it acquires a life of its own. Sensitive energy confers more than contact with bodily, physical sensations. First, we enter a positive feedback loop with the sensitive energy building in us. Our work to increase the sensitive energy returns to us when the energy spontaneously arises and awakens us. This moment of awakening offers a new opportunity for further practice of sensing, which leads to more moments of awakening.

Secondly, by creating a vessel for the higher energies, sensing helps build our soul. As we continue our practice of sensing, the whole of our body becomes robustly filled with the sensitive energy, eventually coalescing into a single field of energy, which we may call the energy body or lower soul. An early taste of this can occur in meditation when we shift our awareness from the experience of being in a physical body filled with the sensitive energy to the experience of being wholly in the (sensitive) energy body. Contact with the energy body creates a strong and stable context in the present moment that permits us to take our place in the next higher energy of consciousness, which is true presence.

The whole of the path resides in the present moment and the present moment can be entered most directly through opening to the energy body within our physical body. The energy body anchors us in the present and opens the door to the spiritual. One frontier of our spiritual work is to make our contact with the energy body stronger, more frequent, and more continuous. At any and every moment, our physical body awaits our attention and intention to deepen our connection with and strengthen our energy body. This in itself affords us a greater degree of freedom. In the energy body, strongly in the present, we are not as prone to identification with past and future, anxiety and fear, greed and anger, nor to the grip of egoism. A natural joy, a celebration of life enters us as we awaken out of identification and into the energy body, into the present.

Relaxation

The development of our soul, the strengthening of our being, and our contact with the spiritual worlds depend in part on accumulating and organizing spiritual energies, such as the energy of consciousness. But tensions of all kinds, particularly muscular and emotional tensions, sap our energies, wastefully burning them up. Tensions create the proverbial hole in our bucket, our leaky spiritual vessel. The amount of energy that accrues to us naturally on any given day would suffice to take us very far, if we could stop wasting energy on tensions. To be sure, we have other holes in our bucket, but tensions wreak havoc with our energies. Intentional relaxation, though, can plug these drains. In addition, work with relaxation can go beyond releasing tensions, for example in relaxing the grip of the inner forces that keep us from our true nature. In these ways, relaxation serves as an essential element of balanced spiritual work. How wonderful to let go and drop all our burdens!

Relaxation practice typically begins with the body. The interconnectedness of the body, the psyche, and the emotions, means that relaxing one leads to relaxing the whole. We could begin with relaxing our emotions, but the subtlety and intimacy of emotions makes them harder to perceive objectively and more difficult to relax. With our inner eye of attention, however, we can with relative ease inspect our body, checking its various parts, noticing the tensions in the muscles, and allowing them to subside. We can relax systematically by beginning with the face, the head, the neck, and gradually moving down through the entire body. In this way we can work at thoroughly relaxing the large and small muscles throughout our body. We do not attempt to bring attention to, or relax, our inner organs, so as not to interfere with their instinctive functioning; as we relax all our voluntary muscles, our breath and pulse naturally follow.

Muscular relaxation provides an excellent beginning for a meditation session, preparing the body for a free flow of energies. Sitting quietly at first, letting go of the day's hurry and flurry, worries and fears, hopes and dreams, we relax as deeply and thoroughly as possible. We may find chronic tensions in some areas, such as the abdomen, the shoulders, or the face. By relaxing our muscles we conserve the energies that we usually lose to tensions, making them available for our spiritual practice, for improving our attention, for creating a broader, more constant awareness.

Relaxation matters not only during formal periods of practice like meditation, but throughout the day. Most activities require some degree of tension in particular sets of muscles: even the simple acts of standing or walking need certain tensions in muscles. Relaxation in activity means relaxing those muscles not required for the action, having the minimum necessary amount of tension where needed, and letting go of fidgeting and unnecessary movements. We refrain from wasting energy. Relaxation is not about lounging around all day doing nothing with our bodies, but rather about not expending energy beyond that required for our chosen life activities, freeing the surplus energy for more important uses in our spiritual work.

Beyond the body, we open to deeper levels of relaxation, ultimately relaxing the grip that egoism and self-centeredness exert on our will. We relax our view of ourselves as separate from other people and from the rest of the world, so that egoism gradually loosens its stranglehold on our thoughts, emotions, and actions.

During the day we often find opportunities to relax emotionally. For example, an aggressive driver cuts us off. We react with anger. We could instead consider his state: perhaps a personal emergency, perhaps he has had some bad news and is full of tension, perhaps he is late for an appointment, or perhaps he is habitually inconsiderate. Regardless of what his actual state might be, we prefer not to let the event drag us into the mud. Not that we release others or ourselves for responsibility for actions, but we do seek to relax emotionally in difficult situations, not to be overwhelmed by our reactions. Such opportunities for emotional relaxation abound. To the extent that we are present, we can respond appropriately and with choice to life's challenges, rather than responding from reactive tension and self-centered views. Of course, it's easy for me to write this, and perhaps easy for you to read this, but for both of us it may not be so easy to actually put it into practice. Dogged, long-term perseverance remains an absolute necessity in spiritual practice.

Please be clear about the fundamental difference between relaxing and suppressing, between relaxing and adopting an attitude that something is wrong with us. Any rejection of tensions, be they muscular or emotional, creates yet another tension overlaid on the first. So if we consider ourselves to be bad or weak, because, for example, we react with anger while driving or grow fearful when we've made a mistake at work, then this attitude of rejecting our own emotionality produces a deeper source of tension in us, a tension in our will.

Instead of rejection, we can base our spiritual work on a radical acceptance of ourselves *as we are*. This calls for the readiness to see and accept whatever arises in us. Such radical acceptance engenders a remarkable shift, an opening toward allowing all things, including ourselves, to be as they are. We still do not permit ourselves to act on impulses toward some wrong or immoral action that would cause harm to ourselves or others. But we accept that such impulses do arise in us. Similarly, we may continue attempts to right some of the wrongs of the world. But we accept, with clear vision, that the world is as it is, and work from that reality as a starting point. Surprisingly, radical acceptance of ourselves enables a radical acceptance of others as they are, opening our being toward love.

Awakening and relaxation support each other. Awakening does not mean sitting on the edge of the chair with bulging eyes wide open, inwardly tensed to pounce on the next perception, in a nervous vigil not to miss anything. Awakening means open, relaxed awareness, not an inner demand to be awake but rather an inner interest in being awake. Being present is not exhausting. In fact, relaxed presence can stabilize for long periods, energizing us in a sustainable manner, not draining us.

Finally, at perhaps its deepest level, we relax our hold on

the known, our insistence on viewing the world in our habitual ways. A glimmer of a deeper way of life begins to open up in us. This requires our perceptions to step beyond our accustomed horizons. Spiritual masters often describe the truth, the reality, the Divine as not far from us, as closer than our own breath, as a medium in which we live and move and have our being. How is this possible if we do not see it? Because our habitual ways of thinking, feeling and sensing, our habitual ways of perceiving, built up over a lifetime, believing we know the world — all this blinds us to the Truth. Gradually we relax this iron grip of the known and begin to recognize another way of living.

Our Body, Our Temple

This miraculous body, given to us at birth, requires proper rest, nutritious food, good hygiene, and adequate exercise not only to support our physical health, but also to regulate our vital energies. This sets the best possible bodily stage for spiritual practice. Bodily vigor can translate to an active, energetic approach to the inner life. Furthermore, responsible treatment of our own body forms a crucial part of a responsible attitude toward life as a whole. Responsibility stands as one of the highest spiritual qualities and begins with our own body. To help maximize our spiritual possibilities, we can work to maximize our physical vitality.

Like everything else in human life, care of the body can suffer many aberrations. Hypochondria, fastidiousness, squeamishness, timidity, vanity, lust, gluttony and laziness suggest the wide range of excessive or obsessive attitudes we can have toward our body. These and others arise from self-centered, egoistic views of life. Given its remarkable resilience, we need

59

not fear using our body, making demands of it. Given the fact of our body, we need to accept it as is, adapting to rather than dwelling on its inevitable shortcomings. The fact of our body also argues against taking the false credit of vanity, or being overly concerned about adorning it. A slovenly appearance, though, shows lack of respect for oneself and others.

Illness presents an opportunity to reassess our situation, our goals, our choices. Any illness can serve as a small reminder of our inevitable death, and as such, can stimulate consideration of the legacy we are creating, of the kind of person we are, of the life we are living, of appropriate use of our talents and disposition. Illness can also teach us acceptance and patience. Sometimes in illness, the depletion of our energies weakens our egoism and allows our more essential nature to shine through. An acquaintance, in the process of dying from brain cancer, gradually underwent a remarkable transformation and became a source of love for all around. Even lesser, non-fatal illnesses, can open our being and our heart.

As our body ages, slowly, slowly, its powers wane. New aches, pains, limitations and challenges enter our life, tempting us to dwell on the decline rather than on continued living in the wisdom, dignity, and warmth of heart that aging can bring.

The body offers a fertile arena for inner work. At all ages, instinctive intuition of what our body really needs challenges our perceptions and fixed opinions. Awareness of physical sensations, posture, gestures, facial expressions, tone of voice, movement, breathing, eating, and all our myriad physical activities grounds us in the present moment, reveals truths about ourselves, and provides a necessary platform for deeper spirituality. A proper object for our love and respect, a cared-for body repays us with well-being, energy, and a home for building our soul.

Managing Bodily Excesses

The spiritual path begins right where we are. As long as we seek to fill our emptiness through addictions of one kind or another, we shall be barred from any progress on the path. If the nascent vessel of our soul leaks, we shall never collect enough energy, enough consciousness to progress. Relaxation of body and heart plugs some of the leaks. But plenty of us have other major leaks, most notably bodily excesses such as those around food, alcohol, tobacco, or drugs. Patching these leaks will conserve the energy we need for our practice. In a deeper sense, stopping these physically harmful habits is an act of respect for ourselves, for these remarkable bodies we have been given, and for the limitations of the Earth's resources. The discipline of working against harmful habits provides us with a truer picture of ourselves, while purifying our will.

The path calls us to forgo excess in favor of moderation, to neither seek nor allow the extremes of asceticism or hedonism, to heal our addictive behaviors. In moderation, we can enjoy life's pleasures without overindulging in them. If we are, indeed, God's eyes and ears, then appreciating the fruits of this life on Earth is normal and natural.

Our fertile minds, however, inevitably look for wiggle room in the definition of excess, the meaning of which legitimately varies from person to person. The basic criterion is whether any particular activity diminishes our ability to be present or to engage in spiritual practice.

Here are a few specific guidelines to consider:

First, in working toward moderation, we work on one thing at a time. Let's say we have two bad habits. If these habits grip us powerfully, our will is probably insufficient to have any effect on both at once. So we start with one bad habit and work seriously on it until we get it right. All the while, we remain watchful not to allow the energy released from stopping one bad habit to flow into making another one worse. For example, we avoid the temptation of being grouchy with people when we give up snacking. Instead we work harder to transform the energy released from giving up snacking into being more constant in our spiritual practices.

Overeating destroys certain energies we need for our spiritual path. The body consumes those energies in digesting the extra, unneeded food. If we feel full when we finish eating, we have probably eaten too much. If we feel stuffed or bloated, we have certainly eaten too much. There is a story of the Prophet Mohammed. A certain king heard glowing reports regarding Mohammed and wanted to support Mohammed's mission. So the king sent his personal physician to live in the Prophet's community and minister to his followers. After a year among them, the doctor went to Mohammed and reported that, during the entire time, none of Mohammed's people had come down with even a mild illness. The doctor asked Mohammed why they were all so healthy. Mohammed replied that their good health derived from the fact that he instructed his followers to rise from their meals before they were full.

To bring the daily act of eating into our spiritual path, we can focus our full attention on our food, on its taste, texture, and aroma, on how full our stomach is, on every aspect of eating. As a side benefit of conscious eating, fully experiencing our food enables us to enjoy it more, to be more readily satisfied, less prone to overeat, and freer in our relationship to food.

Moderation with alcohol means never getting even mildly drunk and not drinking more than once or twice a week. For most people, this amount of social drinking will have no ill effects on their inner lives.

With tobacco and drugs, moderation means none. Tobacco, besides being physically destructive, burns up energies we need for our practice. The same holds even more emphatically about recreational drugs such as marijuana, cocaine, LSD, etc. While a drug may give a temporary high, even one mimicking a spiritual state, in the long-term it burns up an exorbitant amount of energy, weakens our will, and debilitates our spiritual practice. Drugs and spiritual development do not mix. Sincere spiritual practice leads to deep satisfaction and unadulterated joy, much more profoundly and durably than can drugs, alcohol, or tobacco.

For some of us, though, our addictive behavior arises from using drugs or alcohol to self-medicate our psychological problems, depression, stress and so forth. In these cases, we're infinitely better off if we can bring ourselves to seek professional help and face our problems forthrightly. Consistent and systematic relaxation practice also diminishes the need for drugs, alcohol, or tobacco.

Entrenched habits prove resistant to attempts at breaking them. Fortunately, very few actually need to be broken altogether for our spiritual lives to flourish: we need to stop all use of tobacco and drugs, and refrain from excessive consumption of food and alcohol. These create major impediments to our spiritual path. Working against such habits can be extremely difficult, but tremendously rewarding. Persistence, perennially starting over again, eventually pays, clearing obstacles from our way. In the meantime, working on these habits reveals unknown aspects of ourselves and strengthens our resolve. Eventually we learn to respect our body in its service to our higher nature.

Conscious Movement

Reveling in the joy of movement comes naturally to life. We can see it in animals, in infants, and in ourselves. Whether in the fine motor control of the seamstress and the musician, or in the supple whole body movements of the athlete and the dancer, or in the everyday movement of walking, life is in motion. As with every other aspect of life, we can infuse our experience of movement with our spiritual pursuit.

In the practice of conscious movement we establish our awareness in bodily sensations. As a starting point, we bring consciousness to simple, repetitive movements. Examples include walking, running, and exercising. Because we walk so often, walking can serve as an excellent basis for our inner work with movement. The same technique we shall describe for conscious walking applies to any type of movement, from gardening and sawing to typing, cooking, and brushing our teeth.

In walking, we begin with awareness of our feet, of the sensations of our feet touching the ground, lifting, moving forward, and touching the ground again. The practice of walking meditation, in which we typically move *very* slowly with full awareness of the sensations in our feet, trains us in conscious movement. Gradually, we expand the field of awareness beyond the feet, to include the sensations of the legs in movement, the arms, and the entire body. Finally, we transfer this training into awareness of sensations in walking at our ordinary pace, walking through life with full mindfulness, whether for a few steps or a thousand. Rather than mentally arriving at our destination before we get there, we continuously arrive where we are, in our body. Instead of moving from the outside, as if our body were merely an object, we move from the inside, from sensation.

Intention constitutes a crucial element of conscious movement. The complete practice of conscious movement calls for more than sensing our bodies in movement, more even than being conscious of those sensations. We need a third element: the full intention to move, to do exactly what we're doing. Half-hearted, divided intentions lead to half-hearted presence. Whether sewing, cooking, shaving, brushing teeth, bathing, walking, running, driving a car, typing, chewing, combing hair, tying shoes, buckling a belt, buttoning buttons, or carrying out the trash, full engagement arises from the full intention to perform the action. Any movement performed consciously and with whole intention has the potential to transform our life, shining awareness into the dark recesses, enlightening and enlivening us.

Finally, we may enter into sacred movement, which, to have real meaning, must at least be conscious. Sacred movement includes all rituals, gestures, and dances performed as acts of worship. Sacred movement engages the whole of our being. In it we pray, not just with our minds and hearts, but also with our bodies. In those forms of prayer that include movement, we move with particular care, with soft-heartedness filling our bodies, in an all-inclusive offering of ourselves to the Divine.

Conscious Breathing

From the dawn of our birth until the sunset of death, we breathe, always and everywhere. Indeed, breath defines our life and supports us body and spirit. Besides being central to life, ever-present, and connected to the spirit, breathing involves an easily noticeable complex of physical sensations. Thus, the practice of breath awareness was widely embraced by our ancestors in the spiritual pursuit. The Buddha was engaged in breath awareness as his primary practice at the time of his enlightenment. The Christian Desert Fathers, Hindu Yogis, and Islamic Sufis employed variations of breath awareness.

Breath awareness forms a subclass of the more general awareness of bodily sensations. Because the breath always moves, the sensations of the bodily movements associated with breathing remain with us continually from birth to death. The more subtle sensations of the air moving through our nasal and oral passageways also stay with us. To powerfully anchor ourselves to the present, we need only abide in the sensations of each breath, one after another without a break. Since we always breathe, we have the potential to practice breath awareness at any and every waking moment.

A word of caution, though, at the outset: in practicing breath awareness we make no change whatsoever to the physical movement of the breath. We do not attempt to slow it down, speed it up, or alter it any way. We only bring our attention and awareness to the sensations of breathing, as they are, without imposing any changes on the breath. We do not interfere with the vital function of breathing. We simply ease into awareness of it and ride along to stay present.

Such relaxed and continuous awareness of the sensations of breathing creates a sturdy and effective basis for the path of spiritual transformation. This simple method entails a direct attention to, and consciousness of, the actual physical sensations associated with breathing. We might focus on the sensations in the nostrils, the air movement across the upper lip, or the rise and fall of the abdomen and rib cage. Or we might prefer to work with awareness of all of them at once in a more global view of breathing. Each has its advantages. The abdominal region offers relatively large movements, with obvious physical sensations that we can readily engage and follow. The nostrils and upper lip present a small, subtle, and very focused region. The narrow focus can be more difficult to acquire and maintain but enables us to quickly build up a sharp and strong attention. Global bodily awareness of breath readily supports a conscious backdrop to common daily activities. Our situation and state can guide us to the most appropriate style of practice in any given moment.

From ancient times until today, conscious breathing remains among the most powerful, effective, and natural methods for centering ourselves in presence and preparing our being for opening to the spirit.

Energy Breathing

A sea of precious spiritual energies surrounds us. The air, for example, contains such energies, a fact attested to by most major spiritual traditions. The Hindu notion of *prana*, which means breath in Sanskrit, refers to the energies carried by the air. The Hindu word for soul, *atman*, also means breath in Sanskrit. The Latin *spiritus* means both breath and soul, and forms the root of related English words like spirituality, respire, inspire, and expire. Numerous other languages and traditions similarly affirm the close relationship between the air and soul energies, the air acting as a reservoir of energies: Arabic *ruh*, Hebrew *nefesh*, *ruakh*, *neshamah*, Greek *pneuma*, Chinese Taoist *ch'i*, the Christian Prayer of the Heart, Gregorian chant, the Sufi zikr, and the Yoga of pranayama. In ordinary, automatic breathing, however, only a small amount of these energies remain with us after we exhale.

Intentional energy breathing enables more of the energy

to be drawn into us from the air and to stay with us, fueling our spiritual practice and strengthening our soul. In this special form of conscious breathing, we direct our attention to the energies in the air we breathe, rather than simply to the physical sensations associated with breathing. We intentionally draw the energy from the air into us. We can cast our attention as a "net" to capture the energy and carry it into us as we inhale. Alternatively, we can use attention as a "filter" placed in the nostrils to release the energy as the air enters the nose. As we work on becoming aware of the energy in the air and drawing it into us, we discover an unmistakable and wonderful flow of energy in our breath, strengthening our energy body. But this energy flow is never automatic; it requires intention and attention to separate the energy from the ordinary air. Spending time every day on this energy breathing practice proves invaluable in establishing our energy body, the first body of the soul, giving us a sturdy vessel for presence and for deepening our path.

At first your perceptions may not be refined enough to experience the energy in the air. In this case, use your imagination and practice as if fine particles of energy were entering you as you breathe. Work at this as part of your sitting meditation. If, after practicing energy breathing for some period each day for a week or two, you still find the energy flow elusive, please drop the exercise and consider returning to it again at another time. But bear in mind the many spiritual traditions affirming the presence of soul-related energies in the air. If this is possible for other people, it is also possible for you. As your other spiritual practices and perceptions deepen, your ability to contact and absorb the energies in the air will grow apace. Then this vast reservoir of energies will begin to strengthen your inner life and make it more real.

Conscious Speech

Of all spiritual practices, speaking consciously ranks among the most difficult and most rewarding. Even those with long devotion to inner work do not find this easy. When we talk, we have some notion of our intentions, of what we wish to communicate. But typically our awareness of ourselves nearly vanishes the moment our mouths open and we begin to speak. To begin working on conscious speech, we can attempt to be aware of the actual sound of our voice as we speak, during the act of speaking. This apparently simple task proves surprisingly slippery. We may know that we are about to speak, and have full intention of being aware of the sound of our voice as we speak, and then it all disappears in the very next moment when we actually start talking. Yet the difficulty of this practice makes it particularly valuable in improving our ability to stay present, not to mention improving our relationships. We need to extend presence to every corner of our life, especially those that the light of consciousness rarely visits. The act of speaking defines one such dimly lit corner.

Conscious speech means more than simply being aware of the sound of our voice. It extends to awareness of the meaning of our words and our intentions in speaking. So much of what we say comes from ego-centered motives: judgment and criticism of others often enters gossip and difficult emotions lead us to say hurtful words. Self-centeredness makes us think everyone is so very interested in listening to us talk on and on about ourselves, while we exhibit no interest in the other person. All this feeds our egoism. The less we criticize others, the less critical we are of ourselves, and vice versa. The less we hurt others, the less we will be hurt. The less we talk about ourselves, the less we are boxed into our small, ego-centric world, and vice versa. Our ego fears the light of awareness, so the more awareness we bring to the intentions driving our speech, the freer we grow.

Saying only what is true requires consciousness. Of course, this does not imply saying everything that is true, when tact and kindness advise otherwise. Well-chosen, heartfelt words open the gates of relationship, deepening our circle.

Conscious speech also encompasses speaking from the whole of ourselves, so that we mean and feel what we say, and when appropriate and useful we say what we mean and feel.

Speech includes our body language, the gestures, posture, and facial expressions we adopt in communicating. So in speaking consciously, we cast a wide net to include intention, tone of voice, meaning of words, as well as body language within the field of our immediate awareness. To achieve such breadth of consciousness, we need to be fully present. We do not try to dissect the event into its components of tone of voice, gestures, and so on, but rather we reside in presence to the wholeness of the experience of speaking. To prevent this wholeness of presence from disintegrating without warning, we ground ourselves in the concrete and inwardly verifiable awareness of our tone of voice. Listening to our voice as we speak, we listen also for the whole.

Finally, and perhaps most importantly, to speak consciously also means to be fully aware of the person(s) to whom we are speaking, to see them as people like ourselves, to be aware of the potential effect of our words on them before we say the words, to be aware of the actual effect on them after we've said the words, and with open heart and mind to listen to the response. In this way, we honor the humanity of the other person and, in so doing, honor our own.

Awareness of Pain

As long as we have a body, pleasures are possible but pain is inevitable. As our natural and normal response to physical pain, we attempt to alleviate it: jerking our hand from the flame, seeking medical help when necessary. But pain attacks us regardless, minor and brief, intense or persistent. With pain that cannot immediately be salved, we avert our inward gaze, trying to avoid awareness of it; we fear, hate, and reject the experience of pain. Nevertheless, painful sensations do penetrate our consciousness. So we find ourselves inwardly running from our own body, an impossible venture.

As with other difficulties in life, we can bring our spiritual practice to the experience of pain, often with quite useful results. First, we take intelligent and prudent steps to ease the pain; never seeking pain per se, we do not follow the path of masochism or extreme asceticism. We care responsibly for our body and pursue medical treatment for any serious pain, be it temporary or chronic. But the inescapable pain that remains in this moment can become the object of our practice rather than a source of fear, loathing, and obsession. We simply bring our attention to the painful region, becoming aware of it as sensation, aware of our emotional reactions of fear, rejection, shrinking or sadness, aware of the thought patterns that label the sensations as pain. Localized or intense pain offers a strong focus for us, empowering our attention.

In time, we regard the painful sensations as just sensations, without the emotional and intellectual rejection, without reifying the simple sensations into something we call "pain." We see the sensations change and evolve. We learn to watch them with an open and accepting awareness. We learn to let these sen-

71

sations feed our consciousness, strengthening it. The process becomes a meditation on a particular cluster of sensations. The power of attention on these sensations can carry our awareness through inner barriers into very deep worlds.

Such practice of awareness of pain has profound ramifications on the whole of our spiritual life. In learning to accept painful sensations, we train ourselves to work with non-physical pain as well, to accept those aspects of ourselves that we reject. Acceptance should not stop us from seeking medical remedies for our physical pain nor from working to overcome the sources of our non-physical pain. But what we cannot change, we accept with grace. In learning to accept ourselves as we are, we learn to accept others as they are. If we can open our mind and heart to our own body in its pain, we become more able to open our hearts to ourselves and to others, to enter a radical all-accepting, all-embracing, heartful awareness. This is the path toward true transformation.

Fasting

From time immemorial, serious seekers across the spectrum of religious and spiritual traditions have engaged in ascetic practices. One of the most ancient and effective of these is fasting, still practiced in many religions and paths up to the present day. During the holy month of Ramadan, for example, Muslims take no food or drink from sunrise to sunset each day for the entire month. Similarly, on the day of Yom Kippur, Jews forgo food and drink from sunset to sunset. In fasting, we sacrifice our own personal desires for the Divine. However, the true depth of the action of that sacrifice lies beyond our consciousness.

It is, in fact, unfailingly surprising how well fasting invigorates one's spiritual practices, such as being present. With so many aspects of life, wherein we face choices of how to live, how to act, and what to do, those choices do not always involve moral issues, e.g., how much to eat. We need a criterion, a compass to point us along our way, and that criterion can simply be our ability to be present. If certain activities and ways of living increase that, then we recognize them as appropriate for us on our path. If other activities decrease our ability to be present, we work to eliminate or diminish them.

With our ability to be present as a measure of our being, what a remarkable effect a single day's fast can have! Not only does it serve as a personal, small scale sacrifice to our Lord, and not only does it serve to make our body feel more healthy, alert, and energetic in the days following the fast, but it clearly also provides a major boost to our ability to be present. During a fast, the energies normally used in digesting food become available to be transformed into the energies of awareness. Fasting also diverts some of the energy that typically flows into associative thinking and daydreaming, leaving our minds better able to settle into a quieter, more spacious mode. Thus, fasting brings us back to ourselves more often. When we do come back to ourselves during and after a fast, we more readily recognize the importance of presence and abide longer in presence. The sacrifice of fasting increases our commitment to the path. And almost magically, fasting brings us toward that deeper place in us, toward joy, stillness, and love, toward that place where God truly can see through our eyes.

In practice, we see different, effective forms of fasting. Here is one. Choose a period of either 24 or 36 hours for the fast. On the day prior and the day after the fast, eat slightly less than normal. During the fast eat nothing, and drink only water. Drinking water makes the fast easier on the body while not significantly diminishing the beneficial spiritual effects of the fast. Fast no more than once a week. As with any spiritual practice, we must follow our common sense not to harm our bodies, our jobs, our relationships. Medical problems also may prevent us from fasting. If in doubt about this, ask your doctor.

The powerful practice of fasting should be undertaken in a serious manner, not to achieve some high, but as an act of service to the spiritual reality. Consequently, during and after a fast, we make an extra effort to be present as much as possible. If prayer forms part of our path, then a fast day can also be a good day for prayer. Finally, when we fast we can empathize with the hundreds of millions of people who experience chronic undernourishment due to lack of adequate food supplies. Our compassion can grow for the suffering of those who, unlike ourselves, do not have a choice about abstaining from food.

CHAPTER THREE

HEART

Motivation: Our Need to Walk the Path

In response to serious life challenges, people sometimes discover the motivation to seek spiritual transformation. In those difficult times, the basic, unanswerable questions of life spring to the surface. The forces that normally drive us, the petty and banal, temporarily lose their allure, thrusting us into a void of confusion. Unable to fill that void with our usual busyness, we begin again to ask what our life is for, what is truly worth the precious time allotted to us. Love and kindness toward our family and neighbors prove to be a staple of any life of integrity. Beyond that we seek meaningful and productive work.

Still, the unknown depths call to us, an intimation of ulter fulfillment, a whisper of a larger world, a step toward the irresistible and infinite. We begin to suspect that for our life to be whole, we need to do all we can to join our own heart to the Great Heart of the World. We realize that if we wish for fulfillment as we approach our death, to look back on a life well-lived, we need hew to a spiritual path that flows toward the Ocean of Wonder, playing our own small but unique role in serving the Boundless Responsibility.

Again and again, times of trouble or even simple awareness of the passage of our time remind us of this truth, that to lead a substantive life we must work indefatigably to purify and enrich our inner world, while serving the outer. In the storms of time our spiritual life strengthens us and sees us through, becomes our source of hope, our rock in a sea of uncertainty. Our appreciation for the spiritual depths grows.

When the troubles subside and ease returns, we need to work diligently and steadily, to remember the truths we know, to maintain our direction, our search. In times of ease, our energy abounds and our heart may overflow in gratitude, our perceptions may suddenly open wider, pointing toward the Unlimited Joy.

Yet motivation for the path may also be rooted in factors other than life difficulties or the questions they force upon us. Many come to a spiritual path out of an urge to better themselves, to seek self-development, to improve their effectiveness in life, perhaps to improve their image with themselves and others. That is the paradigm of "New Age" spirituality. As we progress in our practice, our motivation may shift to seeking better states of consciousness, to enjoy the delightful tastes of the higher worlds. Deep states of meditation entice us with their refined and rarefied ecstasies.

But as our spirituality matures, we begin to see meditation as a form of service. Our motivation shifts again toward maximizing and fulfilling our ability to love and to serve, outwardly as well as inwardly. Rather than seeking to better ourselves, we seek to go beyond our small self. A profound longing for the Divine, for completion, overtakes us heart and soul. Nothing short of the Real can quench this thirst. Then our inner work embraces a new urgency. We enter a new depth and continuity of spiritual practice.

Motivation is our will and our will is our I. So it can happen that we find ourselves wholly engaged in the path, yet unable to identify our motive or its source. This is rightly called faith. Our will is orthogonal to consciousness, seeing but unseen.

Whatever our motivation may be, the path, held to steadfastly, eventually transforms that motivation and thereby transforms us. So whether we desire to inflate ourselves, or we see the value in deflating our egos, the path welcomes us, loosening our mask, bit by bit, to reveal the unconditioned core of freedom and the choice of true responsibility.

Befriending Yourself: Acceptance

Christian original sin, the Buddhist fetters and hindrances, the lower soul in Sufism and Kabbalah, the inner battlefield of the Bhagavad Gita, and the inner jihad of the Koran — all paint a rather bleak picture of the typical human psyche and the obstacles to be faced on a spiritual path, and with more than an element of truth. For many of us though, an even greater obstacle lies in rejecting those aspects of ourselves that we consider to be liabilities, negative, weak, embarrassing, or just plain unlikable. The rather subtle question of how to approach this side of ourselves requires us to walk a tightrope between repression and indulgence, between severe discipline and passivity, between attempting to eradicate our inner animals and letting them run wild, between engaging in an inner battle and wallowing in a negative self-image. Too many paths focus on the negative in us, while too many others ignore it altogether. Those paths

77

that focus on the negative tend to reinforce the psychological wounds and insecurities we all have, by creating an unnecessary and harmful battle between the "higher" and "lower" in ourselves. Perhaps at one time such an attitude was fruitful, but in the modern cultural milieu we find it inappropriate and destructive of our possibilities. On the other side, those paths that ignore the negative seduce our laziness, feed our imaginary views of ourselves, and pander to our desire for instant spiritual gratification. Both the aggressive and the lazy extremes need to be avoided.

Besides all our inner shortcomings, life plagues us with outer imperfections. Western culture, with its Madison Avenue and Hollywood images of bodily perfection and wealth, engenders a pernicious undertone of self-doubt in the overwhelming majority of us. Not many people compare well physically or financially with the entertainment stars who fill the media. Not many of us can acquire all the attractive cars, homes, baubles, and vacations portrayed as life fulfilling. So our growth-oriented market culture, along with its numerous and very important benefits, perpetuates a life-long hunt for more, a hunt in which we inevitably fall short of the ever-advancing goal posts. We compare ourselves negatively to those who have more beauty or wealth, forgetting that a human being's value cannot be measured in externals, nor can they substitute for soul nourishment. This results in doubting our own competence, worthiness, abilities, intelligence, creativity, and luck. Whether we sink into a depressed hopelessness, grasp at the long shot that one day our lottery numbers will hit, or stay in the race of acquisition, the cultural tendency toward self-doubt persists, coloring our psyche.

The basic and enduring resolution to the whole predicament must be founded on love for ourselves, on a radical, all-inclusive acceptance of ourselves as we are, today. If we embark on a program of self-improvement, we shall never reach its end. Neither our personality nor our body can ever be perfect, nor our financial net worth large enough. Not even great spiritual masters manifest complete perfection in all their actions, inner and outer. Even they fall prey to mistakes; it comes with being human. Freedom lies in transcending our personal psychology, not in totally reforming it, nor in totally indulging it.

Partial reforms, though, typically are needed. Bodily excesses need management. Emotional excesses such as uncontrolled anger, absorbing greed, shrinking timidity, desperate jealousy, and quaking fear must not be given completely free rein. Such excesses impede our spiritual practice and drain our energies. We need to replace our harmful and wasteful excesses with appropriate moderation.

All the while, we respect these tendencies in ourselves as part of our makeup. We respect and accept that this is me, this is how I am made, this is my conditioning, this is my body, this is my mind, and these are my feelings. Some parts of myself I like, some I don't like, but it's all me, and if I am to move along the path, I must open to and accept the whole catastrophe. This sobering act of self-acceptance gradually destroys the false images we have of ourselves. We make the necessary minor reforms toward moderation and move on. Rejection of parts of our inner landscape results from the action of self-centered egoism in the cloak of the pseudo-spiritual. "I will make myself perfect. I will be better than everyone else." Or "I am terrible, weak, worthless, undeserving, and hopeless." These are but two sides of the counterfeit coin of self-centeredness, and we can easily waste years careening back and forth between them.

Self-acceptance and self-respect do not mean complacency. Clear seeing leads us to accept our imperfections as imperfections. Self-respect leads us to work on improving in the appropriate places.

Open-hearted self-acceptance empowers us to transcend the quagmire. We accept and we mend. Just as we care for our bodily wounds, so we take care of our psychological wounds, handicaps, and destructive habits, with concern and a healing attitude of kindness, defusing them. Mindfulness helps. When we fall into anger or fear, we do not turn our backs, but stay facing ourselves with open arms. A good psychotherapist also can help us find this attitude. Then we may move on to deeper spiritual work.

As our spiritual work progresses and we have more contact with the conscious energy, we sometimes see previously hidden aspects of our own makeup, of our personality and character. Often these aspects were hidden only from us and not from others. These shocking new glimpses of ourselves, these realizations that we are not exactly who we thought we were, may bring disappointment. But they arise naturally as a result of our inner work and present us with a choice. We may wallow in self-pity and self-hatred and, thereby, short-circuit the process of practice. Or we may simply accept that the good in us exists alongside the not-so-good, and practice with renewed vigor toward transformation. Not necessarily seeking to change the details of our personality, but rather seeking to change our being.

Loving and accepting ourselves sets the stage for the challenge of loving and accepting others. Knowing our own limitations and problems enables us to have a more compassionate attitude toward others' limitations and problems. Self-acceptance allows us to transcend our overarching concern with ourselves and enter into service of the greater Good.

Difficult Emotions

Only the rare high saints achieve a level of being untouched by anger and other difficult emotions. The rest of us must deal with distasteful, even ugly emotional states in ourselves. For a meaningful and satisfying life, and particularly for our spiritual path, our emotional nature matters dearly, serving alternately as an essential help and a severe hindrance. We need the inner skills to manage our troublesome emotions. The bouts of anger and rage, fear, anxiety and timidity, greed, lust and gluttony, envy and jealousy, arrogance, coldness and rigidity, squeamishness and laziness, worry, hurry, and depression all take a toll. They make us pay by destroying the precious energy of our inner life in a wasteful, self-referential cycle. They interpose themselves between us and the people around us. They distract us from working toward our goals.

But emotions are not our enemy: they are us. Or at least through the process of identification, we believe them to be us. Emotions propel us through life. Our difficult emotions call us to respond to ourselves with kindness, acceptance, and patience. We can learn to neither abandon ourselves to their indulgence, nor to blame ourselves for their arising. Indulging in difficult emotions makes us petty and self-centered, and can even lead to emotional instability requiring professional psychotherapy. The other extreme of unwillingness to face difficult emotions or of condemning them as spiritually impure, leads us to repress them, to refuse and cut off part of ourselves, part of our energy. And ultimately, the repressed energy finds a way to surface, perhaps even more destructively.

With difficult emotions, the most effective spiritual practice, assuming one's readiness to bear it, is to be openly and unflinchingly present to these emotions, to be here within myself in the midst of my inner turmoil, to simply see and not to run away into repression or indulgence, to not identify with or collapse into them. Such forthright presence brings a subtle but crucial new element to bear in our emotional life. Persisting, eventually our presence grows stable enough, large enough, and strong enough to embrace the whole unexpected catastrophe of our difficult emotions. By choosing to participate in an undefended awareness of what we find most objectionable in ourselves, we set the stage for a gradual transformation of our emotional life. By respecting even what we consider lowest in ourselves, we learn to respect others as well. We clear a path for the higher emotions such as love, kindness, generosity, joy, and compassion.

While presence to and awareness of our difficult emotions forms the first requirement, the second crucial element for working with these states is the willingness to let go of the emotion, to let go of nurturing and dwelling on the cause to which we ascribe the emotion. If, in our mind, we keep chewing over the unpleasant event or situation, then we feed the wrong side in ourselves, giving energy to our downward emotional slide. We need to be willing to let the whole thing go, so that we can live in a higher part of ourselves instead of dwelling in our emotional dungeon of identification, which drains the life-blood out of our spiritual work.

Transformation of our emotional life remains one of the greatest challenges confronting us on the spiritual path. We so easily fall into our emotional mud. Another step and we sink up to our necks. Our head then enters the fray as a supporting actor, busily thinking and imagining in ways that only worsen our position. Our breathing may grow rapid or shallow, our heart may pound, our shoulders may slump, and our face may flush or tighten. Our entire bodily demeanor reflects and abets the emotional siren. Our consciousness flees, not wanting to face the disaster. And so, we abandon ourselves to the chaotic whims of the torrent. By this time, there is little we can do but ride out the storm, attempting not to inflict any lasting damage. But even in the thick of it, if we can but open one eye, ever so slightly, and see with a modicum of clarity and perhaps even a hint of compassion for ourselves, we set the stage for the next round not to be quite so dark. Perhaps the next time we open an eye a bit earlier in the process, and a bit warmer. Eventually we may see with kindness at the tempest's beginning, at the first flap of the butterfly wings, the triggering event. Then, before the emotional storm clouds gather, we can choose to let it all be, and let it all go. Out of respect for ourselves and for others, we might choose not to allow this wasteful pain to overtake us again. This forms part of the long-term blue-collar work of the path, wherein our hands get dirty and our heart gets cleansed. We become able to be more present, more compassionate, and more joyful.

In practice, we must find a way to "own" our difficult and destructive emotions. Take the example of anger. As long as I inwardly blame another person for "making" me angry, I am feeding my anger. As soon as I see that the anger is mine, that it has arisen in me, that the other person's actions do not directly arouse my anger, but rather find a ready response in me, that someone else might respond without anger, that I am responsible for the anger, then I may decouple my anger from the outward apparent cause. When I am able to see this clearly, the anger subsides rapidly. Then I am free to take or not take appropriate action in response to the outward situation. But my inner life has been spared the cost of allowing the destructive action of anger to continue within me. Notice that owning my

anger does not mean pushing it away, repressing it, or disown-
ing it. It means accepting the anger as mine and seeing into the
roots of the anger within me. A similar process applies to all our
difficult and destructive emotions: not blaming the outer situation, owning the emotion and, finally, letting it go.

Some emotional storms are short-lived, even less than a
minute. Others can last for days. Recurrent or chronic difficult
emotions that consistently derail us from living a full life, from
loving relationships, and from our spiritual practice may require the help of a good psychotherapist. If that describes our
situation, then the sooner we seek therapy, the sooner we can
move on. We need to be responsible about what we make of our
lives, because our precious time is limited.

So if you see the anger or other destructive emotion, understand its causes, see it as baseless and unnecessary, and yet
despite all that it still has you, then what? Depending on how
thoroughly involved you are, you may be able to turn your attention away, toward something else. One potentially powerful place, if you have a prayer practice, is to turn to prayer, as
deeply, strongly, and genuinely as you can. At that time, rather
than ask for relief, we offer our love for the higher. Opening toward the Divine, with intention and heart, can transform your
state of difficulty into a state of grace. As a byproduct, prayer
releases the energy of the difficult emotion to feed your soul
instead of sapping it.

Another source of help in an emotional storm can come
from remembering the purpose of our life, remembering our
spiritual path. Destructive emotions are so called precisely because they destroy, at least temporarily, our spiritual possibilities. These emotional upheavals burn our energy and entice us
into attitudes and actions that increase our egoism, our sense of
separateness. Remembering that all this flows in the opposite

direction to where we wish to go can help us do damage control, conserve our rupturing energies, and shift our sights toward the path of purification. Every time we fall into some dark state that causes our inner work to vanish, we get up and start again, sooner rather than later.

And what if even that does not help? You are left bereft. Seeing and inwardly admitting to your enslavement, your powerlessness in the face of your emotional state, can empty you, can breach a hole in the darkness of your ego. Your heart and soul lie in ruins. Such emptiness cleanses your heart. Indeed, this emotional emptiness can lead us toward true spiritual emptiness, toward the inner need and openness that relates us to the Ultimate Source of All. The higher can only enter our emptiness, not our fullness. If our need is strong, and if we can orient that need toward the Sacred, the Response will surely come.

The challenge of emotions is not one of taming or controlling them. We need our emotional engine to be strong and vibrant. Our problem arises from our fractured nature. Our emotions, our mind, our body, and our spirit all push or pull us in different directions. The spiritual challenge calls us to integrate our heart into our whole being. Within that wholeness, all our parts find transformation. Then our true consciousness emerges, not identifying with our painful emotions, letting them pass through without singeing us or our neighbors. Clear seeing of our emotional dramas and traumas in action, extricates our sense of self from our narrowly-defined, self-centered emotional pseudo-life and brings us to a wider consciousness. By integrating our emotions into our wholeness, by not identifying or collapsing our sense of self into our emotions, we can rest in the freedom of consciousness and open toward the higher emotions, toward the source of love. Furthermore, the whole of our inner work, all rightly conducted spiritual practice contributes toward freeing us, which, in part, means loosening the grip of our difficult emotions. So by working at meditation, prayer, presence, kindness and the rest, we naturally lighten our emotional burden.

Fear

Fear! The very word frightens us. We all have memories of great or even abject fear. Yet more than we may realize, less intense, less immediate fears and anxieties run our day-to-day lives, both individually and collectively. Low grade, unrecognized post traumatic stress deriving from horrific events in our personal or national life can affect us for many years or even generations. A mild form of this also can result from witnessing violent pseudo events like movies. Our news media specialize in tragic stories because they connect powerfully with our inherent fears and capture our attention. Perversely, such images and stories also feed our existing fears and create new fears. So... we lock our doors, avoid strangers, limit our travels, curtail civil liberties, withhold our generosity, see other people as objects, buy guns and sometimes even use them. Collectively, we formulate policies of lifetime incarceration and preemptive strikes. The more money and attention we spend on security, the less secure we feel.

In point of painful fact, there is no security, there can be no security. The world, from its most basic level of quantum mechanics up to and beyond our human scale, will always be inherently, irretrievably subject to decay and uncertainty. This truth was taught by the Buddha and rediscovered by the great physicist Werner Heisenberg. Nevertheless, while physical death is inevitable, fear need not be. Indeed, through the spiritual path we move toward the deathless, beyond time and dissolution.

More subtle fears, though, commonly lurk behind our habitual patterns of interacting with the world. Fear of rejection leads us to build emotional walls to block potentially close relationships. Fear of failure leads to passivity. Timidity, shyness, being overly ready to please, not voicing our opinions, not responding appropriately when we have been wronged, hiding our unattractive parts, phobias of all kinds, fear of fear — all these and more variations of fear in action cumulatively limit our possibilities, handcuffing us into worrying about and protecting our illusory self.

We can work to free ourselves inwardly. First, we look to understand how fear and its sibling, anxiety, affect us. This requires seeing fear in action in ourselves. But we avoid recognizing fear. When we are afraid, the fear consumes us and we have little energy for self awareness. Furthermore, we fear that seeing our own fear and anxiety will make them even more painful by showing us that the world and our own emotions are out of control and by clashing with our false self-image of fearlessness. We begin climbing out of this morass of fear by practicing fearlessness in regard to our own inner condition, to be willing to see what occurs in our mind and heart, come what may.

Gradually, this self-knowledge leads to confidence, to knowing the best and worst about ourselves and feeling free in front of all that. This works against our egoism, with its inflated self-image. As our ego loses its hard edge of defensiveness, we experience less fear about attacks on our image, we have less to defend. Our growing inner freedom enables us to live beyond many of our former fears.

While our fear of the death of our ego diminishes, fear of the death of our body is another matter entirely. Fear of death, if not obsessive, spurs us to accomplish more, to live more. Of course, this kind of fear remains necessary: our primal survival instinct of fight or flight protects us and keeps us out of harm's way. Our spiritual work does not and should not counteract that instinct: without a body we should find it difficult or impossible to pursue our inner work.

Fear of God's justice leads us to do the right thing. Knowing the infallibility and inevitability of higher justice makes us fear doing harm. The more sublime fear of God's majesty transforms into awe, reverence, and devotion.

As our practice deepens we begin to touch the timeless peace beyond all fear.

Greed

Greed drives us toward external objects, conquests, symbols, status, or money to fill a void within us: the emptiness of our egoism. This ego edifice we build, this grand construction of who we are, this false self-image, when pricked, shows its true colors. Look just beneath its surface and you see nothing there. We desperately try to assuage that insatiable emptiness in a futile attempt to mask our inner abyss with concrete material goods and symbols.

But that ego emptiness reflects the true emptiness inside us: the real void that opens to the depths through which the voice of God approaches us. Greed cannot console that void, nor even approach it. This points toward transforming our greed from grasping at external fulfillment to searching for inner fulfillment, the only real fulfillment, to open our channel to the depths, to a genuine love for those around us and for God.

But even here, the insidious temptation to grasp enters.

Spiritual greed runs after states and experiences, wants spiritual status so that one can brag or preen in front of others or to oneself. Of course, this is just another absurd, ego-centered distortion of true spirituality. We cannot extract wages from God, like a day laborer. We seek a simple life in the spirit for its own sake; love is its own reward. Only the depths of the spirit can fill our emptiness and offer true contentment, as greed transforms into active service for the benefit of our neighbor.

Loneliness, Neediness, and Vulnerability

Loneliness, neediness, and vulnerability all have their roots in our fundamental yearning for spiritual completion. These emotions emanate from the deficit at our core and present us with an uncomfortable glimpse of, and misplaced response to, our central problem: we live our lives cut off from other people, from the higher worlds, and from the Divine. We dwell in a world of separateness and incompleteness, looking outside ourselves to fill our hidden inner emptiness, to assuage our half-formed spirit. We look for relationships and outer security in the false belief that these will solve the problem. Though we always misinterpret and displace it to the outside, our true need is a sacred longing, drawing us into the depths of our being, toward the Divine. Only through spiritual completion can we satisfy this central hunger of human life, by coming into oneness with other people and with God.

Our practice then is to reinterpret into truth our feelings of loneliness, neediness, and vulnerability. When we notice such emotions arising in us, instead of pushing them away or desperately looking for someone to marry, we open to these feelings, look into them, and recognize their source in our spiritual need. We allow our loneliness, neediness, and vulnerability to feed our spiritual practice, by turning their outward orientation and their energy toward our inner work. Working diligently at spiritual practice fills that inner void, brings lasting satisfaction, and opens us to the higher. We let our need become a source of strength that helps drive our spiritual inner work.

We can grow closer to other people and more complete by recognizing our inner emptiness and letting the higher fill it. Then instead of others feeling our grasping for relationship and being repulsed thereby, they can feel our growing wholeness and love, and be drawn by those qualities. In this way we develop our relationships both with people and with the Divine.

Jealousy

Combining elements of egoism, greed, sex, instinct and fear, jealousy forms a potent and poisonous cocktail that drains our energy, enslaves our inner world, harms our relationship, causes suspicion and mistrust, and is sometimes based on a misinterpretation. Egoism's grasping and possessive attitude projects itself onto our mate, endeavoring to turn this other human being into "my" property, not to be shared. Powerful instincts jump into the fray by seeking to protect our prospects for transmitting genes. Furthermore, we fear our mate's infidelity could lead to the loss of the relationship, the abyss of loneliness, and the destruction of trust, loyalty, commitment, and our own self-worth. Given that suspicion reinterprets events and almost inevitably finds or creates hints that justify it, jealousy, like the rapid onset disease that it is, overtakes our heart and mind all too quickly, sometimes even burning out of control with disastrous consequences.

Yet jealousy directed at our "loved" one bears the seed of its own destruction, for jealousy kills love. Indeed, jealousy is a negative love in which we become completely identified with our own needs, desires, and demands. In the grip of jealousy, we entirely forget that the true nature of love is to give and not to demand, to consider the loved one before ourselves, to be united with our loved one, and to share in our loved one's joy, even when that joy involves a third person. This last, unconditional joy in the loved one's joy, is a true and hard measure of love. We can readily envision or even experience such love for a child, but in the context of two lovers it is rare. Yet we can hold in our imagination this potential of unconditional joy in our loved one's joy, and consider it as a sign of the perfection of love. Jealousy, by contrast then, shows us how far we have to go.

To work with jealousy we need, as always with the difficult emotions, to recognize it for what it is, as it occurs. Then we see its various manifestations in body, heart, and thought. This presents us with the opportunity to not identify with it, to not believe the thought "I am jealous," but rather just to see it as a process in our body-heart-mind. We can also perform reality checks to see if the events that sparked the jealousy are truly grounds for alarm, or are they simply exuberant friendliness, for example.

And, finally, what if the reality checks turn out as we feared and our "loved" one actually is moving toward another. Do we fall into depression and anger, desperation and shock? Perhaps we try to remedy any problems in our relationship. And what if that fails? This unwelcome event presents a difficult opportunity. We may open to the inner sacrifice of our self-interest, letting go of the jealousy and seeking our heart of unconditional love. Perhaps you think this is only for the saint, but what is the goal of the spiritual path if not to become that? The relationship may die and we will mourn it. But in the process, our being can grow.

Envy

Things or qualities that we value can easily become sources of envy, dividing us from others who have them to a greater degree than we do. Envy arises from identifying with a thing or quality, or rather with our desire for that thing or quality. Envy closes our world down, narrowing our perceptions to the sliver of life that concerns the object we feel we lack and that others have.

To envy someone for their wealth, charisma, beauty, fame, attainment, or other quality can cause several things to happen. If I actually know the person, an impenetrable barrier may descend between us as I inwardly push them away or withdraw from them. I cannot relate just as person-to-person. I look for faults in them or avoid them or even become obsequious toward them, while inwardly squirming. They become my enemy, a symbol of my failure or lack. If I do not know the person, then the envy may simply color my perception of them and the world. Either way, my mind makes excuses, trying to convince myself that I am not really a loser, that my lack does not matter, and then it proceeds to dwell on my inadequacy. An unhealthy form of self-doubt may descend on me.

Envy may lead us to its close cousin: competition. That may not be all bad, since competition is part of nature's way (the other part being cooperation). Competition might lead me to achieve more than I would otherwise. But if I stake my self-worth on the competition, on overcoming my lack by filling it, on surpassing those I envy, then I adopt a precarious position indeed. My assessment of my life then depends on comparison with others. I can never come to real peace because there is always someone who has or is more.

As the dominant values of our time our culture enshrines the competition to acquire more things and to have a more beautiful body. Our educational system teaches skills for external success, as it should. But where are our schools of wisdom. Our modern media forms a prodigious, mesmerizing machinery geared toward disseminating envy-inducing images. In response we squander our souls by chasing an ever-widening array of things we do not need. But no one has it all, leaving all to envy those who have more. So the economic forces of modern culture conspire to promote the envy on which it is based.

Of course envy also afflicts spiritual circles, where we vie for positions of leadership and tokens of respect. The extent to which envy drives our spiritual work is the extent to which that work goes awry.

It is not so easy to escape from this culture of envy, so deeply ingrained in the fabric of our social environment and the patterns of our personality. Indeed, we might ask: why should we escape? Because envy keeps our focus and our energies turned toward the external and ephemeral, while we neglect eternal values.

If you look back on your life, you might find that the highlights have nothing to do with the things that envy drives you toward. If you look forward toward your future, you may want to stop wasting time and energy on envy and all its baggage. If you look to the present, you may see how envy divides you from others, saps your being, and diminishes your presence.

Our hope lies in the clear seeing that loosens our bonds. Toward that, we work to see how envy operates within us. When we notice one of its many manifestations, we take a long, full view.

Shame

Shame, though never welcome, does manifest in both positive and negative ways. Most of us in this twenty-first century civilization have too little of the positive type of shame and too much of the negative.

The most important beneficial role of shame occurs when it indicates to us that we have acted wrongly. Such shame serves as a channel whereby our conscience, which represents the hidden, higher layers within us, communicates with our ordinary mind. When we feel ashamed of what we have done, and if we face that feeling, we can learn to act more in accord with human dignity and love. This shame, if we do not turn away from it, directly feeds our personal evolution in wisdom and compassion. All too often, though, we squash such feelings of shame and continue with our wrong-headed behavior.

When we feel ashamed of something that is not a result of our own actions, it generally has a negative, debilitating effect on us. If I am ashamed or embarrassed by some aspect of my body, which I genetically inherited or which resulted from accident or illness, then I divide myself, not accepting a part of my makeup. This destroys my possibilities for wholeness. The same holds if I am ashamed of someone in my family, or of my job or lack thereof, or of my lack of wealth, genius, talent, or fame. In a civilization that perversely defines self-worth in terms of net worth and success in terms of wealth, negative shame drives us to waste too much energy in pursuit of the non-essential.

Another source of negative shame lies in the multitude of

destructive, self-centered, greedy, lustful, hateful, and other unbecoming impulses that vie for control of our hearts and minds. Just seeing these in ourselves can make us ashamed. But as long as we do not act on such lower impulses, we have no cause to be ashamed, for they are part of our common human heritage, at least in its present condition. Feeling ashamed of our own harmful impulses only feeds them. We would do better to just accept their presence, not act on them, and move on.

Sometimes the positive and negative kinds of shame mix. If I feel ashamed by my lack of talent, some of it may be due to my shame at not having applied myself in a more disciplined way. From this I may learn to work harder. If instead, the shame just goes into self-loathing, I am even worse off than simply being untalented.

So to turn shame into a help on our path, we need to look into ourselves and see the causes and results of our shame.

Low Self-Esteem

Everyone has limitations. But too many of us take our limitations to heart in self- directed anger, in self-disgust, in revolt against our own nature, and in wanting to have different personal characteristics. But the true transformation sought in spiritual practice is not about overcoming ordinary limitations. Rather, it leads to freedom from all limitation. On their level, our limitations remain, but we can be free nevertheless and not caught by them. When not in that state of freedom, we sometimes fall into self-denigrating attitudes, which burden us with their own unnecessary limitations.

The sources of low self-esteem generally revolve around the questions of what or who is being esteemed and who is doing the esteeming. Low self-esteem's overly negative view of oneself and the self-doubt it engenders are just one side of the coin of egoism. The usual alternative side presents an overly inflated view of oneself, as in arrogance, self-important pride, and misplaced self-assurance. The therapeutic approach toward low self-esteem may involve seeing the negative messages we received in childhood and healing their effects. In deeply rooted or severe cases, therapy may be the only way to overcome problems with self-esteem.

But another effective approach, if we can bring ourselves to it, consists of clearly seeing our strengths and weaknesses without taking them as indicative of our true worth, accepting ourselves as we are, while finding ways to compensate for our limitations, and always working to improve. Spiritual practice leads to greater awareness both outwardly and inwardly, including what can be a rather stark awareness of our personal shortcomings. At that point, care must be taken to foster an atmosphere of sober acceptance of ourselves, whatever we may find. Putting ourselves down only creates new obstacles to our inner work. Truth we need to see. But we need not embark on self-flagellation, nor dwell on our weaknesses. The spiritual path need not and should not exacerbate low self-esteem. In fact, the deeper our inner work goes, the more we discover something inside ourselves truly worthy of the highest possible esteem. That something turns out to be who we really are, our unique sacred core, equal in value to everyone else, equally a particle of the Divine.

Low self-esteem should not be confused with the spiritual state of emptiness. In the former our ego is front and center, beating up on itself. But in real emptiness, our ego vanishes, or at least recedes into the background. Then self-esteem, or the lack thereof, ceases to be an issue, because our ordinary self and the esteem it has or does not have for itself, make way for our authentic Self, which through emptiness embraces all.

In at least two ways low self-esteem blocks our path. It causes us to be preoccupied with our illusory self and it limits our vision of our true possibilities. For example, how can we pray with heart, if we are thinking only of ourselves or if we doubt our potential for contact with the Divine? Look at your attitudes toward yourself. Does low self-esteem undermine your progress, inwardly in your spiritual work and/or outwardly in your engagement with life?

Self-Efficacy in Spirituality

Psychologists define perceived self-efficacy "as people's beliefs about their capabilities to produce designated levels of performance that exercise influence over events that affect their lives."[7] The ultimate influence we seek derives from our ability to establish a vibrant, living connection with the Divine. In this most creative and subtle of human endeavors our beliefs about our personal potential, our perceived self-efficacy, largely determine the outcome. The spiritual path involves long perseverance of practice in the face of difficulties such as dry spells lacking progress or results, setbacks and failures, an unsupportive or even hostile social environment, doubts about the path and its practices, lack of time or energy to devote to our inner work, competing demands, interests, fears, distractions, and so on. To meet and overcome all these formidable obstacles, to redouble our efforts when these stubborn barriers descend on us, we need a very strong sense of spiritual self-efficacy, a confidence in ourselves and our path toward the Divine. Where can this come from?

First, our spiritual practice inevitably produces positive results even at the outset. Perhaps we feel more relaxed after a sitting meditation, or more at peace after prayer, or more centered when we practice presence. As we continue on the path, these and other experiences deepen and prove that we can in fact practice effectively. Confidence grows.

Second, the positive examples of other people engaged in spiritual practice, be they saints, teachers, peers, or friends, provide a convincing view of the possibilities of progress along the way toward the Divine and even of achievement of the goal. The saints and teachers show us the higher potentials and provide guidance, if not in person then through reading their words. But particularly the changes in the lives of our peers and friends lead us to realize "If they can find some measure of happiness, meaning, fulfillment and purpose, so can I." Confidence grows.

Third, the support of spiritual friends or of a spiritual community helps carry us past our obstacles to inner work. When we're down, they raise us up by their example and by their direct encouragement. When we're up, they help us surpass our former limits. Confidence grows.

Fourth, as we continue our spiritual practice, our increasing depth of experience, our more subtle understanding, our more centered presence, our more robust being, all render us able to deal with the inevitable downward fluctuations in energy and commitment to the path. We enter a steadiness of practice come what may. Confidence grows.

Lastly we have the unseen and continuous action of the Divine in the hidden recesses of our soul. This is the realm of faith and the source of spiritual longing. Even as we remain unaware of it, the sacred action in our core draws us forward despite ourselves. Confidence grows.

We ask ourselves: Do I believe in myself, in my ability do

all that's necessary to see my path through to completion? We examine our own degree of spiritual self-efficacy and, if necessary, take the appropriate steps to enhance it.

Equanimity

You hear some bad news. Immediately your heart pounds, your breath tightens, your face frowns. You hear some good news. Your heart jumps, your face smiles. In both cases, your thoughts swirl and you lose your center. You see something disgusting, you feel pain, you notice a horrible thought, or you see your favorite, delectable treat, and you lose your center, rushing toward or fleeing from what you have encountered. All this describes our ordinary mode of pre-programmed, automated, conditioned, and contingent living.

In Buddhism, Sufism, and Kabbalah, equanimity appears as a precursor to and expression of enlightenment, as a wonderful and necessary quality of mind and heart. The spacious mind-heart leaves room for all the difficulties and attractions of life, for everything wanted and unwanted. Within the warmth of this vast inner space, equanimity permits us to live freely, allowing everything to have its place without having us, without taking us. In equanimity, we live in the world of presence, neither fettered nor buffeted by the inevitable turmoil of life.

But equanimity does not build a spiritual ivory tower, insulated from all the cares and woes of living. Equanimity does not mean indifference. On the contrary, equanimity increases our compassion and enables our care to penetrate below the surface of life. While working vigorously toward our goals, while fulfilling our responsibilities for service, equanimity provides a safe harbor, the security of inner peace, the calm in the center of the storm.

As we enter difficult situations, or indeed any situation which we would rather avoid, equanimity enables us to meet life with aplomb. This inner peace and evenness of spirit lets us bring our best to life without retreating or succumbing to inner turmoil as a reflection of the outer chaos.

To work toward equanimity, we let go of attachments. In this we distinguish the normalcy of caring and loving from the slavery of being bound and chained by identification and clinging. The latter may, at any moment, drag us out of presence and down into the world of reactions. Unwelcome events do send ripples across the calm ocean of equanimity, ripples informing us of the need to respond. But it is precisely the quality of equanimity that helps us respond effectively instead of reactively.

By definition, everything in time eventually ends. Our bodies and those of all we love grow ill, age, and inevitably die. All our material possessions fall prey to time. Our raging emotions of the moment and the situations which give rise to them are entirely forgotten in a week or two. Equanimity, however, opens us to the timeless, the deathless. Indeed, equanimity develops through our contact with that part of our soul that resides in the timeless. This peace from the worlds beyond time, embraces the world in time.

Opinions

At first glance we might expect a discussion of opinions to belong to Chapter 4: Mind, rather than here in Chapter 3: Heart. True it is that opinions reside primarily in our thoughts, but our attachment to our opinions lies primarily in our feelings. Our spiritual work with regard to opinions involves seeing and letting go of our attachments to them. Does this mean giving up our opinions? No. A person devoid of opinions would be bland, hardly alive, and lacking energy. We naturally form opinions in response to the riches of our life experience. Our opinions guide us in the waters of life. We need our views. On our path, having opinions is not an obstacle. Being opinionated is.

Being opinionated means identifying with our views. "Here's what I think, and if you disagree, then you are plainly wrong ..." We believe so fervently in our opinions that we become them. "I am a liberal." "I'm a conservative." Our ego, or false-self, forms around our opinions. One telltale sign: we become angry or frustrated when someone disagrees with us. The degree of our anger or frustration reveals the degree of our attachment and identification.

So our problem boils down to this: to have opinions, even to take a stand and defend our position in a discussion or debate, but without allowing our opinions to own us. This middle path requires a perceptive and intelligent approach: having our opinions without them having us. The key is the anger or frustration that signals our attachment to a challenged opinion. We work to see this signal, in a clear, open, and self-accepting manner, without reacting against the anger and frustration, without putting ourselves down for being opinionated. The simple act of becoming conscious of our attachments to opinions gradually liberates us from their grip, leaving us freer to enjoy and elaborate our opinions, relishing debates, without the burden of self-centeredness. As the Third Patriarch of Zen put it: "Do not seek the Truth, only cease to cherish opinions."

Preferences

Someone is speaking to me. A person I don't like. He talks too much. Inside I squirm. Outside I appear attentive and smile. I even nod or grunt agreement occasionally, all the while looking for a graceful and quick, but to my chagrin, nonexistent exit. I am lost in my antipathy to the situation. Anger and resentment rear their heads in me. My desire to reject being here challenges me. I feel stuck in this moment, in this place...

Or I am caught in a traffic jam, frustrated at the interminable delay. Or the bakery, to my disappointment, has sold out of my favorite pastry. Or the drain suddenly clogs and I must clear it somehow and my plans for the next hour or two must be suspended — unhappily. Or I finally get a slice of that cake and as I greedily eat a second slice my belly already begins to protest.

Like opinions, we need our preferences to live a normal, full life. Delicious food is to be relished and appreciated. And like opinions, our freedom may be measured in part by the degree to which we do not cling to our preferences.

Can we relax when held up in traffic? Or do our preferences drive us? Since no one can control his or her life so completely as to never experience an unwanted situation, liberation lies in the direction of freedom in front of preferences. Not freedom from preferences. That would make us and life dull indeed. But rather, we seek the ability to not be driven by preferences when unavoidable situations run counter to them, to not lose ourselves in the inevitable frustration.

If you can be free in the distasteful and awkward moments, then a natural joy can infuse your life and your heart of kindness can open to your neighbor, warts and all.

Art

Over a century ago, the inhabitants of Florence, Italy erected a gallery to house and protect a particular statue: Michelangelo's David. In this seventeen-foot tall work of white marble, the people of Florence could catch a glimpse of the Greatness. To be in the presence of this David, raises one's own stature. The petty in us falls aside as we gaze upon the beautiful representation of David, sling and stone at the ready, about to enter the decisive battle against Goliath, competent, determined and courageous, yet with a furrowed brow of concern at the enormity and uncertainty of the task before him. The David in our own heart reaches toward that same Greatness, toward the destiny that is ours alone to risk and to create.

Master artists like Michelangelo, Bach, Beethoven, Brancusi, Rothko and others create works that uniquely embody intimations of the higher worlds and bestow the timeless on the time-bound. Our role in the presence of such art is to drop beneath the surface, both our own and that of the artwork, to enter that enduring quality of spirit that descends from the Source of all. The essence of great art lies beyond our thoughts about it and beyond our emotional responses to it. If we can listen to the music or view the painting from our own inner stillness, it may usher us into contact with the infinite stillness underlying all. Then, along with the artist, we share the touch of the Ineffable, which the finest art seeks to communicate. Great art occupies a very special place in our world, as a bridge to what lies beyond the creative.

Ordinary art, music, and literature, like the art that some of us as amateurs produce, has its source in the creative force. As such, the artistic endeavor brings us into contact with a profound aspect of ourselves, beyond our self-centered concerns, beyond our thoughts and emotions and into a real world, an unbounded world of freedom. When we allow the creative to flow in us, mingling with the artistic skills we bring to the table, we taste our own possibilities of being, action, and service. Entering the artistic struggle, shaping the materials according to the unknown image taking birth though us, we sometimes find a direct and utter satisfaction in the process. Meaningful work, such as creating art, can make our life meaningful, bring new order to the world, and fulfill our intended role.

Tolerance

All of us who deem ourselves "good" people, consider ourselves to be tolerant. Scratch a little below the surface, however, and we may discover less tolerance than we had imagined. Perhaps our version of tolerance involves outwardly saying nothing, while inwardly we recoil or grit our teeth and fume. Tolerance means allowing, both inwardly and outwardly, others to be themselves, to be different from us, to have beliefs and practices that conflict with our own. We often hear calls for tolerance. Usually, though, it takes the form of one person exhorting another to be more tolerant, perhaps justifiably. In the spiritual path, we look first to put our own house in order.

Intolerance manifests our egoism, our self-centeredness. So reducing our own intolerance lightens our spiritual burden and removes inner obstacles to our path. As with all issues of how we relate to people, we work from the inside out, beginning with ourselves, then our family and loved ones, then others toward whom we are neutral, and finally those toward whom we bear antipathy. And as with all sources of inner disharmony, the healing of intolerance comes gradually through clear seeing. We cannot shed intolerant attitudes without effective preparation, which consists of noticing intolerance operating in us.

We begin with ourselves, with our own "warts." To what extent can I tolerate my own limitations of mind, emotion, and body? Tolerance toward myself does not prevent me from trying to improve. But some things cannot be improved, for example, the basic structure and limitations of my body. As long as I do not accept my unchangeable aspects, I will not accept other people. Certain aspects of myself may be amenable to change, but is it really worth the time and effort to change them? The answer varies. Even with those aspects that can and should be changed, an attitude of tolerance makes the changes more possible. Intolerance simply adds another layer to the problem, a layer that perversely serves to prevent any change in the thing I cannot tolerate in myself. For example, if I need to lose weight and have an attitude of disgust toward my overweight body, the disgust itself may drive me to eat more than necessary. If I can truly tolerate, accept, and embrace the whole of myself, I may then grow more tolerant of others.

To what extent do we give space to, do we truly tolerate our family and loved ones? Can we let our children be themselves and train them properly, while accepting their differences with us? Can we let our spouse be himself or herself, without pushing a program of reform onto them?

Intolerance breeds hatred and violence. Milder forms merely waste our precious energies and keep us mired in its poison. Giving up an intolerant attitude toward others is actually a great gift to ourselves. Intolerance toward individuals or groups, whether of another religion or race, or just someone who has bad manners, saps our spiritual strength. But we cannot simply decide to be tolerant of others. We need to see intolerance whenever it rears its head in us. See it clearly. See its effects on us. See that it is just a feeling or thought passing through, a passing attitude. See that I am more than this ego-centered rejection, this visitor to my consciousness. See, however, how it claims to be me, how it says within me: "I hate ..." See how it says "I," when it is not I, but merely an intolerant attitude pretending to speak for the whole of me.

Why does tolerance matter to our spiritual path? Simply put, one cannot enter heaven while harboring venomous and intolerant attitudes. "Blessed are the pure in heart, for they shall see God." This describes the structure of the higher world: purity of heart is a necessary condition for entry. Whether from individual egoism or borrowed from a group egoism, intolerance blocks the spirit.

Distance and Intimacy

Our inner distance from people continually degrades the quality of our relationships. If I am distracted or preoccupied when I speak with someone, then only a low level exchange is possible. Dwelling on thoughts of what happened earlier, anxieties about what may happen later, or inwardly preparing my response to what they are saying — all this takes me away from the sacred simplicity of listening, speaking, and relating.

If I am distant from myself, not in contact with my body, not really in my body, not in touch with my thoughts and emotions, then I will also be distant from others. But if I am too self-involved, too concerned with my own world, with the events in my life, with what I think and feel, with my physical and mental health, with my interests and opinions, problems and passions, with maintaining my position, and so on, then no room remains for anyone else. If I habitually attempt to present a certain image of myself to the world, then this mask forms an impenetrable barrier between myself and others. If I feel above or below others, different or indifferent, then I live inwardly apart. If I impose demands and expectations on others, I drive a wedge between us. If I am afraid of vulnerability, I run to escape closeness. In all these circumstances, I remain distant, hidden within the walls of my own personal and fractured space.

We crave and also fear intimacy with others. We crave it because intimacy is a basic human need, like food and shelter. Because of the sacred core within us all, closeness to others means closeness the great Self we all share, closeness to the Divine. That is why we experience the feeling of being at home when in intimate relationship, because in that shared space we enter our true spiritual home.

Yet we also fear dropping those walls that both define us and separate us. Without our boundaries, who are we? Do we disappear? The truth is we become more fully ourselves. At first we risk vulnerability in opening our heart to others. But as we grow more whole, the neediness that underpins vulnerability begins to heal. We learn to trust our wholeness. From that we can more readily extend ourselves to merge with others into a greater wholeness.

Intimacy need not be limited to the emotional and physical intimacy of lovers. Emotional intimacy characterizes real friendship. We care about our friends. We set aside our mask and lower our barriers in their presence. Even with acquaintances and total strangers, we can offer a degree of intimacy by meeting them openly. The fleeting, unlikely-to-be-repeated encounter can be an exchange of kind-heartedness.

Despite the record of saintly monks and realized hermits, genuine and effective spiritual work need not be a solitary endeavor. Our relationships with other people reflect, influence, and form an important component of our spiritual life. We share our inner work in spiritual community and find invaluable help there.

But the spirituality of relationship goes well beyond formal prayer or meditation with others. As the great Zen Master Dogen put it, "to be enlightened is to be intimate with all things." To be able meet another human being directly and on equal terms, without our mask, without hiding behind our image, without being so totally enmeshed in our personal world, without being lost in habitual patterns of interaction, without barriers, without demands and expectations, with a presence and an openness of heart that embraces us both, is to be able to meet the simple truth of this unique moment. And that simple truth leads step-by-step toward love and the Divine.

We can work to close the gap between ourselves and others. First and foremost we look to see whether and how distant we are from the people around us. Seeing the distance, we look for its source in us, for the flavor of the barrier. That awareness, repeatedly applied, gradually dissolves our inner barriers and brings us toward the intimacy that makes us whole.

Kindness

The biblical maxim "love your neighbor as yourself" sets a very high goal for our human relationships. Sometimes, for a moment, we may love our neighbor, but as a way of life, love eludes us. We can, though, work to approach love through its practical manifestation: kindness.

Simple, unassuming kindness toward the people and the life around us brings both immediate and lasting rewards. As with any thoroughly right action, acts of kindness bring a special satisfaction to us and a ray of light into the world. Kindness flows naturally from our hearts: we need only lift the veils that hide and block it.

First and foremost, our ordinary self-centeredness precludes true kindness. As long as we measure everything in life in terms of our own needs, wants, and antipathies, as long as we regard other people as objects like pieces of furniture, we leave no room for kindness. We may consider certain people undeserving of our kindness. It may even seem stupid to us to be kind, to give something of ourselves freely for no visible reward. Where is the profit in that? Not seeing the real answer, we may even be unkind or at best neutral toward our neighbor.

But there is a profit in kindness, even for our self-interest, our true self-interest. Being kind removes us from the thrall of egoism, at least temporarily, and ushers us into a more connected and natural world. If we could but see that acts of kindness benefit our own being as much as the recipient of our kindness, our resistance would melt away and we would seek opportunities to be kind. In the meantime, the most powerful medicine for hard-heartedness derives from seeing our own indifference, our own unkindness in actual life events, actions, and attitudes.

Living nearly all the time in the world of pre-programmed actions and reactions, we rarely actually notice anything, including opportunities for kindness. Openings for kindness usually do not appear on our radar, as our habits and conditioning block their perception. Not present to occasions for potential kindness, we sleep walk right past them. As an antidote, we can diligently practice the methods for awakening, for presence, for being fully in this moment. True presence unveils our basic kindness and shows us appropriate venues for its expression.

When our willingness to be kind does break through and our awareness reveals opportunities, difficult questions naturally arise. What constitutes kindness? What is the most appropriate and effective action in a given situation? Most of us have had experiences in which we thought we were being kind, only to have it all backfire because we did or said the wrong thing. We need wisdom to guide our actions. Good intentions alone can lead to misguided actions. Giving the addict money, may only prolong the addiction. Offering our opinions, when the more appropriate stance is to just listen, can easily spoil the moment. Conversely, remaining silent when we should speak truly can be a disservice. Intruding when we should do nothing, clumsily aggravates the situation. To act appropriately and effectively, we need bring all our powers to bear, our intelligence and experience, our insight into the person and the circumstances, our kind attitude, the humility of knowing our limitations, and our developing inner eye for the truth.

We can, however, readily practice kindness in certain simple situations that do not call for deep wisdom. Courtesy is a common and underrated form of kindness, whether in holding a door for a stranger or in driving. Indeed, the practice of kindness while driving can prove a very fruitful field, because it arouses our resistance to giving way, to being magnanimous, to letting the other guy win even when he's rude and greedy.

Work on kindness serves to purify and transform our hearts. Kindness operates directly against self-centeredness, though it can be arrogated by egoism: being kind while preening in an inward mirror. "That was kind of me. I'm such a kind and wonderful person." If we look carefully, though, we find that mirror empty: no separation from our neighbor. The best kindness occurs when we serve another without reflecting that we are performing an act of kindness and without seeking or expecting gratitude in return. This may be a distant goal, so we begin where we are. Far better to take credit for kindness, than to succumb to unkindness or wallow in indifference.

Rightly conducted spiritual practice inevitably leads to the manifestation of more kindness. Outward kindness may even be considered as one measure of a person's spiritual station. Conversely, the practice of kindness, toward both friend and stranger, helps enormously in that most essential task of the spiritual path: the purification of heart and motivation. So we remember to open our hearts and actions toward others both as an expression of the Great Heart of the World and as a method to cleanse our soul. We remember to do this until the day arrives when kindness becomes our nature.

Generosity

It is no accident that every religion places such great emphasis on the virtue of generosity. Not only does generosity enable society to work more smoothly, but it also has a profound spiritual effect on both the giver and the receiver. In practicing generosity with intelligence and openness of heart, we draw closer to the truth of oneness and love, while serving life and the Divine. Acts of generosity manifest that deeper reality wherein we are not separate. In helping our neighbor, we also serve our own eternal welfare by purifying our will. A Sufi teaching enjoins the seeker to help people, to "be their shade in the sun, their cloak in the cold, and their bread in time of famine."[8]

With most of us, our motivations are rarely 100% pure. Self-seeking insinuates itself even when we give. Nevertheless, we practice generosity now, not waiting for that ultimate stage of enlightenment where egoism vanishes permanently. Generosity requires us to see beyond ourselves. It diminishes our self-centered egoism, even when our ego tries to co-opt and take credit for our generosity, attempting to inflate itself thereby. True generosity, by definition, involves giving to others beyond what is required of us, and that outstrips any self-centered motives we might harbor in the process. Ego wants to take and to hold, not to give. But generosity moves against ego, helps expose its illusory nature, decreases its hold on us, and lowers the barriers separating us from others. The more one practices generosity, the more selfless it becomes.

One inner meaning of tithing is to give of our very substance, of what we are, to transfer our merit to those in difficulty. To a person in need, we always have the possibility of responding with a wholehearted wish for their welfare and a prayer from the depth of our being. Indeed, prayer for the benefit of others is a very important form of generosity. The stronger and deeper the prayer, the more it can help. Generosity also lives in the simple giving of our time and attention to others, for example by listening from a place of stillness, compassion, and appreciation.

While giving outward, material help is the time-honored form of generosity, other forms also call to us. For example, our inner work, our transformation of energies, our doing the right thing — all serve the higher world and society.

As always, the spiritual path depends on awareness, not only of the other person, to see what they need, but also of ourselves. We can look inwardly before, during, and after acts of generosity, to see ourselves more clearly, to step toward greater freedom. What feelings, thoughts, and impulses accompany our consideration and performance of acts of generosity? In this seeing, we measure our generosity against the aim of simple, compassionate giving without expectation of reward or recogni-

HEART

tion, the aim of doing right by others because that's what we do.

No discussion of generosity would be complete without gratitude for the loving generosity of the Divine. From the beauty and life-giving quality of Nature to the hidden, inner help that enables our spiritual work, the sacred higher continually bestows on us, personally and collectively, Its bounty of love, energies, and wisdom. To the extent we are prepared to receive it, this outpouring from the timeless Source feeds us heart and soul, and points our personal way toward transformation and service. Thank You.

Finally, in receiving generosity we incur an obligation to live up to our highest ideals, to be worthy of all we have been given.

Patience

Patience! How we hate the unexpected delay, meeting such events, or non-events, with a sinking heart and a desperation to escape. We fall totally under the domination of time, allowing the clock to drive us, rather than calmly living in the richness of every moment. We fret and worry about "wasting" time in line, in a traffic jam, or in some other unwanted situation, but the worrying itself wastes the time. We hurry to save time, but the hurrying itself kills our time. Patience, on the other hand, enriches time, allowing us to breathe, appreciate our surroundings, and open to the inner depths.

Patience both emanates from and increases a calm, steady will. And calm builds presence. And presence builds soul. The practice of patience directly challenges our egoism and identifications. When we find ourselves delayed or our desires thwarted, the act of deliberately seeking a peaceful calm exposes our attachments, as they dash themselves against our intention to be wholly here and now. Thus, the practice of patience brings us right to the front lines of the work to release the core entanglements that block our way. Here you are, directly confronting your own impatience, whose source lies in your illusory "self." Instant by impatient instant, you let go of your insistent, time-bound, self-centered, in-your-face urges and seek to wait in peace and presence. Of course, patience does not preclude moving calmly but quickly when necessary.

Time passes inevitably and everything in the material world changes. Our bodies grow old and eventually wear out. But the practice of patience opens us directly into this moment with all its depth. The more we can relax and let go of all that drags us into slavery to time, the more we live in this moment, the more we live in all our moments, and the more we live our life. Hurry, worry, and impatience eviscerate this moment, depriving us of what really matters, stealing our precious time. But patience overcomes the forces drawing us into the shallows of a future that does not yet exist and lets us be in the reality of here and now instead.

Boredom and resignation entice us as false substitutes for patience. We grudgingly stay or feel trapped in an unwanted state of affairs. Or we hurry through a task we find boring or distasteful. We lapse into ennui, feeling slightly self-satisfied about how good we are to stay with the undesirable event. Yet in boredom and resignation we do not really accept the situation. Patience does not reject our life in that way. The patient heart opens to greet each moment in full awareness.

The unpleasant behaviors of other people often cause us to be impatient with them. We lose ourselves in emotional reactions rather than patiently being with the other person. In this context, patience means accepting the other person, warts and all. This does not preclude taking measured, tactful action to point out the person's shortcomings, but that depends on the situation and on our relationship with them, and is usually inappropriate. A much more effective approach lies in working toward our own transformation and taking other people as they are.

On the flip side, our own shortcomings and difficult emotions often cause us to be impatient with ourselves. Again, we lose ourselves in this second layer of impatient reactivity, rather than patiently being ourselves and allowing the storm to pass. This calls for self-acceptance. On a deeper level, our spiritual practice leads us to see that there is no "self" that has shortcomings or does not accept those shortcomings. Then the whole basis for impatience with "our" problems weakens.

Impatience can become a red flag for us, awakening us to let go, to practice patience, and to be present. When you see yourself in a fit of impatience, look for that peaceful calm within and move with an easy heart. It takes will to develop patience and being to live in it.

Forgiveness

"And forgive us our trespasses, as we forgive those who trespass against us."[9]

To forgive someone who has wronged us runs directly counter to our egoistic impulses and tears at the very fabric of who we think we are. In true forgiving, even if reluctantly, we drop a barrier separating us from the other. Grudges arise out of and feed our self-centeredness, while dehumanizing the vilified other. The net result of keeping accounts against people is to make ourselves less than we might be. But grudges, outrage, and their lightweight cousin, blame, emanate from the core of our illusory egoism, proving tenacious and formidable obstacles to inner freedom.

We can begin the work of forgiveness by examining our anger and disgust with ourselves for our own defects and past mistakes. Slowly we may see that this ingrown attitude of self-disappointment saps our energy through emotional self-thrashing. All this comes from the egoistic proposition that we are or could be or should be perfect. To forgive ourselves means to accept our failings. This act of self-generosity brings greater wholeness and integrity to our inner life.

But some of our misdeeds may have harmed other people. For these, we cannot really forgive ourselves until we have made whatever efforts are feasible to make amends, to repay, to ask for forgiveness. When no such efforts are feasible, or if they fail, closing these accounts may involve repentance and asking God to forgive us. If our contrition is sincere, eventually release will come.

Another stage involves forgiving those who have wronged us. The fleeting misdeeds of impersonal, rude, uncivil, negligent, or incompetent behavior form the first field for the practice of forgiving others. Personally intended offenses, however, create more powerful affronts to our self-centeredness. Our reactions of resentment and animosity can even subordinate our entire inner life for far too long.

Perhaps most difficult to forgive are transgressions against those whom we love. We cannot forgive on behalf of our loved one. Furthermore, such anger may not be egoistic, but well-justified in its morality.

Nevertheless, all blame, rancor and animosity against the

wrongdoers serve primarily to keep us inwardly enslaved to bitterness. So despite the seemingly insurmountable difficulty, we seek to let go our grievance, to forgive, to regain our respect for the humanity of the other. At first perhaps we can only forgive partially, but as we follow the painful practice of letting go our grievances, we may eventually forgive more completely and find our heart's release.

The practice of forgiveness, though, does not imply passivity or non-violence in the face of evil. The greatest kindness to a murderer is to stop him from murdering again, but we need not hate him in the process. Potential future victims also deserve active protection. The saddest of commentaries on our current human condition is that even war is sometimes just and necessary to combat evil. For this reason we practice, because the spiritual pursuit transforms energies and gradually changes the atmosphere on our planet, working against the power of greed and hatred.

Forgiveness requires seeing: seeing our hatred for ourselves and for those who have wronged us or our loved ones. This seeing shows how hatred poisons our inner world and opens our heart to the wish to be free from hatred. Together, the seeing and the wish enable us to let go of the accounts, to let the other person back into our heart.

Gratitude

From infancy through our teenage years, many of us receive a free and nurturing ride from loving parents. We do not question why our parents bother, but rather we take their largesse for granted and expect it. As children we typically show no gratitude for the food we eat, for the clothes we wear, for the air we breathe, for the body we inhabit. The whole package arrives as a given, with no effort on our part. Indeed, as children we look for ways to extend the bounty to luxuries, throwing tantrums when the extras are withheld.

We enter society oblivious to the hard fact that many paid in blood to secure the freedoms we take as our birthright. We turn to the medical profession to heal our body and extend our life. We enjoy the innumerable fruits of science and technology. Yet we never consider how much of this we could produce on our own. We completely disregard the armies of researchers, teachers, and factory hands, farmers and truckers, carpenters and miners, artists, musicians, soldiers, journalists and the rest, whose collective talents and efforts produce this life, this civilization. We even think we own the Earth, rather than the other way around.

In the spiritual path also, we tend to take for granted the treasure houses of wisdom and methods refined over millennia and which give us hope of standing on the shoulders of our predecessors. They have bequeathed to us an invaluable legacy of spiritual practices, ours if we make the necessary efforts.

Do I deserve all this? What do I owe for it? What can I contribute to repay my share? Will the world be better for my having lived?

The awakening of conscience, our hidden seat of wisdom, manifests in the stirrings of gratitude for this magnificent world and our life in it. Gratitude leads us to see our obligations to serve, to accept rather than shirk responsibility. Gratitude pierces the veil of egoism, showing that the world was not made for me alone. Instead of eagerly grasping for what we want and desperately avoiding what we don't want, gratitude brings us a new approach, humility and dignity of heart. We look inside and we look around, and we say to God: Thank You.

Listening

Someone once said that if you want to be interesting, you need to be interested.

The person who rattles on and on and on, regardless of the topic of conversation, demanding to be the center of attention, dragging all the energy to him- or herself, understands little about human relationships and makes others look for a quick exit. Indeed, such people only do monologues, perhaps skillfully punctuated by the feigned politeness of a brief foray into dialogue, but never rising to the level of real conversation. And the fact that they show no interest in you or your views makes them doubly uninteresting. Most people, thankfully, are not so totally self-absorbed as to be incapable of entering into the give and take of conversation, the joy of contact with others.

But rather than judge others in terms of their degree of self-centeredness, we strive to listen well, to let the other person be heard. Listening changes the entire event into a direct relationship, a more essential contact between oneself and the other person.

To really listen, to actively listen to another person, we need to be quiet inside and give our open-hearted attention to him or her. Usually, though, as someone talks to us, we are anything but quiet inside. Instead of listening to the other person, we passively listen to all our own reactions and thoughts. We begin formulating and rehearsing responses. We grow anxious to reply, to rebut, to interrupt, to get our thoughts out before we forget them. But when we can let our reactions and thoughts come and go, listening quietly to the other person, in an open, accepting way, without judgment, we create a space, an atmosphere that produces a profound effect both on ourselves and on others. We postpone the preparation of our responses, our disagreements and disputes for later, for our turn to speak. In the meantime, we just listen.

When you can be so quiet inside that you can rest in consciousness while the other person speaks, consciousness may open to include both of you. In that moment you participate in a deeper communication, beyond words and speaking. You touch the essential unity we all share, healing the divisions. Then the words float on the surface, yet you honor them nonetheless.

The practice of listening helps dissolve our identification with our views and opinions, with ourselves. This practice brings fluidity and sets the stage for becoming able to listen to our intuitive wisdom, to the silent voice of the spirit.

Respect

If we take a careful look at our attitudes toward others and toward our self, we soon come to a whole set of questions. Is my attitude respectful, or not? Whom do I respect? Do I treat everyone with respect? Do I consider anyone to be below me or unworthy of respect? Am I inwardly disrespectful, while outwardly feigning respect? Am I indifferent toward others, neither respectful nor disrespectful? Is indifference a form of disrespect?

Do I respect myself? Do I consider myself to be below others or unworthy of respect? Do I consider every person to be equal, in the sense that we are all children of the One God?

Respect can be seen as two-dimensional: inner-outer and self-other. This makes four general forms of respect: inwardly respectful toward our self, inwardly respectful toward others, outwardly respectful toward our self, and outwardly respectful toward others. One example of being outwardly respectful toward our self is in proper care of our body.

Working on respect has several important ramifications for our path. First, it is a matter of conscience, of doing the right thing. Being disrespectful, whether by our speech and actions or by our thoughts and attitudes, pushes us further from conscience and thus further from God.

Second, respect is a harbinger of, and doorway to, love. We may find it difficult to work directly toward love, to even recognize love or how to approach it. But respect is clear and obvious. Even when we feel disrespect inwardly, we can act respectfully as a first step toward feeling it.

Third, the practice of respect directly confronts many of our attachments and judgments, our self-image, self-criticism, indignation, envy, inferiority or superiority, self-importance or self-hatred, and so on. The way of respect shines a bright light on the self-centered ways of our personality. Thus the discipline of respect leads toward freedom.

Respect for others begins with respect for our self, the quiet dignity that derives from self-acceptance, from understanding our own difficult emotions, and from keeping our word. But respect for others, whether or not we deem them worthy of it, also reinforces respect for our self.

Seeing our own inner lack of respect shows us the path toward cultivating it, toward intentionally adopting a genuinely respectful attitude. And respect, coupled with the rest of our spiritual practice, leads to humility and love. Ultimately we may recognize the one quality worthy of unlimited respect, both in ourselves and others: the spark of Divinity.

Harmlessness

I once witnessed a shy two-year old child enter a room in a city he had never before visited. In the corner of the room sat a little old man whom the boy did not know. Immediately upon seeing the old man, with no words spoken, the toddler ran over and jumped into the old man's lap. The little old man was Suleyman "Dede" Loras, chief Sheikh of the Mevlevi Sufi Order, the Whirling Dervishes. Dede had so steeped himself in love and kindness, that he exuded harmlessness. The child understood this intuitively.

The attitude of non-harming arises out of a humble approach to living: life is not about me, but about what lies beyond me, other people and the spirit. If I do not sit like a king or a beggar in the center of my personality, if I realize the illusory nature of my egoism and thus have no ego to defend, my heart rests in profound peace, letting others be themselves, letting others grow in their own time and manner, letting others flower in the atmosphere of love, letting others rest in the safety of our mutual presence. If I do not seek to take, then others need not defend themselves from me.

Harmlessness need not imply weakness. In the public sphere outstanding examples include the civil disobedience of the Indian independence movement under Mahatma Gandhi and the American civil rights movement under Rev. Martin Luther King, Jr. Of course civil disobedience only worked in those cases because their opponents had not completely lost touch with conscience. One doubts, for example, that Jewish civil disobedience would have proven effective against the Nazis. But while exceptional circumstances can and do militate against harmlessness, such cases thankfully remain very rare and do not impinge upon our ordinary daily life. Responding to rudeness with civility signifies strength of spirit, not weakness: *"the last shall be first."*[10]

The work of non-harming highlights our attachments, shows us where ego still holds sway. "I want that. Get out of my way." "If I am harmless, won't I appear weak?" Non-harming can serve as a mirror guiding us toward liberation and away from such self-centered views, melting the bars of our prison. The practice of non-harming illumines areas and occasions where we consider ourselves to be separate from others, for only then can harmful impulses engulf us. In aspiring to harmlessness, one consciously descends from the "lofty" throne of egoism.

Most profoundly, perhaps, the harmless person enables others to love. Everyone loved Dede.

"Blessed are the meek ..."[11]

Prayer

Prayer is the heart of the spiritual path. When you ponder why this universe exists, you might speculate that the Creator needed beings who could pray, that in prayer a necessary exchange of energies and will flows between the created and the Creator. Prayer engenders a dialogue of emotion between an individual or a group and the Divine, ultimately transforming into a monologue of God (through us) praying to God. The quality of this dialogue ranges enormously from the perfunctory blessing over food to the utter surrender of the saint in mystical union. Four factors determine the power of our prayer: the degrees of our faith, humility, awareness, and intention.

Without faith we would never pray or practice at all. For many of us, faith begins in childhood as a set of beliefs learned from our family and community. As we grow older our spiritual beliefs may be based either in the intellect or in the emotions. Intellectual belief constitutes a reasoned orientation toward the Divine, while emotional belief springs from a heartfelt orientation. But our beliefs typically do not rise to the level of spurring us on to transformative spiritual practice. There comes a time, however, when we are drawn beyond ordinary belief to discover a quiet confidence in the Divine and a silent but insistent yearning to fill our spiritual need. That yearning can grow into a flame that lights our way and draws us ever closer to the sacred. Proximity adds fuel to that flame. So does realization of our distance from the Divine, our separation from what matters so deeply. More and more, our disparate, competing drives align themselves toward the higher. What was once a cacophony of urges and desires unifies into a vibrant, living faith. Then we cross the chasm. The fortunate few attain to the all-consuming faith that emerges from direct and ongoing contact with Divinity. But if you look for the source of faith, you cannot see it. Neither thought nor emotion, faith springs from deep within the will.

Humility, the one essential quality for entering the sacred, arises naturally through sincere prayer and also enables it. But by the time we reach adolescence, nearly all of us see ourselves as the center of the universe; we live at the opposite pole from true humility. Eventually the hard knocks of life show us our actual position as only one of many, and the path toward humility begins. The pure-hearted among us possess enough feeling for people and for all of life to be naturally humble, naturally harmless. The rest of us instinctively gravitate toward that unassuming person, out of respect and trust. Our road toward humility accelerates with an element of fear and trembling before our dim but growing intuition of the Greatness behind the universe.

Thus, we begin wishing for self-abnegation, self-noughting before the Divine. Finally, in moments of true emptiness, we drop
our separateness from the Divine, with none of our self left to
be afraid for, humility momentarily perfected. The truly humble
person remains all too rare, but a treasure for us all.

Our level of awareness during the time of prayer can range
from the dimmest automatism to the brightest love. At the low
end we stay distant, praying in a habitual, superficial manner,
in rote ritual, perhaps lost in thoughts unrelated to the prayer,
adding nothing to the sacred economy. Slightly more awareness brings contact with our thoughts, emotions, body, and
surroundings, imbuing the ritual with feeling. Still our prayer
remains largely self-centered. Another notch of awareness and
the stillness of consciousness itself unfolds before us, opening
the field to a more universal prayer. We pray from the whole of
ourselves and with full awareness of the significance of prayer.
We pray not only as ourselves, but also as one unit of the whole
of humanity. Moving further into the depths of awareness, we
approach what lies veiled behind the stillness: the realm of
the Divine. Then we pray, touched by the Divine Spirit before
Whom we stand in awe and love, and to Whom we address our
prayers.

The quality of petitionary prayer depends on the intention
it embodies. We might ask for satisfaction of some personal
vanity or other desire. Deeper and we ask for fulfillment of a
real personal need, such as restoration of health in times of illness. A higher form of petitionary prayer regards the needs of
others, such as health for the other person, or peace on Earth.

A central factor in petitionary prayer is the awareness that
there is Someone to Whom we pray. We do not pray simply
hearing ourselves in an echo chamber or to an amorphous idea
of the higher. We address ourselves to that Divine One. That

stance changes the quality of our petition, for it confronts us with our conscience.

Beyond petitionary prayer, we pray without a specific or personal result in mind: praying to glorify the Most High, praying to pave our path toward God, praying for help on our path, praying for guidance in our service of Life, praying as an act of service to the sacred, returning our love and intelligence, our energy and will, our selves to God. Our prayer becomes a true act of reverent worship as we pour out our love, awe, respect, and gratitude for Divine largesse in creating this universe and endowing us with freedom.

At the level of conscious prayer, we empty, open, and surrender ourselves to a connection with the higher worlds. We reach inward, outward, beyond space and time, beyond consciousness itself. We reach with the whole of ourselves, with body, heart, and mind, with all of our attention and intention, and perhaps with words calling out to God. Utterly given over to the act of communing with the Divine, we open ourselves to become a two-way channel that sends our hope, gratitude, and love upstream, while enabling an influx of higher energy to descend into us. We welcome this higher energy into the whole of our body. With our attention and intention, we allow that energy to blend with our sensitive energy, refining the latter and helping build our soul.

The differences in these levels of prayer derive from the strength of our intention and from where it is centered: from my false center, to my actual personal center, to the non-center that I share with others, to that vibrant core that I share with All. In the end we pray as God.

All of this applies both to individual and communal prayer. While all prayer springs from individual acts, praying in community *may* wonderfully enhance the efficacy of prayer. The key factor is the degree to which the participants share the same intention and pray in unison. Disorganized communal prayer, where people merely mill about and chat inside a house of worship, has little real value. The deeper the shared intention and the more unified the awareness, words, and actions, the more powerful the communal worship.

Finally, we arrive at prayer that we attempt to extend throughout the day, in which we aim to pray without ceasing. Inwardly, our heart dwells with God; outwardly we offer our actions for the greater good. We find this, for example, in the Christian desert fathers of the *Philokalia*, in the Islamic Sufi tradition, in Hindu yoga, and in Kabbalah. An inner repetition of words of prayer can form scaffolding from which we seek to continuously reach toward the Unconditioned. This very high aim of prayer without ceasing constitutes a worthy life's work.

As for the details of how to pray, a good place to start is our religion, the religion of our parents and ancestors. Because of our lifelong exposure to and relative comfort with it, our native religion may offer us the most direct line toward depth in prayer. We may discover an essential connection with that religion, with its rituals and liturgy, with its people, with its approach to the Divine. From that religion we learn its outer forms of prayer and adapt them into our daily practice. And to those outer forms we bring our inner work, our faith, humility, awareness, and intention, the depth of our being and the constant simplicity of our devotion.

At whatever level we pray, we find a corresponding efficacy of prayer. Even if we cannot pray like a saint, we bring whatever warmth and devotion we can muster. We need no intermediary; our relationship with the Divine is direct. The important thing is to regularly set aside time for that partnership with the Higher, to honestly open our heart and let God do the rest.

Cultivating Faith

Without faith, without that deeply rooted intuition of the Divine, without that inner stirring of attraction to the sacred, the spiritual path would hold no interest for us. We would not move toward what matters most. Conversely, the stronger our faith, the more frequently and deeply we act on our possibilities for inner work. So we need to cultivate faith in ourselves. Of course our spiritual work and our faith form a positive feedback look, reinforcing each other. But we can look toward actions that specifically deepen our faith.

What those actions may be depends on our own individuality, our unique heredity and experience, our propensities and talents. As always, our inner work, to be most effective, must be tailored to who we are in this moment.

Reading sacred and inspirational works can help open the depths of faith. Prayers of various kinds nurture faith. The occasional fast can temporarily break us out of our normal mode of living and remind us of the sacred. By keeping in contact with our own heart, we can allow it to open when it is touched; too often we squash our feelings for the sacred. Music that awakens our need for the Divine can move our faith. Spiritual friends and a worship community are time-honored supports for individual faith.

But most of all, in seeking that direct relationship with the Divine, without intermediary, without past or future, without time or place or thought, we exercise our faith, that perception of and drive toward the sacred.

Awareness of Death

On September 11, 2001 we saw images of an airliner flying into the World Trade Center. We saw the buildings collapse. We heard the silent scream of thousands of people dying in that moment. We saw these atrocities again and again. Like people of conscience everywhere, we were appalled. In the following days we were different than usual. We were traumatized and often in tears. But this was the lesser difference.

As the greater difference, we temporarily lived in a deeper part of ourselves, a part oriented toward the inner. We saw our outward oriented part for what it is: mostly trivial and ephemeral. Indulging in our usual pleasures and pettiness seemed a sacrilege in the face of the death of so many of our brothers and sisters. We were sober, no longer drunk on self-centeredness. An appreciation of our fundamental connection, even with complete strangers, came naturally. Kindness and concern ruled the days. We spoke with solicitude toward all and drove our cars with courtesy.

Why? The proximity and awesomeness of death shook us into seeing truly: that our time on this Earth is limited, that we all share an essential connection, and that what really matters is love.

Gradually, the shock subsided and our changed attitude toward each other eroded. We returned to viewing others as little more than cardboard cutouts of people or pieces of furniture. We returned to our ambitions for money or fame or whatever images fill our personal daydreams.

Standing in the face of death, whether of thousands or of one, can help us remember to live well, to remember that our time is precious and limited. Death reminds us to open our hearts to others and to appreciate all of life. Indeed, we can intentionally remember that both the other person and we ourselves will inevitably die. This is not to be done in a morbid way, to make us sad or melancholy, but rather to awaken and warm our heart toward the other, toward ourselves, to bring us back to the values that we know to be true, that come from our inner depths, to bring us back to the simple joy of being alive.

Awareness of death helps us climb out of the grip of self-seeking egoism and deepens our commitment to spiritual practice. Remembering that our time is limited, that our energies and possibilities will eventually ebb away, imparts an urgency to our inner work, an overarching need to fulfill our highest destiny and not fall short. So in that inevitable moment, when we reach our last breath, we can survey the life we lived with the satisfaction of having given it our all.

Healing the Emptiness

Several forms of emptiness can face us: the more common, lower forms that we can work to heal and the higher emptiness that heals us.

At times the lower emptiness assails us, perhaps as a world weariness or ennui. We fall into the grip of boredom, or the feeling of wasting time, of having nothing or too much to do, of being tired of the routines and frustrations of life, of dissatisfaction with our job, our entertainments, or the people around us. We usually confront this lower emptiness by filling it with busyness, new entertainments, shopping, overeating, substance abuse, or other distractions from our quotidian existence. Yet there it is: that dissatisfaction with life.

A more seriously debilitating form of emptiness arises

through dissatisfaction with ourselves. Self-criticism and self-doubt can draw us into despondency, despair, and even self-loathing. Difficult childhood experiences can create long-lasting wounds that condition us for gnawing dissatisfaction with ourselves. The loss of a significant relationship, a job, or some other major undoing may trigger the descent.

The first antidote to both these types of emptiness is acceptance: accepting our life as it is and accepting ourselves as we are. This does not preclude working to improve our outer or inner situation, but we do so from a base of love and acceptance. Generally this is not so easy, to turn a lifetime of dissatisfaction into acceptance. But it is necessary. We notice the negative attitudes, thoughts, and emotions. While not rejecting them either, we let that awareness prompt us to adopt a stance of acceptance, to let go of our demands and just let ourselves be.

As a further and complementary approach to healing the lower emptiness we turn to spiritual practice, creative work, and right action in service to others. Each of these broadens our ordinary life, opening us to the greater world and connecting us with real meaning. When we find ourselves in the throes of dissatisfaction, we can practice sensing right then and there, knowing that by doing so we strengthen our soul through an effort of lasting significance. Sustaining the practice of presence puts us into a very different relationship with life. Similarly, by entering some creative endeavor or engaging in acts of kindness and service, we touch a region of timeless value.

A different, higher, sacred and unquenchable emptiness lies at our core forms the doorway to the Divine. This emptiness increases our hunger while leading us toward the Source of spiritual nourishment. Along the way, this higher emptiness guides us into the utter peace of pure consciousness, where no thing encumbers us. Stepping further into our empty core, beyond consciousness and peace, all questions vanish; or rather they merge into the singleness of purpose of joining in the Divine purpose. Toward this higher emptiness, our job is to accept, deepen, and surrender to it, while asking, praying for its fulfillment from Above. These upper reaches of emptiness complete the healing of the lower ones, bringing true and lasting satisfaction, contentment, and purpose.

To work at healing the emptiness, distinguish among the forms of emptiness confronting you, notice how you normally respond, and consider how you wish to respond.

Joy

Clouds cannot hide the sun forever; joy eventually breaks through. We discover joy in our friendships, in nature, in loving our family, in spontaneous humor, in delicious food, in meaningful and interesting work. In coming to know joy, we find the important distinction between pleasure and joy by examining their relationship with time. Pleasures always remain time-bound and fleeting, whereas joy transcends all boundaries. Pleasure often contains its opposite, as we dread losing the moment or the object of pleasure, or we desire more — a grasping laden with suffering. Standing as its own timeless quality, joy has no opposite.

In the spiritual path, we may enter true joy that can suffuse our entire life, creating a continuing background of natural and buoyant happiness. Such joy develops gradually over the years of inner work, although we may experience intense flashes of it. But as our contact with the eternal source of joy grows, we relinquish our fears of the inevitable end of every time-bound moment of pleasure, appreciating pleasures as they come, es-

chewing the endless quest for pleasure, and transforming pleasure into joy. The source of joy works both through and beyond
our material pleasures. Even in the midst of pain, joy remains
itself.

The simplest, most ordinary moments can reveal the spir-
ited glow of a joyous world unbound. As our presence deepens,
the veils of our perception grow translucent even before they
dissolve altogether in our maturing soul. The consuming fire
of total-hearted prayer and the hidden worlds of meditation
bear unimaginable joy, surpassing all material pleasures. From
those points of entry, joy works its way into the fabric of our
life. Though sometimes considered a joyless enterprise, the
spiritual path affords true joy where there was little or none. A
few moments ecstasy in a lifetime of labor do not approach the
ever-growing joy nurtured through persistent spiritual practice.
Even a small portion of transformation, a slight loosening of the
bonds of egoism, widens our context of spontaneous joy in life,
in work, in family, in friends, in nature, and in the Source of all
joy.

Recreation

Do spiritual people have fun? Must spirituality and purification follow a puritanical model? A monastic life and a path of
self-denial and even asceticism may be right for some types of
people. However, for most of us who seek to blend a normal life
in society with a pursuit of the spiritual depths, uncompromising austerities only serve to erect a wall around ourselves, cutting us off from friends and family. The walls of piety are walls
of egoism. We do indeed need to be serious, not outwardly, but
inwardly in our persistent and humbling efforts to be present.

As long as we hew to moderation, avoiding attachment, addiction, and destructive habits, we have no problem with play, with fun, per se. Enjoyment of the arts, sports, creative work of all kinds, hobbies, feasting with friends, all are natural to us: recall the biblical admonition to be like little children.

The hidden, spiritual efficacy of fun lies in our letting go, not being so stuck, letting our energies flow freely to recombine in new ways, tapping into our spontaneous and creative core. Spirituality must not become rigid and sterile, for then our path is surely blocked. Instead we cultivate the joy of living and a sense of humor. One clear test is whether we are able to play with children, or play with our friends.

The question of fun also touches on the question of spiritual effort, like the effort to be present. While we do need to persevere in our work of presence as often and as long as possible, there are times when it is inappropriate. The work of presence involves the sensitive and conscious energies. Recreation can involve a higher energy, the creative. So if we try to be present while, for example, making love or making music or laughing at a joke, we may interfere with the effortless presence and creative energy of those situations. Recreation is a type of relaxation that loosens us up, helping to prepare our ground for new spiritual factors to enter.

Since recreation invites a higher energy, should we not just drop our spiritual efforts and focus on enjoyment and creative situations? That would be unbalanced. We would soon be floundering again with little presence and the truly creative energies would not find as ready a vehicle in us.

Periods of recreation, like periods of prayer, meditation, and the work of presence, are a necessary part of a balanced path. We seek wholeheartedness in all we do, including the enjoyment of living.

CHAPTER FOUR

MIND

The Role of Ideas in Spiritual Life

Descartes summed up his philosophy in the famous dictum: "I think, therefore I am." The more a person grows in the spiritual domain, however, the less that person relies on thought. While we may conceive of distant realms, of heaven, of other universes, of higher dimensions, even of God, our thinking itself remains inexorably bound to the world of space and time. As thought junkies, though, we nurture our addiction to listening to, floating in, adding to, and arguing with the ever-flowing stream of thoughts and images in our minds. One cannot think one's way into heaven. The concept trap ensnares many spiritual seekers as we unwittingly substitute thoughts and ideas about the path for the path itself. For actually traveling toward the Divine, thoughts, no matter how elaborate, abstract or holy, are the wrong vehicle. Though words of prayer or a Divine name can orient us in the right direction, only by seeing beyond thoughts and beyond mental imagery can we begin to touch the higher worlds. Thoughts and concepts play no role when we stand before the ineffable.

So why publish thousands of books on spiritual subjects? Right thinking and true ideas offer two invaluable ingredients for the inner life: motivation and guidance. Great spiritual poetry and myths, stories in the holy scriptures, and other written sources contain ideas and images which can serve to raise the level of our spiritual aspirations, moving us to renew our commitment to the path, helping us through our dry spells, periods of doubt, and the inevitable and numerous obstacles we encounter along the way. Eventually, the wonders of the path itself provide ample motivation. But until that door opens, books and ideas can help propel us toward the non-conceptual. The key to avoiding pitfall of concepts lies in not confusing the moon with the finger pointing toward it.

The inner landscape hides a territory unknown to us. The deeper realms lie shrouded within what psychologists call the unconscious. A trail or set of signposts through this land would prove most useful. Unfortunately, such definitive guidance eludes possibility because the inner landscape is not material in the way that streets, sidewalks, and hills are. Books and ideas can, however, provide building blocks for a mental map of the inner realms. Through a difficult and continual effort of map-making, we calibrate, revise and align our conceptual map to conform to the actual landscape, to the experience of walking the path. Understanding deepens.

In certain circumstances, for example on a spiritual retreat, reading can only interfere with our inner work, arousing thoughts and fixing our attention on concepts, rather than moving beyond them. But in most circumstances, in everyday life, our thoughts perpetually cascade through the foreground of our minds. Reading texts of the spirit, pondering their contents, and drawing inspiration from them channel our thoughts and hearts toward actual steps along the path, toward moment-to-moment presence and practice.

Thoughts and Thinking

We collectively glorify our ability to think as the distinguishing characteristic of humanity; we personally and mistakenly glorify our thoughts as the distinguishing pattern of who we are. From the inner voice of thought-as-words to the wordless images within our minds, thoughts create and limit our personal world. Through thinking we abstract and define reality, reason about it, react to it, recall past events and plan for the future. Yet thinking remains both woefully underdeveloped in most of us, as well as grossly overvalued. We can best gain some perspective on thinking in terms of energies.

Automatic thinking draws us away from the present. We wistfully allow our thoughts to meander where they would, carrying our passive attention along with them. Like water running down a mountain stream, thoughts running on autopilot career through the spaces of perception, randomly triggering associative links within our vast storehouse of memory. By itself, such associative thought is harmless. However, our tendency to believe in, act upon, and drift away with such undirected thought keeps us operating in an automatic mode. Lulled into an inner passivity by our daydreams and thought streams, we lose contact with the world of actual perceptions, of real life. In the automatic mode of thinking, I am completely identified with my thoughts, believing my thoughts *are* me, believing that I *am* my thoughts.

Another mode of automatic thinking consists of repetitious

and habitual patterns of thought. These thought tapes and our running commentary on life, unexamined by the light of awareness, keep us enthralled, defining who we are and perpetuating all our limiting assumptions about what is possible for us. Driving and driven by our emotions, these ruts of thought create our false persona, the mask that keeps us disconnected from others and from our own authentic self. More than any other single factor, automatic thinking hinders our contact with presence, limits our being, and blocks our path. The autopilot of thought constantly calls us away from the here and now, and keeps us fixed on the most superficial levels of our being.

Sometimes we even notice strange, unwanted thoughts that we consider horrible or shameful. We might be upset or shaken that we would think such thoughts, but those reactions only serve to sustain the problematic thoughts by feeding them energy. Furthermore, that self-disgust is based on the false assumption that we are our thoughts, that even unintentional thoughts, arising from our conditioned minds, are us. They are not us and we need not act upon or react to them. They are just thoughts with no inherent power and no real message about who we are. We can just relax and let them go — or not. Troubling thoughts that recur over a long period and hinder our inner work may require us to examine and heal their roots in our conditioning, perhaps with the help of a psychotherapist.

Sensitive thinking puts us in touch with the meaning of our thoughts and enables us to think logically, solve problems, make plans, and carry on a substantive conversation. A good education develops our ability to think clearly and intentionally with the sensitive energy. With that energy level in our thinking brain, no longer totally submerged in the thought stream, we can move about in it, choosing among and directing our thoughts based on their meaning.

Conscious thinking means stepping out of the thought stream altogether, surveying it from the shore. The thoughts themselves may even evaporate, leaving behind a temporarily empty streambed. Consciousness reveals the banality and emptiness of ordinary thinking. Consciousness also permits us to think more powerfully, holding several ideas, their meanings and ramifications in our minds at once.

When the creative energy enters into thought, truly new ideas spring up. Creative thinking can happen after a struggle, after exhausting all known avenues of relevant ideas and giving up, shaping and emptying the stage so the creative spark may enter. The quiet, relaxed mind also leaves room for the creative thought, a clear channel for creativity. Creative and insightful thoughts come to all of us in regard to the situations we face in life. The trick is to be aware enough to catch them, to notice their significance, and if they withstand the light of sober and unbiased evaluation, to act on them.

In the spiritual path, we work to recognize the limitations of thought, to recognize its power over us, and especially to move beyond it. Along with Descartes, we live in the realm of "thoughts 'r us." But thoughts are just thoughts. They are not us. They are not who we are. No thought can enter the spiritual realms. Rather, the material world defines the boundaries of thought, despite its power to conceive lofty abstractions. We cannot think our way into the spiritual reality. On the contrary, identification with thinking prevents us from entering the depths. As long as we believe that refined thinking represents our highest capacity, we shackle ourselves exclusively to this world. All our thoughts, all our books, all our ideas wither before the immensity of the higher realms.

A richly developed body of spiritual practices engages thought: from repetitive prayer and mantras, to contemplation of an idea, to visualizations of deities. In a most instructive and invaluable exercise, we learn to see beyond thought by embracing the gaps, the spaces between thoughts. After sitting quietly and relaxing for some time, we turn our attention toward the thought stream within us. We notice thoughts come and go of their own accord, without prodding or pushing from us. If we can abide in this relaxed watching of thought, without falling into the stream and flowing away with it, the thought stream begins to slow, the thoughts fragment. Less enthralled by our thoughts, we begin to see that we are not our thoughts. Less controlled by, and at the mercy of, our thoughts, we begin to be aware of the gaps between thought particles. These gaps open to consciousness, underlying all thought. Settling into these gaps, we enter and become the silent consciousness beneath thought. Instead of being in our thoughts, our thoughts are in us.

Counting

One ancient driver of spiritual practice involves counting. Repetitions of prayers and other practices may be accompanied by counting either mentally or with a string of beads. Such counting practices exist in Christianity, Islam, Hinduism, Buddhism, and Judaism.

Some attention exercises consist solely of mental counting, such as interleaving two counts. A relatively easy example uses one count beginning at 0 and counting up to 100, and another count beginning at 100 and counting down to 0, like this: 0, 100, 1, 99, 2, 98, etc. A more demanding version has one count beginning at 1 and increasing by 3 on each count, and the second beginning at 100 and decreasing by four on each count: 1, 100, 4, 96, 7, 92, 10, 88, ... These mental exercises keep us focused in the present; otherwise we lose the count. Simple counting can support meditation by, for example, enumerating the breaths in the practice of breath awareness. As long as we do not allow the count to become automatic, all these counting methods help us extend our attention through time. The longer we are present, the deeper our presence can be.

A highly effective use of counting in daily practice consists of resolving to repeat an inner exercise a certain minimum number of times during the day. For example, take the exercise of sensing each of our four limbs in turn: cycling through the right arm, right leg, left leg, and left arm. We set ourselves to repeat this exercise a particular number of times during the day – say ten. Whenever we remember the exercise, we turn to it, increment our count, and then leave it until the next time we remember. Instead of sensing we could work on presence, a heartfelt prayer, or some other practice. To simplify, we choose one practice to count for the day and we set the daily number each morning. The determination to turn to inner work at least our chosen number of times provides an extra impetus to our efforts for that day and helps us enter our practice more often than we might otherwise. Over time, we can experiment with increasing the daily number.

If it should happen that we reach the end of the day without having made our self-allotted count, we carry through on our commitment by not going to sleep until we finish. This might, for example, require a period of focused inner work where we allow ourselves one count per minute. Sticking to our commitment for the day keeps the whole process alive. Otherwise the practice of counting our inner work quickly loses its potency.

The inner world defies any attempt to quantify it. Counting our practice provides a clear measure, albeit a somewhat crude one, of our inner work. Crude or not, the objective measure of counting our spiritual practice offers enormous benefits. We see how much practice we actually do, bringing a sober reality to it. Even more importantly, by setting a definite commitment to practicing a certain numbers of times during the day and by gradually raising that number, we can use the count to leverage an increase in our inner work. While counting only measures quantity, a sustained quantity of work may take us to a qualitatively new mode of being.

Repetition of any spiritual exercise works to gradually stretch our attention, open our perceptions, collect our energies, strengthen our will, and dispose us toward the path. Starting anew at a count of zero each morning enlivens our practice by permitting us a fresh start every day, while keeping us humble by the mere fact of beginning again. The count itself ties together our day of inner work, making the separate repetitions into a single act of will. Most importantly, counting concretizes our efforts, moving our inner work from the potential to the actual. Generally we do not remember, nor do something about, long-term goals like enlightenment or transformation of being as often as with our more immediate involvements. Counting our instances of inner work gives us that near-term, actionable aim for today.

Meditation

Meditation, the preeminent classical means of strengthening the soul, opening the heart, entering the spiritual, and serving the Divine, probably predates history. As far back as 4,000 years ago, the Old Testament tells of Isaac meditating in a field[12] just prior to meeting Rebecca, his wife-to-be. Meditation, in its multitude of forms, continues as a core practice in certain sectors of most religions, e.g., the Christian Jesus prayer, Hindu Raja Yoga, Buddhist meditation, Muslim Sufi zikr, and Jewish Kabbalah practice. To our great good fortune, we inherit the treasure of meditation methods refined over millennia and readily applicable even in our fast-paced culture. The numerous styles of meditation include silent and spoken repetitions, visualizations, focusing on a physical object, an idea, or a riddle, movement, relaxation, letting go, opening, delving into stillness, and more.

Simplifying the field, we can view all types of meditation as belonging to one of two complementary categories variously termed active and accepting, or concentration and opening, or doing and non-doing, or directed and non-directed. For proper balance we need both kinds. Indeed, the active prepares us for the open and the open lends meaning to the active. The distinguishing factor between the two categories is attention. In the active forms, we focus our attention on one of the many possible objects of meditation within our awareness. In the accepting forms, we open our attention toward the spiritual reality beyond our awareness. These pages offer examples of both kinds of meditation. Examples on the active side include awareness of bodily sensations, relaxation, and conscious breathing. On the open side we have the practice of stillness and certain forms of prayer. The meditation "Climbing Jacob's Ladder" combines both.

We may judge the efficacy of a spiritual path by whether it incorporates some type of meditation or meditative prayer. Without a direct and repeated action on our soul, a path cannot serve our transformation nor offer the hope of access to the truly spiritual. A path may have wonderful psychological and healing effects, but without carrying us toward the true One, at least not within the limited time we have. The path may be religious, communal, or social, yet lack the power to change our hearts and transform our being. Certainly the outward manifestation of good works is a necessary part of the spiritual path, but a lack of practices for purifying and strengthening the soul limits both the inner and outer value of good works.

To maximize the benefit, we aim to practice meditation every day. Regularity matters because it builds our spiritual commitment. Our attitude toward the daily discipline of meditation gradually evolves from something akin to brushing our teeth into an abiding source of joy in our lives. The duration may range from 20 minutes up to two hours or more. Meditating alone is good. Meditating with others is better. An inexplicable power emerges through group spiritual practices. The palpable effect multiplies far beyond the number of people in the group. A group of two is good. A group of 100 is extraordinary. Participating in communal prayer or meditation fulfills a major aspect of our obligation to life.

All the major religions incorporate some form of meditation. But many leaders within the religious mainstream treat meditative and contemplative practices with disdain or consider them unnecessary or even destructive. Historically, the shunting aside of meditative practices probably served the leadership hierarchy by allowing them to maintain their roles as intermediaries to the Divine. For the congregation, meditative practices bring up difficult issues that many prefer not to face. Who am I really? What actually goes on in my mind and heart? Do I have to change? Am I responsible for my inner life? Do I have to face all this banality in myself? How can I find my way into the unknown? How can I find the time for meditation or contemplative prayer? All of this and more arise when one embarks on a program of meditation. Much easier to leave it alone and continue to sweep the messiness of our inner lives under a carpet of unconsciousness. In meditation we shine a light on our inner world and, little by little, the dust and weeds and broken machinery begin to clear up. Then glimpses come of a deeper world, a more meaningful way of living, of joy, and even love.

One simple, non-denominational meditation practice is as follows. First, before you even sit down, set your intention. Recall your purpose in meditating. Recall that, like all spiritual practices, meditation is an act of service for yourself, for others, and for that which lies beyond. Then sit comfortably, with your spine upright, but not stiff. Use a chair, a bench, or a cushion. Starting at the top of your head, scan down throughout your body, noticing muscular tensions and letting them loosen. Repeat the relaxation scan two or three times at your own pace. Next, place your attention on the sensations of your breathing, wherever you find them most prominent: the nostrils, the upper chest, or the abdomen. Do not change the breathing, just bring awareness to it and keep with it in a relaxed manner. If you find your attention wandering off into thoughts or sounds or sensations, gently bring it back to the breath, over and over and over again. If you have great difficulty staying with the breath, try counting breaths for a while. Mentally count the breaths from one to ten, and then start over at one. The counting is secondary: keep your primary attention on the sensations of the breath. If you lose count, start over at one. When you can stay with the breath continuously for five or six cycles of ten, you can drop the counting and just be with the breath. That's it: simple and direct. Gradually your mind will settle down, your consciousness will start to emerge, your heart will relax, and your soul will grow. When consciousness grows pronounced, you might choose to drop attention to the breath and just be in consciousness itself.

All spiritual practices and methods, including meditation, eventually reach a limit. Usually this limit is merely a plateau. To move beyond it requires something different than what brought you there. Perhaps you need more commitment, a new mode of perceiving, or another meditative technique or spiritual practice. Then you move on. But along the way, real barriers will confront you. When you stand before the ineffable, on the outskirts of the formless, no inner exercise or meditation technique will carry you across. Experimentation, exploration, and commitment help. But only the purity of your heart and intention, along with the grace you receive, will open that door. There can be no method for that. Meditation and other practices may transport us to the threshold of the spiritual, but we must find our own way to step across, empty-handed and emptied of ourselves.

Porosity

In the quiet of meditation, after the mind settles down and we start noticing the empty spaces between thoughts, between perceptions, we can let these gaps grow prominent, bring them into the foreground of awareness, enter them, and become them. Moving out of the content of our mind and into its context, we become porous. Our very awareness becomes porous, open to let all and any perceptions and impulses come and go freely, with no obstacles, no viscosity, no attraction, and no repulsion. Entering this sea of holes, with no holding on, we become free. Even after we step out of the formal meditation practice, the undercurrent of permeability and freedom buoys us, unburdening our approach to life with an ease that allows intensity and joy, nourishes excellence, and meets life's inevi-

146

table difficulties with élan. In this porosity our time expands, enriched. Time flows through us rather than driving or limiting us. We have time to relax, to live and breathe and be in contact with the people around us.

Growing accustomed to the stillness and porosity, we begin to accept and even treasure our inherent emptiness as arising from our true source, as the field of our interconnectedness with all life. The paradox of the spiritual life unfolds: the less we hold onto, the more we receive. Porosity enables us to walk with a lighter step toward our place in the great world beyond our heavily defended self.

Arrogance

Those to whom much has been given sometimes suffer from arrogance; or rather the people around them suffer. Arrogance is doubly a pity, because the talents of the arrogant serve primarily themselves. The arrogant assumes his views and opinions are The Truth. In arrogance, natural confidence goes sadly awry. Rather than the self-assurance born of knowing his own strengths and limitations, arrogance admits no limits. The arrogant brooks no weakness in himself and may even secretly rejoice to find flaws in others. But imperfections are inherent in being human, so the arrogant, like everyone else, always has feet of clay, however well hidden they may be. Fearing exposure, haughtiness forms a hard shell masking inner emptiness.

The arrogant sees first himself. Rather than offering respect to all, arrogance demands respect from all. Dismissive, arrogance poisons all relationships: with himself, with others, and with the spiritual depths. Worshipping the grand but empty edifice of ego, the self-important sees others as less human, as cardboard cutouts, relating as I-It rather than as I-Thou, in Martin Buber's apt phrase.[13]

Like so many self-centered traits, arrogance in others activates the arrogance in us, or its opposite of timidity and self-doubt. Confronted with arrogance, we might erupt indignantly or we might lapse into dwelling piteously on our own limitations. We then infect others and the vicious cycle continues.

A subspecies of arrogance, spiritual arrogance, takes at least two forms. In the first, the victim concludes that he has made progress, perhaps due to having a few deep experiences. Or he prides himself for being part of the in-crowd, or for being friendly with the teacher, or for being the teacher. Whatever the reason, the spiritually arrogant mistakenly determines that he or she is special and then vaunts that assumed eminence over other people. This may be explicit in his outward behavior or implicit in his inward self-image. When a spiritual teacher contracts a case of spiritual arrogance, hubris typically leads to abuses of his unfortunate students.

In another form of spiritual arrogance, the true believer aggressively proselytizes, pushing his own path as the one and only way, browbeating people by claiming that they will not be saved without the chosen path, or that they are misguided. In actuality, this wide Earth harbors many valid and effective paths. The appropriate path for any particular person is a highly individual discovery and cannot be decided by anyone else. It sometimes happens that when people first enter a path, an obsessive infatuation sets in. They may see their path as the one true way and attempt to convert others, even over protests of disinterest. Maturity brings respect for and acceptance of the validity of other paths.

All forms of arrogance lie well beyond the pale of true spirituality. Freedom from arrogance begins with seeing. At first we may only receive hints from how our behavior affects those around us. Then we might glimpse, in action, our overwrought and inflated assumptions about ourselves. Gradually, we learn to allow ourselves, in our own estimation, to be at the same level of importance as others: not higher, despite our gifts, and not lower, despite our defects — just ordinary. This is the antidote to arrogance, and its second greatest fear: to be an ordinary person.

Questions: Doubt, Investigation, Contemplation

Questions forge a double-edged sword for spiritual work. If we never questioned or doubted the conventional science-based world view as the last word on reality, we might never enter the path. If, as a condition for entering the path, we demand proof or direct experience of the existence of God, we shall likely never begin practice. All too easily we cross the line between profitable investigation and restrictive doubt. Their similarities sometimes blind us to their sharply differing effects.

The path requires understanding, which grows through practice, experience, investigation, and contemplation. Investigation begins with a question, or a set of related questions, and seeks answers, sometimes by performing experiments. We might ask, for example, what is the nature of the sensitive energy in the body? Perhaps we try practicing sensing more diligently and in new ways, through active sensing and through opening to physical sensations. Investigating this seriously over a period of time, our understanding grows. Answers come, along with new questions, and we progress toward deeper layers of the mystery.

But when questions slip into questioning, investigation

turns into doubt. Doubt poses questions, demands answers, and then refuses to accept any answer. The doubter questions everything, except his own questioning, his own refusal to accept the answers presented, even by his own experience. Because the spiritual path ventures into inner realms where concrete, material-world proofs cannot be had, the seeker must learn a new kind of verification: to trust inner experience, inner events. Doubts seduce us precisely because of the non-ordinary nature of the spiritual. The other extreme of blind faith also stymies our path. We need a healthy doubt, a searching, investigative flair.

Some of the big questions, like "Who Am I?" or "Where is God?" or "Why am I here?" lead our investigations into a blind alley. We cannot see the answers. We might even find the questions themselves disturbing or frightening. By staying grounded in our ordinary day-to-day reality, such questions will not overcome us and we will not be deluded into accepting facile, clever, or false answers.

Yet the essential questions persist in tugging at our heart. Gently and humbly, without expectation or demand, we approach the question through contemplation. We contemplate the unanswerable, the unfathomable. We contemplate the questions that matter most, the questions that drive our search, that enflame our very soul. Worthy questions propel us into the unknown, opening doors whose existence we had not perceived. We welcome the question into our heart and mind, like a Zen koan, bypassing the would-be and trivial answers, seeking the realm of truth beyond all questions and all answers.

Layers of Reality

What you see is what you get. And with limited vision, life seems flat. Yet it can grow immensely richer, if we develop the ability to live in its higher as well as its lower levels. Above the many layers of our physiology we find the level of the pre-programmed automaton in us. We walk, we eat, and we perform numerous other complex physical tasks without needing to consider or even notice the minute details of every little movement. The conditioned, automatic layer also includes our personality, the whole complex pattern of thoughts, emotions, and mannerisms that comprise the person we believe ourselves to be. Living in our personality, we react in our typical and idiosyncratic fashion to all the events of life. Our personality operates as a restrictive, deterministic program, reacting automatically to sensory inputs while harboring an illusion of initiative and freedom. Yet all these necessary skills embodied in our trained and habitual behaviors serve us quite well at a functional level.

At the next higher layer we find the sensitive energy, through which we can be aware of our thoughts, emotions, and body. At this level we already have some limited freedom from our pre-programmed personality: we can make real choices. The sensitive energy serves as the substantial basis for much of our inner work, as we collect, contain and transform it into our soul.

True consciousness announces our entry into the next layer. This level of stillness and cognizance enables us to be both fully ourselves and fully in touch with the world beyond ourselves. Consciousness underlies and permeates everything, everywhere. Like the air we breathe, we can open, through stillness, to this unbounded yet immediate and substantive vastness which makes us whole. When we feel ourselves to be fully present, we begin to touch consciousness. Through consciousness we can organize and refine the lower levels.

The layers beyond consciousness include the creative energy and love. By emptying ourselves of ourselves, forgoing our egoism, surrendering to the Divine, we may come into contact with the new, the invigorating, the purifying forces of creativity and love.

All these layers of reality impinge on the here and now. Though we spend the bulk of our time in the lower levels, through spiritual practice we aim to open to and gain a foothold in the higher levels. But the lower does not evaporate, it remains. Only it does not have the same exclusive claim on our hopes and imagination. Being in consciousness, we still see the automatic and sensitive at work in us, assuming their proper roles in our personal ecosystem. Touching the creative and love, consciousness itself begins to unwind the knot of egoism. The more fully human we become, the more fully we live on all the levels.

CHAPTER FIVE

I AM

Attention

The single most important tool we bring to our spiritual work is our attention. This fundamental ability to direct our awareness toward an object and steadily hold it there forms the foundation of most, though not all, spiritual practices, as well as many of life's ordinary activities. A focused and sustained attention enables us to see our attachments, our clinging, offering hope of releasing their hold on us. A focused and relaxed attention equips us to contact, collect, and organize our inner energies, and to support the emergence of consciousness from the lower energies. Attention enables us to relate to other people and endows us with the possibility of opening our hearts. It animates our life in the present moment. Directing our attention toward the Divine, as in true prayer, creates a channel through which higher may flow into us.

As the lowest and most recognizable form of will, attention can direct our perceptions and thoughts. Attention exemplifies the character of will by entering into nearly every aspect of our lives, yet remaining unnoticed, subjective. In response to the question "Who am I?" we can rightly answer "I am my attention." Inexplicably, our culture woefully neglects training our attention, approaching it indirectly, incompletely, and inadequately. Correcting this one shortcoming of education would produce enormous benefits, materially as well as spiritually, by addressing this most fundamental aspect of the person.

Of the three primary forms of attention, we typically think of the first: active attention. Yet the passive and open forms of attention also merit careful study.

Take the example of watching a television program. Our attention works *passively*: we just sit back, consumed by the program, allowing the TV to run our inner world, to drive our thoughts and emotions, to usurp our place, to sap our alertness, initiative and energy. Such involuntary, passive attention characteristically operates with the automatic energy and sends us onto a downward slope with respect to our humanity. TV may be useful for a short respite of relaxation, but the negative consequences of overindulging in television carry over into the rest of our lives. This holds at any age, from early childhood on up. Yet our attention need not be passive in watching TV: we could inwardly work to be more conscious. But TV's inherent design lulls our consciousness into abeyance and set us on a subconscious, automatic, consumerist track. The couch potato does indeed sink from the human toward more vegetative qualities.

In contrast with passive attention, both active and open attention work with the conscious energy. Both may be directed toward a single object or non-directed, i.e., related to the whole of the present moment. The differentiating factor between the active and open forms of attention lies in the inner movement of our will. In active attention, we move outward, as in speaking.

In open attention, we move receptively toward our inwardness, as in listening.

We need to exercise both active and open attention. Actively, we enliven and collect the sensitive energy in our body. In the other mode, we open to the sensation already present in our energy body. Actively, we train our children, while openly listening to and loving them. Actively, we seek to understand where God is, while opening beyond our uttermost depths. Our progress on the spiritual path depends in an essential way on understanding and training attention in both its active and open forms.

Commitment and Confidence in the Path

Commitment means that we know, in our heart of hearts, that we shall persevere in a course of action, come what may. Good parents are defined by their utter commitment to the welfare of their children, regardless of whatever challenges may arise. On the ground, when we meet the unforeseen events brought by time, creativity and compromise may be necessary; we may need to bend without breaking our commitment.

What causes us to commit ourselves to a course of action? In the case of parenting, it is love and conscience, knowing intuitively what's right, what matters. In the case of the spiritual path, it is the same. Love and intuiting the truth about our world bring us toward a stronger, more all-encompassing commitment to the spiritual journey. The circumstances precipitating commitment vary as widely as people. The "how I got started on the path" stories always fascinate, with their coincidences and unexpected episodes.

The spiritual quest begins with the excitement of a new discovery, a new love, a new world. We eagerly learn the methods and practice them with zest. Our teachers inspire confidence in the possibility of transformation and arouse our hope that our own sincere efforts will carry us far along the path. Early results of our practice surprise and delight us, confirming the rightness of the approach and establishing our confidence in the path.

Then a dry spell enters. With no noticeable progress or evident movement, we seem to be treading water. Seeing how we are inwardly, always identifying with thoughts, emotions, and body, gradually builds a weariness of this ordinary way of living. We cannot stop our quest, but we also cannot see our way forward. The weariness, however, leaves us nowhere else to turn. Faith and commitment enable us to persevere through such spiritual deserts. Then somehow we bridge the abyss. For example, we realize that we practice because we must. And furthermore, that the source of this "must" lies beyond our consciousness, in the unseen realm that gives faith. This realization leads to confidence that we shall not stop, shall never give up. Our inner work reaches a new tempo and depth, allowing confidence in our own eventual transformation to take root, further bolstering our practice. We reach unexpected experiences of higher states and intimations of possibilities of deeper forms of service. This reinvigorates our commitment to the path toward greater being.

A new difficulty arises, however, where despite our continuing best efforts, we reach another plateau of no further progress. Our confidence in our practice and in our own future transformation evaporates for a time. At a loss, we turn toward the higher and ask for help. Then our confidence shifts from ourselves to the Divine. We discover the faith that eventually the door to love and the higher worlds will open even to us.

And so we continue. Sometimes our movement is passionate, even desperate. Commitment and desperation form two wings of the same force, the flame of longing for the Real. Desperation combines this intense longing with the dissatisfaction of separation and the fear of failure in the quest. Desperation burns urgently and transports us to new peaks, but soon flickers. Commitment, however, remains to warm and sustain us through the inevitable droughts. The basic longing behind both commitment and desperation moves us, offers us tastes of new worlds, and brings confidence in ourselves, in the path, and in the Higher.

Determination

What determines who succeeds and who fails? Certainly luck, preparation, and circumstances shape our possibilities. But none of these are either necessary or sufficient. The one indispensable factor in success is determination. In the spiritual path, even more than in material pursuits, our degree of determination makes the crucial difference between fulfilling our spiritual potential and falling short.

Material success arrives in tangible, obvious forms. Progress on the spiritual path? We may not even recognize it. Long years of uncertainty confront us. Determination sustains us through the droughts and doubts.

Determination results from our sense of purpose. And our sense of purpose, at its best, is a projection of the Great Unconditioned Purpose into our limited world. Thus, our determination to pursue the spiritual path day-to-day and moment-to-moment is a direct manifestation of our openness to and connection with the Divine. The greater our determination to serve and practice now, the stronger our relationship to the

Source, and vice versa. Our need for spiritual sustenance and connection originates in the particle of the Divine Will placed in us at birth. This need manifests in us as a longing, as an unwavering determination to practice, to open, to win our way through to that Perfection and utter fulfillment that await us.

In any (or every) given moment, determination enables us to work on awareness, sensation, presence, kindness, and all the other practices which form our path. This is the essence and touchstone of the reality of the path: practice in this moment, in every moment. The more we practice, the more our determination to practice grows. Our repeated recognition, particularly in times of difficulty, that the spiritual is the source of all meaning, renews our determination, returning us to focus on our practice.

Imagine the determination we would need to practice unabated, moment-to-moment, in continuity of awareness: great determination indeed. Fortunately, we find help from another direction. Determination emanates from the active, forceful side of will. On the open, accepting side of will, we have our commitment growing apace. With determination we push ourselves and our practice, probing and extending the boundaries of our familiar envelope, our assumed limitations. Commitment draws us to practice, attracts us into this moment of heartful presence. Together, determination and commitment create a natural synergy directed toward liberation, love, and service.

Determination is the ramrod strength of will to see the path through, come what may, even in our weakest and most distressed moments. Yet the truth is, it waxes and wanes. At times when other interests, cares and burdens distract us, our inner work and determination to practice may weaken. But rather than merely flapping about in the breeze of life, we can, even then, reach beyond our usual self, into our own core and find that which will not let go of the path, which holds to the most basic source of meaning, which remembers why we are here. This, our second and hidden determination, picks us up from life's muddle and sets a clear course. Then we find our bearings and begin to walk the path again.

Seeing

The faculty of seeing truth, in particular the truth about our own behaviors, both inner and outer, illumines our path toward liberation. This inner seeing, if accepted, repeatedly exposes the manifestations of our egoism, which withers slightly each time the light of seeing strikes it. The faculty of seeing has this power because it intuitively knows right and wrong. Seeing penetrates our illusions and recognizes any hint of egoistic self-centeredness, not only in our speech and actions, but also in our hidden thoughts, emotions, and desires. Seeing sees all.

Why then, with the benefit of our ability to see, are we not already free of egoism? Because seeing the manifestations of our egoism for what they are means seeing many of our motivations, thoughts, and actions revealed as unbecoming, unattractive, petty and ugly. These sobering revelations cause us great discomfort, because they clash with our carefully constructed and well-protected self-image. At that point we brush aside, reject or ignore what we see, effectively insulating ourselves from the power of seeing. So, although this faculty continually sees, it lies buried under layer upon layer of self-centered attitudes, desires, and attachments. And with our egoism hidden from view in our very center, we remain identified with the surface instead of reclaiming our depth.

Seeing depends on consciousness, but the conscious energy

is not the essence of seeing. For that we must look to our will, to the one who sees in us, who sees us. This willingness to see, this seer is none other than our own conscience, our deeper self.

To reopen this channel, to regain the light of the seat of seeing, we must leave the darkness of the seat of egoism, for we cannot sit in both places at once. When we lapse into ego, we want no part of seeing, for it only interferes. But when we relinquish our ego priority, we inevitably begin to see our self-centered actions, inner and outer, and thereby weaken their hold on us. The key is to be ready to take note of and accept what our seeing faculty shows us. The more we open to seeing, the more we see. The light dispels the darkness and makes us whole. The very event of seeing our own attachments and identifications loosens their grip.

Seeing is crucial to our path. If we honor it and continue to honor its promptings by changing our inner and outer actions accordingly, it will do its work of purification. By actually reforming our inner and outer behavior in the light of what we see and know to be right or wrong, we eventually become the one who sees in us and take a great stride toward our perfection. In that process, we shift our emphasis from the seen to the seer. The stronger our will to see, the more established as the seer, engaged in seeing, the more we rise out of entanglement with what we see and even with what we do not see.

In the book of Genesis, the primordial act of creation occurs when God says "Let there be light." Discoveries in modern cosmology indicate an immense explosion of energy and light at the moment of creation. In seeing we connect with that light, both the well-known outer form of ordinary light, as well as the inner light by which we see within ourselves and see in depth. In the penultimate stage of the spiritual path, the realized person sees uniquely in the utter glory of the Divine Light.

But along the way we must not ignore the basic difficulties we see. If we see we are doing something that is wrong, or that we are feeding and nurturing egoistic thoughts, attitudes, and emotions, then we need to let go these unbecoming manifestations. By doing so, we honor the one who sees, we establish true inner integrity, and we respect and move toward our higher self.

Obstacles

Without obstacles, it seems that our path to the higher would be smooth and fast. We are constructed in such a way, however, that obstacles abound and even proliferate. The spiritual usefulness of obstacles is that by working against them or despite them, we gain strength, wisdom, and humility.

Each religion presents a view of the obstacles to spiritual freedom and love. The Buddha taught about five hindrances on the path: grasping, ill will, sloth and torpor, agitation, hurry and worry, and doubt. To those five, the Buddha added the core fetter of belief in a separate self: egoism. The Christian seven deadly sins present a similar view of the obstacles: pride and vanity, envy, gluttony, lust, anger, greed, and sloth.

In the context of the spiritual path, sloth is perhaps one of the least obvious but most detrimental hindrances. Its source is a lack of need for liberation and love. This lackadaisical attitude stops us before we begin. If we do not have a strong spiritual hunger driving us to practice, then spiritual sloth rules and we do not move. We remain lost in our daydreams and thoughts, in unbecoming emotions and desires. Fortunately, the more we practice, the more we see the truth about ourselves, the more we taste the higher possibilities, and the more our longing and determination grow. Furthermore, the realization that our time is limited and relentlessly vanishing also mitigates our inner laziness.

When we lack presence in the here and now, we may fall into haste and anxiety, focusing on our fears and desires for the future. When we live in our superficial layers, not in contact with who we really are, nor with the peace in our depths, we may fall into pride, vanity, envy, gluttony, and greed. When we lack real connection with others, we may relate through anger, jealousy, lust, domination or submissiveness. All of these difficult emotions divert our energy and attention from the path.

The doubts that block the path come in several flavors, all centered on asking for assurance and certainty before we have earned them. We doubt the reality of higher worlds, of the Divine, of the possibility of perfecting our soul. We doubt the efficacy of the spiritual path. We doubt our own ability to awaken, to live in presence. All such doubts can only be answered by our own deepening experience, by our own devotion to spiritual practice, come what may. Nothing that we are told or that we read can erase our doubts. The only way to dissolve the knot of doubt is to see the deeper realities directly for ourselves. But in the meantime, doubt need not block our inner work because we need not be certain. Our heart's intuition, faith, and determination can substitute for certainty until, through our continuing practice, we reach the stage of where doubts abate in the face of our growing realization. The more we see, the more certain we become.

If we look carefully at our own experience, to see what keeps us from awakening, to see what distracts us from our inner work and from being more present, we will discover our own personalized set of obstacles. We need to know them very well and experiment with how to overcome, avoid, reduce, or neutralize them. This requires true intelligence. Butting heads with deeply ingrained patterns may exacerbate some. Patient, unflinching, and clear seeing can undercut many obstacles. But others do call for active opposition. Bringing intelligence, creativity, discernment, and determination to bear within our daily rounds empty of practice pays handsome dividends.

A Meditation: Earth and Sun

The Earth and Sun are repositories and generators of spiritual energies. In this meditation, we seek to open a channel to those energies, so they will feed our being and enable us to pursue our spiritual work more deeply.

While this meditation involves contact with the Earth and the Sun, it is typically practiced indoors. The contact called for is an inner contact and does not depend on physically touching the ground or having the Sun's light shining on your body. In fact, it can be practiced when the Sun is not visible, on a cloudy day or at even at night. You only need to have a rough idea of where the Sun is. For example, if you were to practice this at midnight, then you would know that the Sun is below you, beyond the opposite side of the Earth. If in the morning, then you know the Sun lies above you and toward the east.

Sit comfortably with your eyes closed. By way of preparation, spend some time (say 20 minutes or so) relaxing deeply, letting go all the tensions, and then awakening your contact with sensation throughout the body.

Recall in your mind and heart that the Earth is your mother, caring for you, nurturing you and providing for all your needs. Like every living creature on this planet, you are a child of the Earth, you are a part of the Earth, partaking in its bountiful kindness.

Now send your attention directly below you, deep down into the Earth. Let your attention form a channel to the depths of the Earth. Open that channel to allow the Earth's energy to flow directly into you. Do this repeatedly, sending your attention down, down, down into the Earth, and opening to the flow of energy welling up from that great reservoir. Let the energy merge with the sensation already present in your body.

When your body is saturated, stop. Evoke a feeling of gratitude toward the Earth. Rest in awareness.

Recall in your mind and heart that all lives on the Earth, including your own, depend on the continued beneficence of the Sun. While the Sun is not the Divine, it serves as a model or reminder of the Divine outpouring that creates and sustains this universe.

Now turn your attention toward the Sun. (Note: eyes are still closed. You're not looking toward the Sun.) Send your attention out toward and into the Sun, to form a channel to the Sun's immense reservoir of a very potent energy. Allow this energy to flow into you, letting it merge with the sensation in your body. Do this repeatedly.

When your body is saturated, stop. Evoke a feeling of gratitude toward the Sun. Rest in awareness.

The Illusion of Presence

As long as we believe ourselves to be fully present and awake during our everyday life, we have no reason to try to awaken nor to practice the methods leading to presence, and the spiritual life will not take root in us. But the construction of our minds keeps us under this very illusion that we are present

164

all the time. If someone asks us if we are conscious, then we correctly and perhaps indignantly reply "Yes, I'm here." For that moment we are indeed present, because the question suddenly prods us into a more complete awareness. But the moment passes in an instant and we return to our automatic, autopilot, pre-programmed, personality-driven mode of living.

Take the example of our storehouse of memories, out of which our entire personality and self-image form. We only remember moments of presence. So if we look back on our day, on our week, on our life, we recall events only to the degree to which we were present for them. If someone asks us what we had for dinner on some random evening three weeks ago and how it tasted, we do not remember. This fact of incomplete memory indirectly shows our lack of presence, at least in the past.

Even true presence itself perpetuates the illusion of continuity. When we happen to enter a state of presence or consciousness, its timeless quality and its organic naturalness delude us into thinking that this is our usual state, this is how we are all the time. "Here I am, awake as always." Again, though, that state of presence evaporates almost immediately.

To see our lack of presence in a given moment, we need only work seriously at any of the practices in these pages intended for use during our daily routines. One of the very first things we see in the effort, for example, to be continually aware of our physical sensations, of our energy body, is that we can only achieve it intermittently. Our conceit of the continuity of our consciousness proves empty. That cracking of our illusion of continuous presence ushers in a major step toward the reality of the spiritual path. Only when we truly understand our lack of awareness, can we begin to work in earnest toward developing presence.

Presence

Presence... The very word evokes a sense of depth and potency of character, a gravitas, a charisma based on inner substantiality rather than outward flash, a simple and quiet dignity. All of that, however, only describes the outward indicators of presence. Our path addresses its inner manifestation.

True living absolutely requires presence: more presence, more life. Without presence, life passes us by: we neither participate in nor experience our life. Presence means being at home in ourselves, being here, not only in contact with our sensory experience, but also doing what we are doing, not just letting life happen passively. Presence means inhabiting our bodies, inhabiting our space, inhabiting our actions and inhabiting our life.

Consciousness, the basic foundation of presence, is a timeless energy of wholeness and peace. We may develop strong sensations of our body, emotions, and thoughts, even while consciousness remains weak and dispersed, submerged and mixed with the energies of sensation. Our sensory perceptual experiences, including thoughts and emotions, cover and obscure consciousness. The foreground of life, the perceptual picture on the screen of consciousness, captivates our attention and we remain unaware of the screen itself. But we cannot find consciousness by focusing on its contents, on the ever-changing play of sensations. Consciousness possesses entirely different qualities: spacious, timeless and unchanging. However, our contact with consciousness does change. Presence is always available, but by habit, clouded perception, and lack of choice, we are not always available to it.

Perhaps you have seen the drawing of a black vase on a

white background. You shift your focus to the background and suddenly see two faces kissing, the vase having merged into the background. This foreground-background perceptual shift presages exactly what we need with respect to consciousness: to bring consciousness to the foreground, as the basic container of our experience.

We can approach presence from the front or from behind. From the front, the side of sensory perceptions, we approach through quiet relaxation and meditation, letting thoughts, emotions, and sensations settle down, until we become aware of the gaps between them, and then aware of the consciousness filling those gaps. As our energies settle, consciousness may coalesce like beads of water joining to form a pool. We rest in the still pool of consciousness, not entangled with its contents, not lost in sensations. Then the foundation for presence grows strong.

Approaching presence from behind, we search deep within ourselves for that vibrant space beneath all our sensations, thoughts, and emotions. As we step behind our ordinary perceptions, the vast continuum of consciousness gradually unfolds in a new mode of perception.

Yet consciousness alone is not enough: we need the will to be present, the will to be. If we do not intentionally choose to be present, presence will be rare and fleeting. That is our role in the work of presence, to make that choice again and again, to take every moment of awakening and decide to be. If there is no one home in us, it matters little how much awareness we may have of bodily sensations or anything else. The degree of someone being there, someone (will) who actually does the seeing and moving and thinking, determines the degree of presence, the quality of our life. Thus, our will-to-be is the central component of presence.

The will-to-be can pervade our entire body, our entire being. Acting through our attention and intention, our will entrains the energy of consciousness, carrying it into our body, into our energy of sensation, where the two energies blend to help create our soul. The key to this begins with being present in our energy of sensation, which resides in our body, not just being present in our body. The difference is subtle but significant.

This simple will-to-be supports our presence, giving us life. Our will-to-be suffuses our presence with a force, the force of will, like the wind filling the sails of a boat. When we accept to become our will-to-be, we raise ourselves out of the thrall of associative thoughts and our other automatic and reactive processes, and we abide in presence. We experience this will-to-be as "I," as "I am," as "I am here." Yet this "I" is not separate from others, but rather an element of the Whole.

This will-to-be, this wind filling our sails does not begin in us. Its source lies in the higher worlds. The challenge is to open ourselves sufficiently, so as not to block or divert that wind flowing through us from Above. God may see through our eyes and act through our hands, but only to the extent that we are present, that we engage in this moment, in being here, and in opening to the higher will. Our will-to-be thus takes on a two-fold character. First, we are active toward the outside, toward full sensation in the body, toward full contact with sensory experience, toward activity in the world. Second, we are open to the innermost, the higher, allowing it to warm our very being and infuse us with proximity to the Ultimate. Between them, in consciousness, the two act in harmony as simple, relaxed presence. Thus not merely a personal matter, the effort to be present itself fulfills a sacred duty incumbent on all human beings, to serve as a bridge between heaven and earth. Presence sets the stage for love, good works, and the transformation of energies.

Presence has several measures: frequency, duration, intensity and depth.[14] Frequency connotes how often we return to ourselves, how often we remember to be within ourselves and make the effort to be present. We aim to decrease the lapsed time between falling out of presence and coming back to it. Every activity in life transforms into an opportunity for practice. Former sources of frustration, such as waiting in line or being stuck in traffic, become openings into which we pour our spiritual effort. Whenever we notice that we have fallen out of presence, out of consciousness, we immediately rouse ourselves back to the moment.

Duration reveals the stability of our presence. It indicates the length of any given period of presence, how long we are able to stay within our awareness before we fall back into sensation or down into autopilot. We may effectively gauge our day by estimating the percentage of our waking hours during which we were present. Our goal is 100% unbroken presence all day, every day. But as with every other aspect of the spiritual path, we start where we are: somewhere less than 2% on a good day. Being honest with ourselves clarifies our situation. If we remain under the illusion that we are present all the time, we shall never come to the necessary effort and determination.

Intensity of presence depends on two factors: the quantity of energy and the strength of our will-to-be. The more energy brought together in our being, the more intensely present we can be. The more steadfast our will-to-be, the more intensely present we are. Intensity of presence should not be confused with tension of any kind. Presence comes with an inner relaxation. An intense will-to-be does not imply an experience of tension, but rather a strong, vivid, and current intention to live in presence, which enables us to actually be here at home in this body, in this place, in this very moment.

Lastly, depth results from the combination of the degree of

stillness and the clarity of will in our presence: the quality of energy and will available. Is our presence underscored by the deep silence underlying everything, conferring a conscious, unifying wholeness to presence? Am I actually here in this silence? Is the whole of my attention and intention engaged in being in this moment? Our external will-to-be opens inwardly to an alignment with and devotion to the higher world. We open the very core of our being to the higher. In the center, between the open will toward the inner/higher and the active will toward the outer/lower, we stay relaxed in being conscious.

Presence builds on awareness, awareness encompassing physical sensations, emotions, and thoughts. Strong contact with sensation throughout the whole of the body serves as an excellent foundation for consciousness to arise. Contact, in turn, with the pure, underlying screen of consciousness serves as the foundation of presence, a vehicle to carry presence, an invitation to presence to reside in us. Into this basic consciousness, we, our true will, can enter. To really live, means to live in presence. Without presence, our time passes, lost like yesterday's sunset. With presence, we bring the timeless to time, transforming it, as well as ourselves and our lives.

Stabilized Presence

In the wilderness of the spirit, how can we know the true direction and limit our wandering missteps? One way is to establish a clear goal, against which we can measure ourselves and toward which we can see how to move. Continuity of awareness, continuity of inner work can be such a worthy, even necessary, long-term aim for our practice.

Every spiritual path puts forward some notion of stabilized

or continuous conscious presence. In the *New Testament* we find Christ's admonitions *"Watch ye therefore: for ye know not when the master of the house cometh ..., lest ... he find you sleeping,"*[15] and *"watch ye therefore, and pray always,"*[16] as well as Paul's *"pray without ceasing."*[17] The *Philokalia*[18] and the *Way of a Pilgrim*[19] offer powerful examples of the Christian approach to continuous prayer. Like the Jesus Prayer, the Sufi zikr, or remembrance of the Divine, moves from the mind and the tongue to become the perpetual zikr of the heart. Sufis, from the early, great masters known as the Khwajagan down to the modern day, have pursued and taught the constant practice of watchful awareness. In Kabbalah, the goal of devekut, or cleaving to God, comes about through continual remembrance of the Divine. Some of the devout Kabbalists consider it a sin even momentarily to lose their connection to the sacred. Buddhism counsels its advanced practitioners to enter the effortless effort of continuous mindfulness. Zen Buddhism, as well as the Tibetan Buddhist teachings of Dzogchen and Mahamudra, extol the wonders of an open, spacious, continuous awareness. Hindu traditions such as Patanjali's Yoga Sutras and the teachings of Advaita Vedanta present the liberated person as residing in stabilized awareness. Buddhist monks and Hindu yogis go to great lengths to attain that station. Taoist practice leads toward non-doing in unbroken presence.

Yet the fact that many generations of seekers across the entire landscape of spiritual ways have worked to develop stabilized presence does not make it any less challenging for us. If there can ever be a critical mass of humanity from whom stabilized presence could spread to the rest of us, it obviously has not yet been achieved. So this incomparable challenge stands before us.

First, let us look at what we mean by stabilized presence.

We use the term stabilized in the sense of a stable equilibrium: a state to which a system will, of itself, return after being perturbed away from it. When a person established in stabilized presence gets distracted and falls out of presence, the fall is short-lived and self-correcting. Their natural tendency is not to stray far from presence and to revert to it very soon. For most of us, the opposite holds: our presence is unstable and momentary. When we get distracted we tend to move further and further from presence, typically returning to it only after a lengthy sojourn on autopilot and passive attention, lost in rambling thoughts, emotional reactions, and half-noticed sensory perceptions. But consciousness is not in time and need not be destabilized by events in time and space. Our ordinary thoughts and emotions need not distract us from presence, which subsumes all events brought to us by our senses.

We can have early, sporadic episodes of unbroken, stabilized presence that last for varying durations. All movement toward higher worlds occurs in this way: initially as an intermittent experience and later as an enduring change in our being. When our entry into presence grows frequent enough, and our sojourns there grow long enough, episodic presence merges into continuity. But to realize such a steadfast and fully stabilized presence, one that does not diminish and remains continuous throughout our day and night, even while we sleep, marks a very great transformation of a person's soul, a major milestone in their spiritual journey, and a blessing for us all.

Many seekers falsely believe in and search for some hidden secret practice or magical formula that will speed their progress on the path. Yet the real requirements stand open for all to see and belong to the realm of will. The key factors in working toward more continuous presence are (1) how much it matters to you, (2) actually deciding to do it now, (3) opening to higher energies, (4) opening to a higher will, and (5) accepting to live in a new way, in the full light of awareness. Any of us can be present for a moment. So we know presence through our momentary tastes of it. The crux of the matter is: at what point do we allow some alluring or repulsive item from the never-ending stream of potential distractions to grab us? If, with the whole of our being, we have truly decided to anchor ourselves to presence, not just in some future but right now, if we wholeheartedly commit ourselves to be here, if this becomes our overarching priority for every moment, as important to us as our next breath, and if through deep meditation and prayer we can open to the transformative action of the higher energies and the higher will, only then is continuity of presence possible. The absolute commitment attracts help from the spiritual depths. That help, in turn, increases our commitment to presence, our love for the Divine, and our attraction to the sacred spirit hidden within.

Those of us who aspire to a spiritual path tend to wish we could be more present, but generally that wish falls short of wholeheartedness. We fear that real commitment to continuous presence will interfere with the duties and pleasures of life. But it is not like that. Perhaps we would spend more time in meditation and prayer, but certainly not to the point of irresponsibility toward our material life. We quickly realize that presence is a parallel process that occurs as we move through our ordinary daily experiences. We can learn to be present at any and all times and places. Presence can even help us be more effective in life, enable a stronger appreciation for the pleasures of life, and serve as a robust framework from which to meet life's challenges.

Our first forays into working at presence show the difficulty of it. At that point, the danger lies in assuming that because presence is hard to maintain, it must be impossible to maintain.

But that is not so. All the great paths point to the necessity of continuous presence. If we allow our assumptions based on past experience to limit our future, we box ourselves into the world of automatic, self-perpetuating thoughts and emotions, which control our life and of which we remain only half-aware.

Another danger with presence lies in pseudo or illusory presence. If we believe ourselves already present, we shall make no effort toward real presence. But our habitual inattentiveness, forgetfulness and distraction expose as false our presumptions of presence. Persistent and intentional work at presence gradually teaches us the difference between living on autopilot and being awake.

The practice of awareness of bodily sensation offers major help in moving toward continuous presence, because sensation creates a platform for consciousness. The more we work on establishing and increasing the sensitive energy in our body, the more that energy stabilizes. Sensation can then come back to remind us to be present at moments when we are lost in our personality, our pre-programmed mode of functioning.

Continuity of presence does not depend on continuity of effort to be present. Of course, such effort is most necessary, but not all the time. Instead, we can relax into sensation, relax into consciousness and find a natural stability there, a new home in the light of full awareness. Letting go of tensions and distractions carries us more and more into this one, eternal present moment.

Traditionally, those who were serious enough to pursue continuity of presence did so in the context of monastic-style seclusion or retreat. Removed from many of the cares, duties, and distractions of ordinary life, perhaps surrounded by reminders of the practice and by the intention and energy of fellow travelers on the path, the seeker could work out his or her salvation

174

with diligence. It still holds true that a spiritual retreat, during which one works to establish continuous presence, proves its possibility.

While the retreat approach certainly remains valid and powerful today, we look toward a path within life, a way to purify and build our soul in the midst of modern society. Fortunately, to meet this challenge, a remarkable array of spiritual practices, hitherto hidden, have become widely available during the past century. Any of us can find genuine and personally-suitable ways to pursue inner work seriously during our typical days. Perhaps we begin the day with prayer and/or meditation. During the day, we frequently come back to presence through awareness of bodily sensation, through conscious breathing, through prayer, or other practices that build presence. The more we practice, the more we wish to practice, the more we are drawn toward the spiritual worlds, and the more we can and do practice. Aiming at continuous presence, in itself helps move us toward it. Depending on our understanding and determination, a state of presence begins to become the norm rather than the exception for us. The foreground of our ordinary awareness of thoughts, sensations, and emotions opens out to merge into the background and wider context of consciousness. Events in time and space stand in the silent midst of the higher dimensions. And love finds a home in the clarity of our presence.

As our presence grows we come to the barrier of egoism. Why do we seek presence? Is it to be better than other people? Is it so we can congratulate ourselves for it, boast inwardly, if not outwardly? Is it to form our soul for our personal salvation? In the end, all self-oriented motivations fall short. Self-centeredness inevitably moves from the desire for spiritual advancement to some other attractive item, making continuity of presence based on an egoistic posture impossible. If, instead, we approach presence as an act of service to our neighbor and to the Divine, then we have a chance to live in presence. If we realize that the true answer to the question "Who is present?" is not me, but rather the sacred higher will, then we have a chance to live in presence. If we recognize that without opening to the higher, sacred energies, we cannot move toward continuous presence, then we have a chance to live in presence.

Bring yourself into full awareness of body, heart, and mind. Open to your whole presence and be here. This state seems so natural, so right for us. Our challenge lies in dropping the assumption of impossibility and working diligently, strongly, deeply and frequently enough to transform our presence from an intermittent and short-lived state into our enduring level of being.

Participation

What does it mean to participate in our life? Isn't that what we do all the time? Looking carefully at how things are with us, we may notice that we rarely adopt that combination of responsibility and presence that defines true participation. We sleep-walk, allowing the acts of our body to occur by happenstance and habit, with perhaps our passive consent. When you stand, do you have the direct feeling of "I am standing here," or is your body standing on its own and anyhow?

Participation means actually doing what we are doing, purposely, not just letting everything happen by default, autopilot, habit, and accident. To participate means to be the source of our actions: from simple acts like walking, to more complex ones like thinking and speaking. When you participate in walking, you have the sense that you own your body. Otherwise your body owns you. When you participate in thinking, you direct your thoughts rather than abdicating to random associations.

The hallmark of participation lies in the unspoken, unthought, direct sense that "I am doing this." This state can be contrasted with observation, witnessing, or mindfulness. Mindfulness sees, whereas participation does. Observation can be from a distance, while participation lives in the midst of the action with full awareness and full engagement. Participation sees like observation, but also takes the further step of being the actor, the agent of our being. In any given moment, participation means entering our body, our life and our time as the doer.

The first impediment to participation is passivity and the second is egoism. Being the doer, the agent of our actions, does not necessarily imply letting ego control. Indeed, participation clears us of egoism and self-centeredness because it arises from a deeper place in us. The process begins with becoming the one who lives our life. And the path of becoming ends in the ultimate goal of spirituality: allowing God to be the One Who participates in us, through us, as us.

The Illusion of the Ego

What in us blocks our connection with the spiritual depths? If heaven is real, why am I not in contact with it? All religions and paths address this central question, under a variety of names, the most common today in the West being "ego." The term ego, in this context, alludes to our deeply ingrained self-referential, self-seeking disposition, our well-hidden and highly adaptable attitude that life revolves around me and mine. Ego cuts us off from other people, from Nature, from God, from our

THE SACRED ART OF SOUL MAKING

authentic self, from our true responsibility, and from fulfilling our destiny. Our ego is the great usurper. It focuses on our local independence, falsely presuming it to be a global independence. The ego convinces us that we are truly separate beings with ultimately separate will, having no inherent connection with other people or with God.

Our ego installs us at the center of the universe, separate from all and enslaved by time. Dwelling on our past history, our conditioning, our grudges, our manufactured identity, our personality, or on our future hopes, dreams, fears, anxieties, desires, and pressures, ego creates a constant torrent of mental structures, each of which proclaim "This is me." In childhood we become so involved and enamored with the growing arsenal of our ego, that we unquestioningly assume it is who we are. That insidious assumption constitutes the ego's iron grip on us.

This ego, this false pretender, whenever it arises grabs the seat of honor at the core of our being. It purports to speak for the whole of us, even though our various parts lack integration. It adopts the voice and desires of whatever part of us pushes itself temporarily to the top of the heap. So for example, our ego, under the influence of one part of us, "decides" to do something, but later under the influence of another part, we find ourselves doing just the opposite. I may think "I am going to quit smoking tomorrow." But tomorrow my hand, not caring what my mind thought yesterday, reaches for a cigarette. The pretender to the throne does not bear the royal seal, does not have the power it ascribes to itself.

Why is it that the ego, or separate self, produces such a major difficulty in the spiritual path, indeed THE major difficulty? The answer can be found in the subtlety of the place occupied by ego and I. That place is not readily visible, even to our inner eye. It lies in the realm of Will, beyond all thought, emotion, and sensory experience, beyond awareness or consciousness itself, beyond our mind. Ego and I reside in the place of who we are, that in us which chooses and decides, or abdicates choosing and deciding. A thought that says, "I will ...," masquerades as the source of decision. When this does represent an actual decision, the true source is will itself. Our will, however, usurped by the self-centered ego, an aberration of will, enters into a wrong and self-referential mode of working. Our true I does not act by force, but rather by cooperation. The uncooperative ego can thus come and stand in the place of the I, hiding and splitting off our authentic I from the rest of us. Under the influence of ego, we believe ourselves to be our own source. It turns out that, although we are indeed our own source, that very source is the Source of All.

Religions and paths portray the nature of our egoism and how to deal with it in one of two quite distinct modes. Usually, and to our misfortune, the ways reify and solidify ego into a something, an enemy, which must be overcome, which must die, which inherently resides in our tainted nature, which must be purified. True enough. One cannot argue with the accumulated wisdom of great religions. For our modern culture, though, the notion that our ego must die seems frightening. More importantly, the notion that we harbor inherent spiritual taints gets interpreted by our self-bashing, insecure psychology to mean that we are bad — something that we in the West have been trained to believe since childhood. We believe we are not good enough. So we don the knowledge of being corrupt to our core as a mantle of supposed wisdom, and flock to those that teach it. Then the religious teaching about egoism simply gets co-opted by the self-denigrating side of our ego, eagerly adopted and accepted as yet another weakness. We hang our heads and beat our breasts and feel the better (or worse) for it.

Unfortunately, all this only strengthens our egoism and leads us into an endless cycle, akin to a dog chasing its tail.

Casting our ego as the enemy in an inner holy war and winning that battle is an exceedingly difficult proposition, primarily because the ego proves to be a most subtle adversary. In fact, the ego will even join the battle against itself. It will take it on and say "this is wonderful, I'm going to battle against ego, I will become free, I will be wonderful, I will be better than I am now, and I will be better than other people, because I will be a highly evolved spiritual being." The ego joins our forces. As an enemy, it infiltrates our lines, wearing our own uniform, its soldiers and officers indistinguishable from ours. How does one fight a battle against such a devious and resourceful enemy? For most of us, it comes to nothing but an increased layer of suffering as we merely fight ourselves in the name of spirituality and sink more deeply than ever into the morass of self-centeredness. Only the rarest of souls find a way through this conundrum.

An alternative, but also traditional view casts ego in an entirely different perspective, not as an enemy, but as an illusion, and invites us to see our ego for what it is: an empty, ephemeral sham, a hall of mirrors, a self-referential web. The rise of Buddhism in the West is, in no small part, due to this kinder yet no less incisive and perhaps more tractable formulation of the problem of egoism.

Our belief in our ego, or separate self, is to a large extent learned from society. All the people around us labor under a self-centered perspective on life, which naturally devolves to impressionable children. Repeatedly shining the light of awareness directly on this sense of separateness gradually disperses it. But if we look carefully for our ego, for this separate self that we think we are, we shall not find it.

Am I my body? I can control my body, I can be aware of

my body, and my awareness is greater than my body. So I am probably not my body.

Am I my feelings? I can be aware of my feelings and have some rudimentary influence on them, so I am probably not my feelings.

Am I my thoughts? My thoughts claim the title of I, thinking "I think," "I am hungry." But that "I" is just a thought, having no more substance than any other thought. It fools me though, this thought "I." I believe in it. I believe it refers to something real and substantial, to the real me. But if I look at it clearly, I see it as only a thought with no real referent. At best, I may have a vague idea that I am some combination of my thoughts, feelings, and body. Again it proves empty to the perspicacious observer.

Am I my knowledge and experience, my habits and desires, my style — in short, my personality? But I can see all this at work in myself. And clearly, the one who sees seems closer to me than this whole complex of acquired patterns and inherited predispositions that I call my personality. So no, I am not my personality. I need my personality because only through it can I function in life, but I also need to remember that this personality is not who I am.

How about my awareness? Am I my awareness? Two problems here. First, I have some control over what I am aware of. So there must be something deeper. Second, the deeper I go into awareness, the less it is centered in me, so how can that be me as a separate entity, as an ego?

How about my attention? How about that in me that decides, my will? This is the subtlest of all. Yet again, the deeper I look into my will, the less it is centered in me, and the more it opens beyond me.

So wherever we look, we do not find this self, this separate person that takes our name, this self-important actor on the stage of our life. The more carefully and persistently we look, the more this once-compelling ego, this self disappears. Or perhaps we see that it never existed to begin with. Gradually, our belief in our ego assumes a porous quality, which rather than cutting us off from others, merely clouds our relationships intermittently. This separate self never was. Our devotion to it shrivels and we are left to truly be ourselves, to play our unique role in the larger story of our common life. When moments come in which we fall back into that trance of selfness, we feel uncomfortable, like in a shoe that no longer fits, and we let it go.

Our ego, this illusory pattern, however, endures with remarkable resilience and persistence. Complete freedom from ego comes only at a very high station of spiritual development, something to which we may aspire and work for with diligence. The best approach lies somewhere between the two outlined above. Seeing and letting go can only work insofar as we are able to see. The depth and subtlety of our seeing must increase. For this, efforts of various kinds are necessary. These efforts may include grappling with some of the propensities of our separate self. Doing so can illumine the tentacles of egoism, while creating energy for seeing more. Only we must not have the idea that such struggles will, by themselves, reform our recalcitrant self-centeredness. A project of reform by force is doomed to fail. Efforts at reform can only be useful to the extent that they help us to see. Sensing the energy body and working at presence also help us see. And seeing, it is said, leads to liberation: liberation from the illusion of the ego and into the freedom of interconnectedness.

Humility

"...Blessed are the meek ..."[20]

Full of myself, I leave no room for God. Worse still, as long as I harbor even a shred of egoism, my will remains tainted and largely unavailable to the Divine. I put my pseudo-self in the place that rightfully belongs to God, ascribing everything to myself. This basic truth places humility at the essential center of the spiritual path.

But because we fill our sacred emptiness with self-centeredness, egoism, and even arrogance, we cannot work directly to develop a humble heart. Egoism, however much it pretends to don the mantle of spirituality and disappear, remains in the shadows, unwilling to relinquish its control of the actors on our stage, unwilling to depart, always ready to be the agent who we incorrectly believe ourselves to be. So instead we work indirectly toward humility, toward clearly seeing our inner and outer manifestations as they are, against the objective measure of a pure heart. This is the approach from below.

To approach humility from above, we pray and we feel our utter dependence on other people and on God. Try this little exercise. Look around yourself. How much of all these things you see could you make on your own? Your clothes, your food, the furniture! Perhaps none of it. Even on this material level, we completely depend on other people. Spiritually, our situation is still more dramatic. Even a fleeting hint of a taste of the reality of the Divine fills us with awe and humbles us before the Unfathomable. Our entire hope and all our possibilities come from the fact that every effort we make is more than matched by grace. Indeed, the Prophet Mohammed tells us that for each step we take toward God, God takes ten steps toward us.

I learned about humility from my uncle, who repaired shoes for a living. A simple man of kindness, he lived happy and content with his place in life. With unwavering devotion to family and a great capacity for friendship, he inevitably greeted everyone with a warm and genuine smile.

The humble, unassuming person immediately puts us at ease. We can just relax and be ourselves in their presence, a zone of no competition, no judgment, and no fear. The heart of the humble knows love. Humility realizes we are all in the same boat, all human, all equally children of the same God. Humility gladly honors others and, except for reasons of conscience, readily and without rancor gives way.

Yet humility should not be confused with weakness or passivity, with a bowed-head timidity or inactivity. Rather humility arises out of acceptance, out of understanding our true position in the world, as a part of humanity, and a part of life. Humility knows we bear a Divine spark, which is the unique individuality given to each of us, but which remains inseparable from the greater Whole. Our destiny can be found in being fully ourselves, while fully a part of the Whole. Only in humility can we find our way toward that Wholeness.

But what does humility mean in practice? We live in our conditioned part, our knowledge and experience, desires and tendencies, habits, style, and patterns. We can refer to the whole of this as our personality, the mask that hides our authentic self, the instrument we acquire and use to make our way in the world. Our personality can change, but not transform. Spiritual transformation lies deeper than personality; it concerns the user, the one who drives our personality. As long as our personality serves our self-centered ego, we prevent the sacred from entering our core. The practice of humility then is not to change our personality, but to open the agency behind it, to stop placing ourselves above others, to stop claiming our little corner of the universe for our illusory ego, to set aside our adolescent hold on separateness, on me-firstness.

If we really wish to be able to love, then we must empty our heart in humility.

Group Egoism

Like the personal egos that enclose our hearts, minds, and spirit, but even more destructive, a group of people can create an illusory boundary around themselves. Combining their individual egos, group members strengthen the illusion of separateness by layering the group identity onto their own or, even worse, substituting the group ego for their own. History offers too many examples of large scale, horrible manifestations of group egoism: rabid nationalism and tribalism, predatory corporatism, and violently zealous religiosity. Every major religion has at times fallen prey to this malignancy, causing abject misery, with the extreme examples ranging from massacres within and by the early Hebrews, to Christian crusades and the Inquisition, to the Hindu-Muslim conflicts of South Asia, to recent Islamic terrorism. Surely God must weep to see such evil committed in the name of religion. Extreme nationalism leads to the carnage of war, dictatorships, and untold suffering. Corporate predators defraud their stakeholders, pollute the Earth, and buy undue influence over governments, all in the name of the corporate good.

Most groups, however, do not succumb to the extremes of violence and immorality. Religions typically refrain from violence. Nations usually keep their identity without making unjustified war on others. Many corporations restrict themselves to ethical business practices. Even so, milder, nonviolent group egoism still divides the world into "us" and "them" with an absolute, uncaring wall in between.

That wall belies our complete interdependence. Outwardly, humanity shares closer connectedness than ever with the increasing complexity and globalization in the arenas of economics, politics, culture, and impacts on the Earth. Inwardly, an even more remarkable unity unveils itself as our perceptions develop. But all of this shared humanity splinters before the onslaught of egoism, whether individual or group-based.

As participants in the great enterprise of seeking spiritual completion and because of our need to share our search and to worship in community, we depend on having a clear vision of what is and what is not spiritual, of the pitfalls of group spirituality. The overriding principle may be formulated as follows: the degree to which the religion or group emphasizes a difference between members of the religion or group and non-members, between "us" and "them," is a direct measure of its lack of true spirituality. We are all children of the same God. No religion can rightfully claim exclusivity of God's beneficence and compassion. The rain falls equally on all plants.

One illustrative example is the Judaism of the Old Testament. In the first five books, God appears as a partisan for the Hebrews, favoring them over other tribes. But later developments in the Hebrews' understanding of God overcome such partiality. By the time of Isaiah, the Bible says that one day all nations will flow into the mountain of God, walk in His paths, and beat their swords into plowshares — all this not by violence or coercion, but by voluntarily being drawn to the truth of the One God. Clearly, Isaiah recognized the Divine as the God of all humanity, welcoming diverse religions and modes of worship.

Today we look for Christians, Jews, Muslims, Hindus, and Buddhists to tolerate and accept each other, to be able to pursue their faiths and lives in peace and freedom. We hope that ordinary people of all faiths will not allow ourselves to be drawn into blanket condemnation or vilification of other faiths or nations. Arab media portray the U.S. and Israel as forces of darkness and majorities in many Arab countries agree. What a shame, for it is not so. Americans and Israelis, like Palestinians, want peace, both for themselves and others, and understand full well that the road to peace lies through establishing a decent life for all. Some Americans today portray Islam as a religion of violence and aggression. What a shame, for it is not so: truly devout Muslims are as spiritual, tolerant, and peaceful as any people on the Earth. Yet Muslims and Hindus in Kashmir kill each other in the name of religion. What a shame.

When we first enter a spiritual path, we can be amazed by its power, beauty, and truth. We become true believers, thinking that ours is the only way to salvation. Again, it is not so. Gradually, we outgrow our limited, exclusive view to see that other true paths exist and that no one path has a monopoly on the spirit.

Group egoism endangers us in ways that individual egoism cannot. Because we adopt the group identity, perhaps even born into it, and because the group interest seems more objective than our personal agenda, we tend to believe unquestioningly in its validity. The division into "us" and "them" appears natural, appropriate, and true. The delusion of separateness, of being special, seems so right that we cannot even conceive of the need to escape our bondage to it. Compounding the problem, groups naturally wield more power than individuals, so a group ego gone astray can create a dangerous, even evil force.

True spiritual practice loosens the bonds of both individual and group egoism, helping us become both more independent and more connected with others.

Who Am I?

A cursory take on the question "Who am I?" leads us to believe that we are our personality, the sum of our typical patterns of thinking, feeling, and acting. A more careful and perceptive look, however, reveals that the question is not so readily answerable. Indeed, the great Indian sage Ramana Maharshi made contemplation of this question a central practice in his teaching, because for him it had opened the door to a deep spiritual transformation and he saw that it had the power to do the same for others.

Asking ourselves "Who am I?" can guide us in contemplating our true nature, in backtracking through our experience, beyond sensory impressions, beyond emotions, beyond thoughts and mental images, beyond the energy body, even beyond consciousness, toward our source. The question "Who Am I?" followed persistently and honestly, brings contact with that in us which decides, which directs our attention, which intends, chooses and commits. That I is not physical, not a place, not our personality, not an energy and not even our consciousness. It is our will. It is who we really are. We cannot see our I, because our I, when present, is the one who sees, the one who does what we do, the one who thinks, the one who feels, the one who looks for him- or herself, and the only one who can truthfully say "I." That I can direct our attention, effectively choosing what we will be conscious of. This fact shows that our I is deeper than our consciousness.

Asking "Who Am I?" creates an inner mirror that we hold

up to look for our I. But look as we might, we find the mirror empty. We cannot touch or see our I, but we can become it, become our self fully, and "embody" it. To do so, however, our inner mirror must indeed be empty. When the false I of egoism shows up in that mirror, our true I recedes to await our next opening. Presence, by seeing truly, weakens the ego, makes it porous, and permits our authentic I to shine through.

Although it may sound far away and difficult to attain, it is not, it is simple. It is simply and directly being oneself: un-distracted, naturally, and now. It is who we are without our baggage, without our thoughts and feelings about who we are, without our attitudes, opinions, and indulgences, without our desires and fears. It is our unique, individual wholeness. This I is who we are when we say "here I am" and mean it. We cannot manufacture or develop it, for it is already here in us. To be in contact with it, all we need to do is to really be ourselves more often, to be in our own center.

Yet although our I is our disarmingly simple core, it is also unfathomable, because it opens out into our participation in, and ultimately our unity with, the Divine will. That is why a clear conscience is so important: when we willingly engage in inappropriate, unbecoming actions, we distort and pollute our will, centering ourselves in egoism rather than opening toward the higher. The distortions of egoism effectively bar us from contact with the sacred. Thus we see the emphasis on morality in all the great religions.

So we can answer the question "Who am I?" by saying "I am," by being the one who is present enough to be able to say "I am" truthfully. This is not a mystery; it is simply and wholly being oneself here and now. We can directly see the difference between saying "I am" when it is just words and saying "I am" when it has the fullness of our intention and presence behind it, our will-to-be, our will-to-act. This difference shows us the direction our inner work needs to follow to become more fully ourselves.

Our response to the question "Who am I?" shows us our current level in terms of identification with the patterns of our personality, of integration of our disparate impulses, of wholeness of our presence, and of submission to the Divine. First we seek to become ourselves, then to let God become us.

What to do about this? Again and again we ask ourselves "Who am I?" Again and again we return to be that central core of ourselves to which the question directs us. Persistently returning to our center, we find our true home of wholeness, joy, and meaning.

Non-clinging: Letting Go of Attachment

The whole of the spiritual path may be summed up in the term non-clinging, because through non-clinging love comes, through non-clinging the door to the Unconditioned opens, our heart and our will purified and prepared to receive the Will of God. The Buddha taught liberation through non-clinging: not clinging to anything as me or mine, not grabbing something or pushing something else away. Most of our human problems and all our difficulties in the spiritual path result from clinging, from attachment. We take anger as me, as my anger, rather than simply a feeling that will pass, that I can let go of. We take the desire for more as my desire, to be acted upon, rather than as simply a thought or feeling that will pass. We take all our thoughts and feeling reactions far too seriously, as if we were just thoughts and reactions. When we cling to a thought, we become that thought.

On the road to freedom, we must let go of everything as me or mine. One wonderful aspect of the practice of non-clinging is that partial results accrue to us, even early in our path. If we learn not to identify with just a few kinds of thoughts or emotional reactions, we discover a little freedom and lightness, more joy as we walk through life. Non-clinging serves as its own reward.

Non-attachment should not be confused with detachment. On the contrary, non-attachment is the antithesis of detachment. Through non-attachment we free ourselves to love, to be wholly engaged in life, with family, friends, and profession. In non-attachment we disengage from the barriers that separate us from others. Detachment, on the other hand, fortifies the cold walls of separation.

If someone slights me, a whole train of thoughts and emotions may ensue and persist for hours. If I am awake enough at its beginning or even in the midst of it, I see how I cling to the hurt feelings and thoughts. If through that seeing, I am able and willing to release the grip of my reactions on me and release my grip on them, then they subside on their own. I am left breathing easier, unburdened and free to respond or not to the original situation. My energies are conserved for better uses, such as joy and mindfulness. My will is a little less caught in the habit of a self-reflexive stance, in creating a false sense of myself as a person who was hurt by someone's slight.

Paraphrasing the Buddha, non-clinging is an invaluable practice at the beginning of the path, in the middle of the path, and at the end of the path. The price of admission to the spiritual depths, to the Unconditioned, to the presence of God is to give up our clinging. The gate to the deep place only allows those to pass through, whose hearts are purified, at least temporarily. We might catch a glimpse of the Divine though, if even for a moment we can relinquish all attachment, all grabbing and all pushing away.

Because approaching the Divine requires complete non-clinging, life itself serves as a strict, uncompromising taskmaster and teacher on our path. For example, whenever anger arises in me and I identify with it, justifying to myself why I should be angry, I need to notice this situation and let it go. This can be very hard indeed, but very necessary if I am to free myself of clinging. This is not to say that I shouldn't take appropriate action to defend myself. On the contrary, we need to love and respect ourselves, as well as others. But to respect ourselves is to let go of clinging to anger, to greed, to fear, to wanting and to not wanting. This is our situation and our difficulty, where we must bear the true heavy-lifting of the spiritual practice of non-clinging, a heavy-lifting which consists of relaxing, relaxing the ties than enmesh us in mud, relaxing our attitude, releasing our grip on the lower to reach for the higher.

Mindfulness

Mindfulness, the direct awareness of present perceptions, is one of the primary wonders of being fully human. Yet our ordinary mode of being lies somewhere below the level of mindfulness, with a largely unrecognized but terrible cost. With inadequate mindfulness we live a shortened and impoverished life. Shortened in the sense that we experience less if we are not in a state of mindfulness. Impoverished in the sense that what we do experience remains less vivid, less alive, less real. Mindfulness is the authentic state for a human being: a relaxed, open awareness of our inner and outer perceptions in this moment.

While mindfulness may be the birthright of all humans, to

our misfortune we sell it cheaply. We spend the great majority of our time unmindfully, our awareness non-voluntarily collapsed to some minute fraction of the whole, drifting along in a passing reverie or TV or radio, captured by anger, envy, lust, boredom, fear, or greed. Our lives go on without us. Time passes us by, leaving us unmoved, unfilled, unaware. Fortunately, the remedy for our situation exists. And it is an easy one, easy but requiring perseverance.

Coming to, bringing our awareness back to the riches of this one moment can be as simple as basing ourselves in awareness of bodily sensations, in the breath, or in consciousness itself. We can readily enter mindfulness, at least for a moment or two. The more often we try it, the more we acquire a taste for it, and the longer we are able to stay in it.

Mindfulness means being aware of the constantly changing cavalcade of thoughts, emotions, sensations, sights, sounds, tastes, and aromas, without becoming lost or attached. We become the stream rather than the sticks, leaves, and other debris carried by it. Mindfulness can also be called choiceless awareness, to emphasize its non-clinging, non-grasping, open quality. Mindfulness is inherently compassionate, both toward ourselves and toward others. If we do not reject what we see in ourselves, if we can just open into the seeing, our heart also begins to open toward our neighbor.

Mindfulness can be grounded in the sensations of body or breath, or in consciousness itself. These can serve as our home base while seeing the flow of experience. To practice mindfulness we begin by finding that comfortable home within ourselves, e.g., in awareness of bodily sensations or the breath. Then we allow our awareness to expand to include any and all other elements of our current experience, while maintaining awareness of our home base. When we notice, inevitably, that we have become attached, clinging to or rejecting some thought, emotion, pain, etc. and collapsed into it, we gently and gratefully return to bodily sensations or the breath and start again. Repeat until mindfulness becomes our normal way of being. In quiet moments we return fully to basic mindfulness itself: unencumbered, without boundaries, featureless, whole, the background of all experience.

The enormous dividends of this simple practice more than repay our efforts. On a personal level, mindfulness dramatically enriches our quality of life and offers healing, meaning and wholeness. On the level of the Earth, mindfulness opens us to a profound connection with other people and all of life. On the universal level, the practice of mindfulness serves the Great Whole.

Stillness

Stillness acts as a gateway to the spiritual, a gateway of three successive forms of stillness. The first, stillness of the body-heart-mind, develops in meditation when we sit quietly long enough. The body's fidgeting, itching, and restlessness settle down gradually as it attains rest and stillness. Our heart may recall a situation in life that brings into play one of the many hues of emotion. Or a totally imaginary event in our daydreams calls forth an emotion. But gradually, in quiet meditation, the waves of emotion also settle down to a peaceful state of equanimity. Our brain can be pouring thoughts one over another in a cascading stream. As we watch our thoughts, unmoved, not participating in them, just listening to them pass, they slow down. In some cases, they may cease altogether for periods.

Often in meditation, thoughts grow lighter and the gaps

between them widen, so that we can touch what lies beneath the thoughts, the second form of stillness. Stillness of awareness, stillness of consciousness differs from stillness of the body-heart-mind. When we enter the place of pure consciousness, the screen upon which thoughts, emotions, and sensations manifest, when we sit back from all the perceptions arising and falling, when we drop beneath all the inner and outer sounds, and settle into that simple awareness, simple consciousness, we discover consciousness itself as inherently still and silent. Pure consciousness offers us a more profound form of stillness, in which joy naturally arises and through which energy can flow into us, spontaneously infusing our whole being and body. This stillness of awareness forms the shoreline of the spiritual. Beyond it lie the worlds of the spirit. We find contact with the stillness of awareness most readily, but not only, in meditation. Rather, this stillness comprises the background of all our experience: always there, awaiting our greater or lesser alignment with it.

Of even greater subtlety, the third form of stillness, the stillness of will, means letting go of our attachments and intentions, desires of all kinds, even the desire to be in a state of stillness. We open our will, our intentionality, thereby allowing our core, the place of our will, to be approached by the higher will, the Will of the Transcendent. As long as we remain firmly fixed on our personal agendas and desires, we block the entry of the higher will.

Neither stillness of consciousness, nor stillness of will depend on stillness of the body. Thoughts and emotions can be streaming, the body moving, seeing, hearing, and speaking, and yet, simultaneously, underlying all these more external perceptions, we can stay in touch with the more interior, the stillness of consciousness, open in our will, fully present.

Stillness of will, openness to the Tao, should not to be confused with passivity. Instead, it calls for an alert, awake, open way of being. It involves the action of non-action. Not placing oneself in the loop of action, but allowing the action to flow through us. In this way we can be responsive and responsible, very active, yet free of our personal agendas, open to a more universal agenda. We see and act without the overlay of our attachments to distort our actions, but rather through the instrument of our wisdom, our knowledge, our skills, our particular talents and character. Ultimately, we aim to serve as a conscious, cooperative instrument of the spiritual force. While living a truly moral life, stillness of will involves not inwardly taking credit for our successes, nor blame for our failures. Stillness of the will brings true inner peace and fulfillment. Have you ever been utterly content?

We Are: The Illusion of Separateness

We live alone within our personal shell. We relate to people as if appearances were real, as if the ultimate truth dictates that I am here and you are there and an impenetrable wall separates us.

When I look at another person I see the outside. I see a body clearly separate from mine. But when I look at myself, I see the inside; I see my awareness, my consciousness. I know, rationally, that you have awareness, consciousness in you just as I do, that you have hopes and dreams, knowledge and fears just I as I do. But when I look at you, I do not see all this. I know the whole glory and catastrophe of being a human resides there in you, but I cannot see it. And so I assume and act as if consciousness is mine alone, as if consciousness stops at my skin. My perception does not show me your consciousness. You remain hollow to me, just an animated body, not real in the way that I am. How can I bridge this gap between us? How can I operate from the reality that I know must be true despite the limitations of my perception? How can I see you to be as real as I am?

The source of this illusion of separateness lies in the illusion of the ego. Relaxing with friends or family we may lower our inner barriers. In the underlying context of awareness, in the silent pool of consciousness we discover spaciousness without limits. Beneath our thoughts, beneath our emotions, we let go into simple awareness, into consciousness, the field in which we live and experience, the very substance of experience. Consciousness knows no boundaries, does not end at our skin. Space embraces us all, as does consciousness. Space penetrates all and walls cannot limit it. Likewise, our bodies do not define the limits of consciousness.

To rest in awareness, in consciousness, we drop our shell of separation, our false identity and enter the larger world, the great present. As we drain this moat of egoism, we see others in a new way: just people, neither more nor less than ourselves. Sharing in consciousness, knowing that others experience a full inner world just as we do, we begin to bridge the gap. We become simultaneously an entire universe in ourselves and just "one of the guys." The "guys" become one in consciousness, even though we continue to experience this peculiar fact of life: that we directly know only our own thoughts, emotions, sensations, and not anyone else's.

The more we enter into the stillness of simple awareness, the more we drop our fences of separation and identity in the consciousness that we share. This brings us to the first level of unity among people: unity in consciousness. Prior to this level, we can speak of cooperation and relationship but not unity.

Will offers a field for another kind of unity: shared intention and common purpose. The levels of unity under commonality of will depend on the depth and breadth of the sharing: from family, to community, to nation, to all humanity, to all life, to the Great Purpose of the Universe. We all enter into shared purpose with others in many types of communities: the corporation, the school, the sports team, the orchestra, the worship community, the political party, the military unit, the construction crew, the city, state, or nation. In all such cases of associated intention, we act in a coordinated fashion as part of a unit larger than our individual self. The result can be true and deep fellowship along with a sense of fulfillment. Shared intention, at its most effective, does not entail loss of individuality, but rather our fully individualized and unique participation in a greater whole.

We know in our hearts that our aim for a meaningful life depends on becoming fully ourselves while transcending ourselves. Both unity in consciousness and unity in will enrich and transform us with a spirit that eventually approaches Love.

Peace

Like water drawn to the ocean, peace beckons us toward its palpable presence. Substantive peace bears its own positive quality, not merely an absence of non-peace. But the practice of letting go of non-peace dredges the river of our inner and outer actions, so we more readily flow toward the ocean of peace. Peace offers the perfection of contentment, freedom from wanting. When our contact with the higher confronts and dissolves our attachment to the lower, the reconciling embrace of peace warms our heart and suffuses our soul.

The paths to peace include both action and non-action. Care for our body through proper nutrition, exercise, and relaxation, while not indulging in the harmful, removes roadblocks to a peaceful body. As-is acceptance of oneself, others, and the world, builds the foundation for a peaceful heart. Accepting the inevitability of change releases our grip on the non-peace of fear and desire. This does not preclude working for positive change, but such efforts occur in a context of tolerance, not rejection. Awareness of thoughts leads us out of our mental morass and toward a peaceful mind. Thoughts float by like clouds in the sky, but the sky itself remains unperturbed. Being rooted in open, accepting, non-identified awareness of body, heart, and mind, ushers us into the peace of presence.

Peace of body, heart, and mind sets the stage for meditation leading to contact with the ocean of blissful ease, within and beyond all sensory experience. This peace of being supports us in seeking peace of will through right action and surrender to the higher. We earn a clear conscience by invariably doing the right thing, fulfilling our duties to family and society, keeping our promises, giving our best by practicing excellence, and persisting in our spiritual practice and prayer. All this brings a deep sense of purpose, true satisfaction, fulfillment of spirit, and the peace of conscience.

Inner peace leads to outer peace. Our personal attitude of non-harming and acceptance of others creates an atmosphere of peace. While fear, hatred, and violence are infectious, so is peace. The surest way toward a peaceful world, a world without war, without violent crime, is for each of us to manifest our own aura of peace.

Non-Dual Awareness

In certain remarkable Eastern spiritual teachings the entire path revolves around entering our inherent pure awareness, pure consciousness, pure being, and residing there. Seer and seen merge into a global awareness which excludes nothing, has no center and no separation between observer and observed. The ego, at least temporarily, evaporates. Unfiltered, unfettered consciousness replaces ego as the organizing structure of the person. Seeing reveals the pseudo-self of ego as an empty and illusory construction, instantly dismantled by the unifying wholeness of consciousness in which nothing can be truly separate. Instead of our awareness collapsing in egocentric identification with some distraction or problem, we remain in the authentic fullness of consciousness. At first, this realization of the non-dual might only be intellectual. When the true seeing opens, however, it is both a magnificent surprise and patently obvious. Problems dissolve, joy, wonder, and compassion arise naturally.

The extremely rare saint may, on the occasion of this first taste of non-dual awareness, spontaneously enter a stable, lasting and completely effortless abiding in pure awareness, in clear seeing. Such people inspire us with their teaching that enlightenment is at hand, is our true nature, that we need only let go and be fully in the moment.

The great majority of us, though, are not so spiritually gifted that we attain enlightenment on our first contact with pure awareness. We sink back to autopilot. We cannot learn to ride the bike of non-dual awareness without training wheels. If non-dual awareness is our only practice, we either find it rough sledding, fragmentary and momentary, or we delude ourselves into thinking we have been conscious when we have not.

We need an inner structure to enable us to balance between falling out of the present moment, back into the self-centered view on the one hand, and falling off into a semi-conscious absent-mindedness on the other. We need to contact, build, and organize our sensitive energies into a vehicle capable of supporting pure consciousness in a stable manner. So we focus on practices that involve the gradual cultivation of attention, contacting and organizing energies, body awareness, radical acceptance of ourselves and our situation, seeing the processes of attachment and identification operating within us, prayer, and the rest.

Non-dual awareness is not difficult to experience. We need only simplify into the moment, coming to rest in pure awareness itself by backtracking within our ordinary awareness to its natural, wide-open clarity. We go behind sensory experience, behind emotion, behind thought, behind our very self, into the now. We allow the clouds of thought and emotion and pain to float by without obscuring our presence, and we become that vast sky of unadorned awareness. Pure awareness precedes all; it forms the substrate that receives experience. This clear consciousness appears both wonderful and seductive because the relative ease of momentarily entering the utter satisfaction of non-dual awareness is matched by the ease of falling out of it. Non-dual awareness draws us to seek it directly. But to establish ourselves in awareness, we need a balanced path of cultivating our soul, our wholeness.

This conundrum has been widely debated in spiritual circles for millennia. In early Chinese Zen, for example, the discussion took the form of gradual cultivation versus sudden awakening. The wise, like the 12th century Korean Zen master Chinul, taught the necessity and complementarity of both. Sudden awakening into non-dual awareness bestows a first release from the ego-centric grasping and rejection of experience. With this weight lifted, we can breathe freely the air of the Present. When we return to our usual state, our understanding has changed. From then on, the recognition of clear awareness as our own essence informs our pursuit of practices in the gradual cultivation of our being. Doubts dispelled, our faith and confidence in the spiritual pursuit grow unshakeable. Awakening recurs more frequently and for longer periods, and we discover the satisfaction of living in Presence. No longer divided inside, no longer focused on the division between our self and the rest of the world, we arrive at rest in the non-dual wholeness of awareness.

Yet non-dual awareness, pure consciousness is not the ultimate goal. We are here to serve a great Purpose. Living in awareness accords with and supports that Purpose in important and subtle ways. But our obligations do not end there. Respecting both the traditions of the East with their focus on being and those of the West with their focus on doing, we see that being is not enough. Purity of being, awareness, promotes the purification of our will, the letting go of attachments and egoism. Gradually opening our will to the Divine Will and our heart to the Great Compassionate Heart of the World enables us to discover and create our destiny through our own unique service to the All.

Promises

In Judaism, the holiest day of the year is Yom Kippur. And on Yom Kippur, the holiest prayer is the first one: Kol Nidre, a prayer to declare null and void all personal vows that do not involve other people. Why is this? Why should this ancient religion place such seemingly inordinate emphasis on a prayer regarding vows? Of course, other religions also proclaim the importance of keeping one's word, but the thrust of that Yom Kippur prayer illustrates the point particularly well.

Suppose I tell someone I will do something, and then I fail to do it. That person may be disappointed, may think less of me, and may be inconvenienced. Serious enough, but what about me, what are the consequences for me, other than a drop in my polls? If my word proves worthless, then what am I?

We can frame this in terms of responsibility. If my word is worthless, then I am irresponsible. But why should this matter to my spiritual path? Can't I be both present and irresponsible? Perhaps so. Does irresponsibility interfere with presence? Perhaps not, but the path consists of more than presence. In particular, will, in all its aspects, constitutes a major and crucial factor. If my word is worthless, it reveals my will as weak, fragmented, or twisted. How can God's Will possibly find a home in me, unless my own will is whole and wholesome? I must be undivided and pure in my will before I can wholeheartedly open to God.

Thus, if I fail to keep my word, if I disregard my promises, my path surely remains blocked. This holds whether the promise is to another person, to myself, or to God. If I neglect a promise to myself, then I lose self-respect. If I breach a vow to God, I have no reverence for the Awesome. If I violate my word to you, then I hold you to be less than me. All of these seriously impede my path. However, if I always keep my word to you, to myself, and to God, then this transparency of heart and strength of will accelerate my way.

Now we might attempt to bargain in front of this requirement. We may reason, "well, if I don't promise anything to anyone, I'll never break my word." But dodging a situation by not giving our word, by not responding, by not accepting an obligation, by shirking our rightful duty when called upon, also defines irresponsibility. The more responsible we are, the further we can go. Not that we must overburden ourselves and clutter our lives with many responsibilities. Rather, we choose those that matter the most and that we can fulfill within our limited time and power. If we treat every promise as if it were a promise to God, then we shall not stray far off the mark of how to live in respect, by our word.

Complications arise. We make promises in reaction to some outer stimulus, from a part of ourselves and not from the whole. Later, we regret the promise. Perhaps someone goads and pressures us into agreeing to something we oppose, and we give in rather than stand up for what we see as true. Perhaps the heat of a moment moves us to promise something, from which quiet reflection would have diverted us. Perhaps we have no time for reflection; we must make a snap judgment, possibly based on our emotional reactions and habits rather than on our deeper intuition. These and other complexities of life form the gray area, the cutting edge of our work to become whole in our will, to keep our word, to serve truth, to be responsible. For despite our sneaking desire to let it pass, the buck does stop with each of us.

The Sacred Vow

At our innermost core, we are our will. Attention and intention, actions and decisions, love and compassion all emanate from will. As such, will defines our true spirit and our relationship with the spiritual. So the purification and strengthening of will form the heart of our path.

One time-honored method for work on will consists of making and keeping vows, solemn and sacred vows that we inevitably carry through, come what may. At the outset, it behooves us to understand that vows bring us into direct relationship with God, deriving their sacredness thereby. If we imagine God as a mountain of purpose, the Purpose behind the universe, we will not be far from the truth. In making a vow, we partake in that immense Purpose by infusing an aspect of our own life with a definite purpose, that of keeping the vow. As befits any action relating us to the Divine, we treat a vow with the utmost respect and care.

What vow to make? Like New Year's resolutions, a vow should neither be too easy nor too difficult: the former has little value and latter leads to the disaster of a broken vow. Vowing not to get angry is a recipe for failure, beyond our capacity. A true vow should never be broken, although it may well incorporate a time limit. For example, we might vow to perform or to refrain from some action every day for the next month.

Furthermore, the specifics of the vow must yield clarity. Vowing not to get angry can only lead to confusion. "I didn't yell, but I felt perturbed. Was that anger?" Better to vow some easily verifiable, outward action. A well-chosen vow will exercise our will and stretch our being in a steady and meaningful way.

When to make a vow? Timing can help. Consider choosing a propitious moment for making the vow: New Year's, our birthday, a holy day in our religion, winter or summer solstice, a new moon, a special event like a marriage, a birth, or a death. Besides choosing a suitable time, we need to prepare inwardly for the act of making the vow. Meditation, fasting, and prayer can help establish the appropriate attitude within us, reflecting the seriousness and sacredness of entering into the vow.

The making and keeping of vows strengthens our spirit,

creates positive self-confidence, diminishes attachment and clinging, organizes our energies, develops our soul, unifies our will, and serves the Sacred. A completed vow increases both our freedom and our potential to play a more useful role in the drama of the evolving world. But we must not take a vow lightly. The utility of a vow grows in direct proportion to wholeheartedness and resoluteness of our commitment to it.

From the Center

Physics denies the existence of a privileged location, theorizing instead that every point in space is equally the center of the universe. This radical notion also holds true in the spirit: the center is everywhere. To be more accurate, though, we should say that the center lies beyond space and time, so that it touches every point in space and time. We humans have been endowed with nervous systems whose complexity enables us to serve as vehicles for the higher energies: consciousness, creativity, and even love. These higher energies, in turn, confer on us the potential for a very different relationship with the spiritual center than is possible for other animals. Unfortunately, we remain largely out of touch with that core, which lies hidden within us, just beyond the range of our minds and perceptions. Spiritual practice gradually unearths and establishes our relationship with it.

But what kind of relationship can we have with the spiritual center of the world? Is it possible for God to see through our eyes, to love through our hearts? In deep meditation, in the silence, we may relate to the center in at least two ways. In one mode, we can turn toward the center, opening ourselves to it, letting go the shackles of being centered in our outer selves to stand ever closer to the true center, to prostrate ourselves in submission to it, with the whole of our being to beg admission to that hallowed ground, and finally to give it all up and let ourselves be brought empty-hearted into the Great Presence.

Still, there is another approach: to be from that center, to be that center. In the deep silence, we allow the purposeful will emanating from the center to move through us unobstructed. We open ourselves to the center, letting the center see through our eyes, perceive through our senses, be through our being. This act makes us whole. The movement originating from the center strengthens us like a wind at our back, affirming our steps. That movement through us reintegrates our tiny, personal, yet important part of the universe with the center, thus expanding and amplifying the center, the source of all.

A Meditation: Climbing Jacob's Ladder

In this meditation we climb as far as we are able up Jacob's Ladder, the ladder to the higher worlds. We might work at this meditation when in a particularly good state, for example after a fast. Or when in difficulty. Or when we feel an especially strong need to delve into the depths of being. We do not expect to climb all the way up. Indeed, this meditation can be a measure of our being and of how thoroughly we can release our grip on self-centeredness and all the rest that keeps us mired in unfulfilling modes of living. Working to climb this ladder, to operate in progressively higher energies, gradually strengthens our being and purifies our will.

To fully enter this practice may require an extended block of time: an hour or more. Give each of the stages its due. They cannot be rushed or pushed. Let each phase take as much time as it needs to ripen into fullness. You will know when that happens.

We begin with a thorough relaxation, letting go the tensions, large and small, in every corner of our body, our thoughts, and our emotions.

Next, we open to the energy of sensation in the whole body. Energy breathing can help build the sensation. We sit in the midst of this remarkable body of ours, in full awareness of the whole of it through sensation. We continuously direct our intention, our will to support and strengthen the full-body sensation, which grows more and more and more substantial. Our will-to-be manifests through this whole body of sensation.

We become aware of ourselves, of who we are. We become ourselves. We experience ourselves as wholly and firmly present, as I Am. *"Here I am, sitting in this body of sensation, in robust presence. I am here. Unique. Wholly myself. I fill the whole field of awareness with my intention to be. I am making an act of being, of being here, of being whole in the fullness of my current experience. I sit. I am. I am complete. I continuously renew this act of being."* These sayings are not intended as affirmations to repeat to ourselves; rather they describe what we do, what we create and experience in this stage.

After some time, we notice the growing spaciousness around and in our awareness. We naturally shift into that fundamental, spacious awareness behind all sensation, thought, and emotion. While maintaining the full-body sensation and the experience of I Am, we rest in consciousness. No longer entangled with random sensations and sensory perceptions, we let them be. We let all the sensory input be embraced in the context of our consciousness, our pure awareness, the field and background within which sensory perceptions flare up and fade out. This transparent awareness forms an empty vessel, through which all the sensory perceptions, thoughts, and emotions pass freely, unhindered, appearing and disappearing. Behind it all, we rest in conscious awareness, as I Am. We may notice a new relationship with time: we are partially released from its dominion. Our perception of space also changes at this level, where the categories of inner and outer no longer apply.

Gradually, consciousness itself grows porous. Then, with the whole of our being, we simultaneously reach out toward and open to a greater world beyond ourselves, beyond consciousness, and begin to perceive the world of light. Inwardly calling out to the Divine, we repeatedly open to that ultimate, creative light until only it remains. All separateness, all the ten thousand things merge into that Primordial Sacred Sun. That light is part of our nature. We become the light, basking in unimaginable joy.

Next, we become aware of the other side of I Am, of the source from which it arises, within a stillness of surpassing quality. We see our I as a knot that blocks off the depths, a knot that makes itself the source of our will, intentions, choices, and decisions, including the intention to meditate in this moment. Gradually we loosen the knot until it gives way, until I let go entirely of being myself, of being my own source.

Silently and wholeheartedly calling out to the Ultimate, completely and utterly opening the very core of who we are, we reach beyond the world of light, into the unbounded emptiness, which is also an overflowing fullness, an intimacy with all, with the All.

This is the Sacred Will of the World,
Of Whom I am now a particle,
Who lends me the will to be myself,
Who lends me my I,

Who is my very Self,
Whom I hope to become able to serve by emptying myself
Unconditionally,
In Whom we are all united,
And Who continuously creates and sustains this universe
In love.

This last stage of the meditation comes only as an act of grace from Above. It lies well beyond our ability to make happen. Attempting to enter here, prayer may help. If you are so inclined, silently repeat one of God's names, one close to your heart, one that both expresses your yearning and brings you peace.

Transmission and Initiation

Inner exercises, meditations, and their related states belong to realms beyond sensory experience, beyond thought, and beyond the possibility of being well defined or adequately described by words. How then can one person learn such inner acts from another if their only means of communication is through words? Physical gestures, facial expressions, and external body language cannot help. Well-chosen words can be evocative, pointing the hearer in the true direction. But real understanding of the exercise or meditation communicates directly and simply, through the atmosphere created by the person showing the exercise.

Such a transmission is not necessarily a high and esoteric event, requiring the presence of a fully enlightened master. It happens any time someone thoroughly-practiced in an inner exercise or meditation teaches it to another. The instructor brings him- or herself into the inner state of the exercise and that state transmits itself through the teacher's atmosphere to the student. The will of the instructor demonstrating the exercise can directly inform the will of the student who is ready to learn. Because we are not typically quiet enough inside to clearly perceive the direct transmission, the instructor must also use words. This combination of direct demonstration supplemented by words of guidance may enable the student to recognize what is required, to taste the desired action and state. Such transmission is the traditional means whereby inner work of all kinds passes from person to person, generation to generation.

Does this mean that inner exercises and meditations cannot be learned from books? Not exactly. While the direct help of a competent instructor is preferable, it is not always effective. The student may not be ready, may not have the required subtlety of perception, and thus may not be able to receive the transmission. Conversely, if a student is well prepared, perhaps through having practiced other forms of meditation, then just reading about an unfamiliar form may be enough to enable the student to enter that new meditation. Furthermore, certain basic types of inner work are simple enough not to require the presence of an instructor to be rightly understood. A good instructor can, however, provide invaluable help by validating the student's understanding and responding to the inevitable questions.

In some circles, the transmission of a spiritual practice is called initiation: a ritual or ceremony ushering the student into the practice, into the tradition, sometimes accompanied by vows of loyalty or secrecy. For those whose inner perceptions have opened sufficiently, another kind of initiation sometimes comes, not from any person, but directly from the depths of being. Such unmediated initiation can begin simply as our intuitive adjustments and adaptations of practices to our own uniqueness. Later, new depths and their corresponding practices may be revealed to us from within. At that point we no longer depend solely on teachers to show us the way. We still seek out people of wisdom, however, to learn from and to be drawn further toward the Real. But for those dedicated to the path, the creative source of initiation unfolds new avenues toward the Heart of the World.

Integrating Body, Heart, and Mind

How often do you feel what you think or think what you feel? In the light of growing self-awareness, we may notice that our body, heart, and mind typically do not act in unison. Instead, they often work at cross-purposes to each other. For example, our body wants to eat the ice cream. Our heart recoils at the prospect of gaining weight. And our mind dwells on cholesterol counts. Or, our mind wants our body to exercise to stay healthy. The body, though, is lazy and resists. Meanwhile, the heart prefers puttering about the garden or conversing with friends. Such inner conflicts and lack of coordination sap our energies and hinder our effectiveness. In most activities we are not wholly there, because one or more of our parts refuses to cooperate.

If we could act with the whole of ourselves, the quality of our life would change dramatically. Our inner battles and contradictions would diminish. Our fractured sense of self would begin to heal. Our confidence and effectiveness would grow. Our presence would deepen and stabilize. A dynamic force would enter our inner work, simplifying and accelerating our path.

How can we evolve toward this? The surest way to work

toward integration of body, heart, and mind is through seeing. First we need to see our actual situation, our lack of coordination, and our inner contradictions. In the face of this disturbing revelation, we do not lose hope, because seeing both reveals and heals. Seeing is the action of the conscious energy, the energy of wholeness. Seeing alone can bring our disparate parts under one umbrella, merging them within the fullness of our being, permitting each to play its appropriate role in the enterprise of life.

But this transformation occurs slowly and fitfully, with ample room for misunderstanding. For example, what we feel often drives our thinking: our thoughts just slavishly following the emotion. At other times, our thoughts drive our emotions. We may daydream a scenario in which we are insulted. Then our feelings wax indignant in response to the imaginary event. But these examples do not portray integration, rather they speak of the automatic operation of our parts reacting to each other. True integration derives from the conscious energy, not from automatic functioning.

The work of consciousness, of seeing, is not so easy to jump straight into. The sensitive energies allow us to approach it constructively, however. By practicing sensitive awareness of each part of ourselves, we move toward sensitive awareness of all parts at once, which builds a foundation for true seeing in conscious wholeness. Simultaneously sensing our body, kinesthetically, viscerally and directly, coupled with awareness of our emotions whatever they may be, and of our thoughts and daydreams, expands the domain of our attention and opens the way for consciousness unity.

To be sensitive to all three parts concurrently is also not so easy. We may enter spontaneous moments wherein we find ourselves conscious, with will strong enough to unify our parts into a whole. But such moments do not last and cannot be repeated intentionally. To live in an integrated way, we train in the practices of awareness. We begin with establishing awareness of the sensitive energy body, as strong and as stable as possible. When in that state we can, at times, branch out to incorporate awareness of thoughts and/or emotions. In this way we train our attention and awareness toward the wholeness that integrates our parts, toward unity of action, toward the ability to act with the whole of ourselves.

Purification

Every major religion and path addresses the requirement of purity of heart, purity of action. Impurities literally bar our entry to the higher realms. But what are these impurities? If they are in my heart and in my will, are they not a part of me? How can I become purified in heart and will? A whole gallery of nasty thoughts and petty emotional reactions course through my mind and heart. Do I need to somehow stop all that? Is that even possible? If I am impure, how can I purify myself? Won't there always be some taint? Isn't impurity inherent in dealing with this imperfect world? Isn't life full of tradeoffs, so that nothing is totally pure?

If we truly aspire to open to the depths, these and other questions about purification cannot be ignored. Yet confronting them presents such difficulties that we take every opportunity to avoid them.

The first thing to remember is that it is not all up to us to do the purifying. The Christian model says that through grace we are forgiven our sins. In Buddhism, final enlightenment comes as the ultimate letting go of attachment, and all the remaining fetters drop at once, revealing the spotless purity of being. In both representations, a willingness to be purified, repentance and equanimity, enable the purification to come. The general principle is that, for each level, the higher purifies the lower.

This willingness to be purified grows gradually in us as a result of all our spiritual efforts. We become wary of succumbing to the temptations offered after we make an effort: temptations to rest on our laurels, to enjoy the self-aggrandizement of increased energy, to strut and brag about our practice, to compete with our fellow seekers and be jealous of their progress, to follow a fast with overindulgence, to fall into extremes and disregard the middle road of moderation in all things, to look only outward or only inward instead of both. We stand ready to be purified — except for our own unique set of special attachments, such as certain resentments and grudges, a propensity to angry outbursts, self-pity, self-glorification or self-loathing, laziness or avarice, worry and hurry, a surfeit of doubting or a naïve readiness to believe, strongly held opinions or weak-kneed vacillation, arrogance or timidity, stubbornness or refusal of commitments, and whatever else lurks in our personal psychological menagerie. True willingness to be purified means the willingness to not be attached to any of our personality traits, the willingness to let them go, to not be ruled by them, to stop looking to our thoughts, emotions and the momentum of our life experience as who we are, to come from a deeper place instead, to see the stream of thoughts, emotions, assumptions and reactions without floating away in it.

Perhaps you have known someone who struck you as a simple person, simple in the sense of guileless with nothing to hide, harmless with no one to hate, content with nothing to grasp, happy with nowhere to go, and childlike with maturity earned. The spiritual path leads to simplicity: the simplicity of presence here and now, of action directed by the intuitive and immediate wisdom of conscience, of a loving and joyful heart untroubled by the chains of time, ruminating thought or emotional reaction. Simplicity is purity.

Several stages delineate the path of purification. Early on, we may need to actively engage against our destructive habits of body, mind, and heart. As our contact with consciousness grows, clearly seeing our patterns of attachment weakens their sting, their sway over us. Drop by drop, the murky waters of our psychology are distilled and cleansed. The mud sinks and settles to where the winds and currents rarely disturb it. As we open to higher energies, our mind, heart, and will gradually grow transparent to motivations in accord with kindness and wisdom, supplanting the detritus of egoism and guiding us through the thickets of life's many dramas and dilemmas. Laughter and tears still accompany the ebb and flow of life, but leave fewer traces, as the tar of identification gives way to the air of freedom.

We may pray for purification and we struggle to see wasteful and disruptive patterns. But in the end we must choose whether to keep ourselves living in a narrow-hearted way, or give ourselves over to enter our place in the Great Heart of the World.

One-Pointedness

The exercise of will lies at the heart of any spiritual path, because it addresses the very core of our spirit. One important mode of this exercise involves focusing our attention on some object, be it a phrase or an image, a feeling, the breath, or the body as a whole. We aim our attention toward the object and place it on the object. Focused attention, however, tends to dissipate quickly. So we add the effort of sustaining our attention on the chosen object.

This demanding work of sustaining attention, keeping to the chosen center of focus, requires the willingness to leave behind all distractions, all our automatically arising, associative thoughts and emotional reactions, at least temporarily. We are so enamored and identified with our usual patterns of thought and emotion that we loathe the very idea of letting them go, of doing without them for a time. This letting go, with its associated weakening of distracting thoughts and emotions, is itself the act of purification required to deepen our work on attention. Sustained, focused attention entrains and unifies all the disparate impulses of body, heart, and mind, bringing wholeness to our being, a wholeness centered around our attention.

While a focused and sustained attention is necessary, it does not prove sufficient for true one-pointedness. We also need a focused and sustained intention: the intention to connect with, open to, surrender to, and serve the Sacred. This one-pointed intention, like our one-pointed attention, must be immediate, in this very moment. Gathering every fiber of our being, every wayward intention, we gravitate toward a higher world.

Particularly in periods of meditation, the effort of sustaining attention and intention gradually gives way to stabilized presence and the readiness to move deeper still. Together, our one-pointed attention and one-pointed intention merge into the wholeness of unified will, the source of who we are and our true connection with the Sacred. Simultaneously focusing and opening toward the higher, with everything else left behind, we discover our most direct approach to our deepest possibilities, to the Source of all meaning.

Total Engagement

To engage fully in whatever we do is an important method and goal of inner work. By this we mean to act not only with wholeheartedness, but also with our whole mind and body, with total attention, and every ounce of our intention. We aim to bring our entire being and will to bear on the action at hand.

A prime example occurs in prayer. Whenever we pray, we work to engage wholly, unreservedly, with nothing held back, nothing left to feed stray thoughts, and nothing lazy or unco-operative dragging behind. We give ourselves utterly over to relating to the Ineffable. Prayer like that bears fruit.

In the wake of the death of Pope John Paul II, a public television program showed some remarkable photos of the Pope kneeling in private prayer before a simple cross. His eyes shut, his face a study of unmitigated, intense, and total devotion, his posture of permanent surrender, all combined to reveal John Paul's proximity to the Divine. This was a man whose silent photographs could teach true prayer. Amazing.

In a more ordinary way, we can also learn total engagement from the virtuoso musician or the world-class athlete at the peak of their performance. In such moments, we see a person completely absorbed in their music or sport, body and soul. We see joy and freedom manifest thereby.

In working at presence, we seek all-embracing engagement and singleness of purpose in being and acting in this moment. We enter presence with a seamless awareness of body, mind, and heart, and with a profound will-to-be, to be here in this moment, to be ourselves.

We wish to live our life to the hilt, with the greatest depth of being and the utmost strength and devotion of will we can muster. To each action in life, we bring the appropriate fullness. When we relax, we really relax. When we eat, we savor the taste. When we think, we focus on the issue. When we brush our teeth, we exert just the right pressure. Interacting with another person, we mean what we say and we listen in stillness and respect. Throughout it all, we seek a robust presence as our foundation. We wish to engage totally in our life, to give ourselves unconditionally in serving our highest destiny, in kindness and in love.

Being

When we ask "who am I," the answer lies in the realm of will. When we ask "what am I," the answer belongs to the realm of being. Sometimes we just sit and be; we have a sense of our own being, of our inner collectedness, of what we are. We also sense that our being waxes and wanes; we can be more or less strongly with more or less stability. Extrapolating, we see that being can grow. While our body weakens with age, our being can strengthen, especially if we persevere in our inner work.

We can most readily understand being through its role in determining the quality and subtlety of our perceptions: how aware we are and the kinds of things that can enter our awareness. To what degree am I aware of my body, my thoughts, and my emotions? Do I perceive other people as people, in the same sense that I am a person? Am I aware of my own presence, of being here in this moment? Am I aware of the Divine presence, the Always Here? These perceptual states and abilities change throughout the day and even more over the years.

Our being fuels our perceptions and depends in turn on the quality, quantity, and organization of our inner energies.

The quality dimension of being refers to whether we operate primarily on the automatic level of energy, or on the sensitive, the conscious, and so on up. With the automatic energy we are only half-aware of the world around us and inside us. With the sensitive energy we open to the reality of our outer environment as well as our inner world. With the conscious energy we discover a global, holistic view of life, a view not as bound to our usual self-centric, time-based orientation. With the energies beyond consciousness we open to creativity, love, and the higher spiritual realms. As our being grows and we ascend the levels of energy, we find new modes of perception which subsume the lower modes.

The available quantity of any particular energy also has a crucial effect on how we live and experience. The more of an energy we have, the longer we can experience and the wider the reach of our perceptions at the level of that energy. More of an energy also means more inner stability and a responsive container for the next higher energy. That container of energies is our being.

The degree of organization of our personal reservoir of energies is the third factor of being. If consciousness is available to us, and not just mixed up with, lost in, and driven by our sensory experience, then we can be more than otherwise.

All spiritual practices depend on and affect our energies and thereby our being. Some practices raise the quality of our energies, some the quantity, some organize our energies, and some do all three. The U.S. Army's recruiting slogan "be all you can be" works very well as a motto for those aspects of the spiritual path that concern transformation of our being and formation of our soul.

While being certainly has its own intrinsic value, its true significance lies in its role as the enabling medium for will to act in the world.[21] Being is the transmitter of perception and action. Perceptions flow from the perceived through being to the perceiver. Actions flow from the actor through being to the acted upon. Recalling the saying of the great 14th century Christian mystic, Meister Eckhart, that God "is a nothingness beyond being,"[22] we recognize that the ultimate, universal actor is God.

Because we can only act effectively in regions where our perceptions operate, will depends on the perceptual abilities provided by our being. As our being grows in strength and subtlety, so does the reach of our actions. We cannot act on what we cannot perceive. As a consequence, the level of our actions depends on the level of our being. Thus, a central requirement for a truly fulfilling and effective life is to be more.

Spirituality engages both perception and action, being and will. The deeper our being, the less easily we are entranced by the multitude of inappropriate, destructive, or unbecoming impulses passing through us. Furthermore, the deeper our being, the more possibility we have of opening to the higher energy of love and compassion. In the peaceful pool of being we can more readily recognize the voice of conscience. Thus, growth in being, in what we are, enables purification of our actions, our will. A person of great being is a person of great heart and a refuge to whom others can turn in the storms of life. So we work very hard (frequently, deeply, and with duration) to be more.

Living As Intention

When beginning any new activity, some traditions embrace the custom of invoking the sacred to set the stage and the intention. For example, Muslims may say "Bismillah ir-Rahman ir-Rahim" (In the Name of God, the Merciful, the Compassionate).

Christians might say "In the Name of the Father, the Son, and the Holy Ghost." In Kabbalah also, the notion of *kavanna*, intention, plays a central role. The Kabbalist might say: "I am prepared to fully engage myself in what I am about to do." Unfortunately, good beginnings do not always carry through the whole event. The opening invocation may well be quickly forgotten as the action proceeds by momentum.

We seek instead to bring intention into everything we do: not just at the start, but sustaining our intention throughout. We seek to live in intention, to become intention itself. At any time, even in the middle of some action, we can intend to do that action, and continue intending it as we continue doing it. Naturally, if we find ourselves doing something we had not intended to do, we can change course. But the main thrust of this kind of inner work is to become intention in action. To rephrase the Zen teaching: when eating, eat; when sitting, sit; when walking, walk; when talking, talk; when thinking, think; and when doing anything, do that very thing. Keeping our attention to the task at hand is only part of this: we also continue intending the action.

Intention is an often-overlooked part of presence, a key part because it is the central part. In addition to the energies of sensation and consciousness, presence needs the intention and will to be, to do what we are doing, to engage in life as we live it. Without intention, presence is hollow and unstable. With continuing intention, there is someone in our being who is present.

If we work seriously at this, we will find that acting with intention, that becoming intention, conveys a profound and surprising potency into our inner world. Why? Because free will is both our gift from and our participation in the Divine. Intention in action, moment-to-moment intention, brings us into that invisible stream of will, closer to who we really are, to our own "I am."

In working with intention, the question eventually arises: whose intention? And the answer is put succinctly when Christ, addressing the Lord, says "... *not my will, but thine* ..."[23] The perfection of intention comes when we can be clear enough of our egoism and open enough to the higher will so that it can act through us. Simultaneously open, in our deepest core, to the higher and active toward the more external, we approach the true meaning of life.

Will and God

We are our will. Yet Will enshrouds a mystery, a mystery so hidden that we fail even to recognize it as a mystery. Will so fundamentally, so intimately constitutes our very self that we stay utterly unaware of it. In fact, we cannot be directly aware of our will. Find the wind. We cannot see the wind itself, yet it possesses a sometimes awesome power. Will forms that part of us who genuinely says "I", the one who sees by means of our awareness. More subjective than awareness, will is the user of awareness. We can be aware of our awareness, but we cannot be directly aware of our will, because will originates beyond awareness. At best we can, so to speak, ride it, open to it, become it.

The easiest way toward recognizing the action of will in ourselves consists of acquiring the taste of its lower modes of operation. First among these stands attention. Our attention moves our sensory awareness from object to object. Yet we do not investigate this innate mechanism. How is it that I am able to switch focus from noticing what I see with my eyes to noticing the sensation in my hand? Working as attention, our will directs the energies of awareness.

Noticing how we make choices, also enables us to recognize will. Typically we have an emotional and thought process of weighing the pros and cons of a choice confronting us. Informed by this process, we choose. But the choice itself is no mere thought or emotion. When our thoughts or emotions "choose," then it is not a real choice and carries no staying power. When a thought says "I think I'll lose five pounds," the "choice" soon evaporates. Real, effective choice rises to the level of decision and commitment. Our will engages the situation and we know it. We stand behind our choice. Then we see it through regardless of the time or effort involved.

For years I have contemplated the question: Where does attention (Will) come from? I do not take this as an intellectual, psychological, physiological, or philosophical question. Nor do I strive to think up the correct answer or try to reason it out. That proves totally useless, like venturing to describe the Grand Canyon without ever having been there. So it is with this question: What is the source of attention?

To take it practically, we ask whether we can approach the source of Will in our own direct experience, within ourselves. This appears impossible, because Will cannot be objectified. Will can never be the object of our awareness, because Will is always the subject: the seer rather than the seeing or the seen. To move into the seer and behind the seer, we can use attention as a kind of a rope, guiding our steps back along itself toward its source, back beyond consciousness. The Korean Zen master Chinul coined an apropos phrase: "tracing back the radiance."[24]

We might ask: So what? Why bother with this will business? The reasons to bother go even beyond the fact that our will is who we are. Will is the link through which we serve our Creator, through which we participate in our Creator, through which we can be an instrument of the Higher Power. In fact, one could go so far as to say that God is Will. What can be everywhere, yet not be recognized? It is Will. Will is in us. The tree has the will to be a tree. The car has the will to be a car put into it by its human creators. The people of a nation share the will to be a nation. Yet we do not recognize Will. We may be familiar with the workings of energies and the functioning of physical bodies. But what drives these, the Will, we do not notice. And indeed we can view the Lord as an infinite mountain of purpose, of Will. The universe has a Purpose, an immense Purpose beyond us, beyond our scope, beyond our consciousness, beyond our pay-grade — at least for now.

The reality of will goes far deeper than our usual definition of it. Typically we take will in the sense of will-power, determination, uncompromising attitudes, and even aggression. We think of God's will as an all-powerful and capricious source of actions impinging upon and controlling our lives. We recall Christ throwing the moneychangers out of the temple. Yet will lies behind all actions, human and Divine, including acts of kindness, generosity, humility, meekness, service, and, above all, love.

To understand this in another way, consider a simple but astonishing and well-known fact of modern physics. A photon of light acts as both a wave and a particle. In a particular experimental arrangement, the photon, wavelike, follows all possible paths from its starting point to its end point. But when an experimenter makes an observation, the possible paths suddenly collapse into one, as if a particle-like path is being chosen retroactively by the act of observation. This act of observation is an act of will on the part of the experimenter. The physicist's will, in effect, creates the path of the photon, creates the photon as a particle. Until the act of observation, the photon remains in the wavelike realm of possibilities and becomes actual only when looked at by the physicist. This fact about photons also holds true for the rest of the world, because all elementary particles exhibit some wavelike behavior. The remarkable upshot: our collective will creates our world, moment by moment. Because God puts the freedom of God's own will into us, we participate directly in the continuing creation of the universe at every instant. We should deeply contemplate this co-creative role of ours.

This mysterious Will matters to us profoundly and immediately. For our personal journey through life, our relation to Will is crucial. In particular, to go very far along the spiritual path requires more and more resolve, for example the resolve to be continuously present so as to develop a stabilized presence, and the resolve to let go of our many attachments along the way toward that stabilized presence. As the force behind a state of true presence, Will allows God to see through our eyes. Opening to Will, beyond consciousness, opens us to our higher soul and to love.

According to the sacred traditions, Will enters the ultimate choice of a human being at the culmination of the personal phase of the spiritual path: the choice to surrender our will to God's Will, to return our will to the Great Will as a free and independent servant of that Greatness. God introduced Himself to Moses as "*I AM THAT I AM*,"[25] a phrase that openly embodies the deepest of all truths. God is the true I within us all, the Source of will, the I of the universe and beyond.

So, will emerges as the crucial factor in our personal and collective spiritual work. Everything that happens has will behind it, even if it is the capricious will of random chance. Most importantly, will not only includes the active, forceful determination we usually think of, but also the non-force of loving, giving, connecting, allowing, and harmonizing. Our will can be fragmented and conflicting, weak and passive, overbearing and timid. Nevertheless, our will determines the course of our life and what kind of person we are. One way to look at the spiritual path is as a process of unifying and purifying our will, and making it a vehicle for the higher will. Toward this we can begin our study of will by looking directly and carefully at our own attention, intention, decisions, and will-to-be.

A Meditation: The Eyes of God

Let each stage of this meditation take the time it needs.

We begin by relaxing thoroughly.

Next we open our perceptions to full awareness of bodily sensations, awareness of the whole body, of the sensitive energy in the body.

Next we open to our basic awareness itself, to the stillness behind our thoughts, behind our sensations and emotions.

Now imagine God as a vast emptiness, supremely intelligent, and utterly compassionate. Imagine yourself looking directly into the eyes of God, without personifying them into the shape of eyes, but rather opening yourself to be seen clearly by that vastness.

In looking into the eyes of God, you and God see all your impurities, all the places you hold onto separateness. And in that seeing, in God's seeing you with supreme compassion, you forgive your defects and mistakes, you begin to let go of those impurities and all smallness of heart. Let go of owning all the limitations. Let go of being distinct from God so that God sees through your eyes. Bask in the radiance of that limitless compassion, that living stillness.

CHAPTER SIX

BEYOND OURSELVES

Our Relationship with Time

Time: the open field for evolution and hope, but the constraint of the daily grind. Have you ever noticed that when you anxiously await a letter (or phone call or email) it tends not to arrive? Then you give up hope and voilà - it appears. Have you ever noticed that hurrying frustrates you, leads to mistakes, and even slows you down compared to simply moving quickly and with focus? Have you ever noticed that worrying about what might happen (instead of simply taking appropriate preventive measures) only serves to waste your energy? These few examples typify our difficult relationship with time.

Time is both our limitation and our opportunity. Time, with space, serves as the hidden but all powerful gate that limits our reality to actualizing only one event at a given time and place. We cannot do two different things at the same time; we must choose. This simple fact both defines and impoverishes existence. Time also serves as part of the field in which we may create and fulfill our destiny. The other part lies beyond time.

Some say that time does not exist, calling it a malleable psychological construction, a social convention. This contains a kernel of truth that we may recognize as we live more wholly in the present and thereby taste the dimension of being, no longer entirely trapped in time. As we enter into consciousness and thus into the timelessness of the present, our perception of time seems to disappear, psychological time vanishes altogether. In our ordinary, less conscious state, however, time assuredly does have a psychological reality: we certainly believe in it unquestioningly. But the more awake we are the more strongly we experience and the more fully we live, with the result that we have more time, more life. Days on which we are relatively more awake, more present, are full and even seem to last longer than our typical days.

Time has a physical reality, not simply in the movements of clocks and planets, but also in limiting experience to only one event at time. The aging of our bodies reminds us that entropy and decay define time as the condition of impermanence. So while time does not comprise the whole of reality, it forms a major ingredient.

Time's three great domains of past, present, and future, each serve up their own set of obstacles and opportunities. We can profitably examine our relationship with them in terms of whether we are active, passive, or open.

Passive toward time, we succumb, enslaved by it. Passivity toward time means lying there, pinned to the mat by the weight of the past and future.

Passivity to the past means living full of regret about opportunities missed, dwelling on prior wounds and stressful situations, ruminating over and over about what he said, what she did to me, or "I'll never love again." Passivity to the past means living on past glories: "when I was young I could ..." or "I remember the time when I ..." Passivity to the past means being condemned to act only out of our conditioning, with no possibility of loosening the fetters of old traumas, habits, and attitudes. We passively accept our belief systems, our character, our personality, our entire identity based on our personal history. All this combines to create the persona that we think we are. We cobble together all the pieces of our history, forge them into a pseudo-self, and then utterly identify with the result as "Me," defending this would-be self against all comers.

Passivity toward the future means worrying about what's going to happen in some situation, even a totally imaginary situation, imagining all the things that could go wrong and recoiling from them. Passivity toward the future means hurrying to get someplace, hurrying to complete some task, impatience with waiting in line, inaction toward our true goals, not even formulating goals, lack of determination to create a better future. Passivity toward the future means living in expectation, waiting or hoping for that event when our ship will finally come in. This attitude toward time shields us from the fact that each day brings us closer to end of our life, lulling us into a spiritual lethargy.

Passivity toward the present means sleepwalking through life, only dimly aware and only intermittently and briefly awake to our inner and outer surroundings. Passivity toward the present means fear of what's in front of us, rejecting what's happening, or on the contrary, insatiably grasping for more money, objects, and experiences. Passivity toward the present means letting whatever emotions are uppermost highjack the whole of us, ruling the moment. Passivity toward the present means being identified, inwardly collapsing into whatever prevails in or colors our awareness, allowing ourselves to be carried along rootless in the stream of thoughts and experiences.

Rather than living as a slave to time, we can seek freedom by two approaches: the active path and the open path.

Activity toward the past means consciously mining our storehouse of experience to discover the wisdom there. When we confront difficulties, activity toward the past means remembering what we have faced before to see how prior experiences might inform our current dilemmas and choices, and coupling that with our intuition. We have habits of body, mind, and heart ingrained through past repetition. Some habits are wasteful or even destructive. Activity toward the past means working against the wasteful habits, one a time. Activity toward the past also involves our collective, cultural past, understanding what people have done before us in history, science, literature, art, business, and spirituality. When we mine the past for wisdom, we can look at our personal history as well the past of our culture, civilization, and the whole human race.

Activity toward the future means working in the present to create a better future, placing a positive influence into the future by what we do now, creating the conditions so that future events in our personal and collective lives will flow in the direction we wish them to flow. As a minor example, if we want good health in the future, we stop smoking now. If we wish for a better job in the future, we might pursue further education now. If we wish to grow closer to the Divine, we practice diligently in the present. If we want our children to grow up to be happy adults, we treat them with great kindness in the present. Activity toward the future does not wait, hesitantly hoping for a miracle, but rather works actively now toward a better future, but without living in expectation of results.

Activity toward the present means practice, not being identified, not being lost or asleep, awakening to the now, doing what's possible now to repair our past by overcoming wasteful habits and harmful conditioning, and creating a better future by working along intentionally chosen lines. Activity toward the present means living in presence, working to strengthen and deepen presence in ourselves, an inner willingness to face all aspects of the present, inner and outer, with eyes and heart wide open. The spiritual path is not in time, but rather outside of time, in the depth. However, it unfolds in time as our changing states fluctuate and our being waxes and wanes.

The open path toward the future means being agile, listening to intuitions about our potentialities for the future and then acting accordingly, listening to how those intuitions might change. Openness toward the future means choosing the highest among our many possible futures, noticing and taking the appropriate windows of opportunity. Openness toward the future means opening to a vision of the evolutionary possibilities for ourselves, for humanity, for all life on the Earth, and working in our own small way toward the realization of that vision.

Openness toward the past means a willingness to allow the past to inform our intuition, letting the wisdom of the past enliven our hearts, accepting and learning not to repeat past failures. Openness toward the past means providing an accepting and loving space in which past psychological traumas may be recalled and may heal. This is best approached in collaboration with a professional psychotherapist. Openness toward the past means forgiving those who have wronged us, healing that rift in ourselves.

Openness toward the present means listening to the people around us, to the situation we find ourselves in, and responding appropriately. Openness toward the present means living in awareness of that overarching, timeless stillness underlying everything, that eternal realm opened to us through conscious

233

presence.

Our path through life wends its way through space and time. We move from moment to moment, event to event, each defined by its time and place. But we do not typically recognize that, in a profound way, the quality of our presence also defines each moment. So our life path lies not only in space-time, but simultaneously in another dimension. Our location in that dimension depends on our presence, higher or lower. Our experience of time itself changes with our height in this other dimension, the dimension of presence. The more present we are, the stronger our experience will be. A day full of presence is so much richer and seemingly, satisfyingly longer than a day of wistful thoughts and dreams. We call this the dimension of being.

A Contemplation: The Dimensions of Emptiness

How can we understand, even if only in theory, the idea of emptiness as the root of spirituality? Consider for a moment a geometric analogy:

A line measures its size in terms of length. A point has no length. So from the perspective of a line, a point is nothing, empty. Yet, if it could think, the point might consider itself to be something substantial.

A flat surface measures its size in terms of area. A line has no area. The line is empty, nothing from the standpoint of the surface. Yet, if it could think, the line might consider itself to be something substantial.

A solid measures its size in terms of volume. A flat surface has no volume and therefore is nothing from the point of view of the solid, even though the solid may touch the surface at every point.

To relate properly to the higher realms, we must accept and enter our own emptiness with respect to the Greatness that surrounds and permeates us. The Infinite is not merely larger than the knowable universe, but has more dimensions. Emptying ourselves of our self-centered view enables us to take our proper place in the greater world, in our true home.

Conscience: the Perception of Wisdom

How is it that despite our ongoing accumulation and occasional contemplation of experience, wisdom continues to elude us? True wisdom cannot be developed or acquired; rather we open to it through the quality of our being. The ultimate source of wisdom lies in the Divine realms. It devolves to us to discover our own direct intuition of the Divine wisdom. Our one tool for this purpose is a kind of inner sensitivity, a mode of perception that we can call conscience. Ordinarily we think of conscience as the moral sensibility instilled in us by our parents, teachers, and others. But conscience holds the potential to extend far beyond anything taught or experienced. The knowledge of right and wrong that we learn as children often fails before the moral ambiguities of life. However, wisdom-based conscience can serve us as a reliable moral compass in any situation.

But knowing right from wrong will not carry us far enough. How can we fulfill our destiny, realize our highest potential? How can we best help another person? What opportunities should we create and embark upon? Should we marry the person we've been dating? A moral compass alone cannot address such questions, but conscience can. Conscience enables us to perceive wisdom as it applies to our own circumstances, with our own particular set of possibilities. But to hear the voice of conscience, we must be prepared to serve, for conscience does not pander to our egocentric view of the world.

How can we open to our conscience? How can we distinguish between the voice of our conscience and the voice of our egoism? We find a way to gradually develop an intuitive sensitivity to our inner perception of rightness. The instability of our hearts and the clutter of our minds present problems in this regard. So many urges and thoughts vie for our inner spotlight that to hear the voice of conscience amid the cacophony sorely challenges our intuition and discrimination. But spiritual practice quiets our mind, pacifies our heart, and supports the emergence of conscience out of the noise.

Conscience sees. It sees our own behavior, inner and outer, from an objective viewpoint. When our thoughts, feelings, or actions fall into the unseemly, conscience sees the truth and causes us embarrassment at having been seen, at having caught ourselves in manifestations we would rather keep hidden, even from ourselves. But if we can open to this seeing of our ego-based behavior, conscience becomes our hope and lifeline to purification and freedom. This is how our higher part speaks to us, by seeing us as we are, and showing us the way toward cleaning up our inner world. Conscience reveals our attachments and illumines areas for letting go.

Openness to conscience also requires a readiness to follow its promptings; otherwise conscience withdraws. After checking to ensure that a particular intuition of what we deem conscience does not violate our ordinary moral and practical sensibilities, we need to act on it. A further test comes in hindsight: do we consider our action to have been the right one? The process of listening to our innermost intuition of rightness and applying the reality test to where it takes us gradually refines our ability to perceive conscience, to discern and "hear" the voice of truth within us.

Our conscience is nothing less than our truest self, our own deeper will, and our connection to the Divine. The more we follow our own unique conscience, the more intimately and fully we become ourselves. This is not easy. Conscience, as we well know, often conflicts with our desires and appetites. In the path to liberation, we face an ongoing series of choices, sometimes hard choices that challenge us to let go of our egocentric attachments. Conscience, if we can accept its promptings, will guide us through. Living in conscience is like inviting God to see everything we do, inwardly as well as outwardly.

The next few sections explore several aspects of the path of conscience.

What Is Our Responsibility?

The Divine Purpose, awesome and unimaginable, creates and sustains the universe. We cannot "know" that Purpose in the way we know other things. The Purpose cannot be formulated in words, because it abides beyond words, beyond images, beyond our minds, beyond knowing in the ordinary sense. If we could know the Divine Purpose, we would know God; indeed we may rightly consider God to be that Purpose itself.

Although we cannot know the Unconditioned Purpose, we may participate in it more or less consciously, more or less intentionally. The Sacred Purpose communicates itself to all of us through our intuition of the rightness of a course of action. Faced with a choice, we have an opportunity to do the right thing, to be responsible. Thus, by following our conscience, we

enter into a partnership with the Great Purpose. We can follow our sense of appropriateness, rightness, and opportunity
to pursue the spiritual path, to serve others, to serve the future.
Imagine how great must be that Will that is responsible for the
entire universe. It offers us the opportunity to be responsible
for our personal universe. Following what our heart tells us
to be right establishes an authentic connection, a commonality of purpose with the Divine Purpose. Through us, through
such connections, the Divine reaches into the life of the world.
Responsible action based on conscience strengthens our link
with the Universal Purpose. That link serves as the essential
mode whereby the world is gradually spiritualized, whereby life
on the Earth will ultimately realize its destiny.

What obstacles do we confront in becoming responsible,
in serving the Great Purpose? First, our self-centeredness, our
egoism deludes us, at times, into choosing dishonorable and un-
principled actions, as well as actions which do not lead toward
fulfillment of our own potential. We take the easy, shirking way,
the selfish way, the wasteful way. In the parlance of religion, we
sin, we miss the mark. We ignore the promptings of our conscience. The siren song of egoism beguiles us into believing that
wrong is right. "If I want to do it, that makes it right." Following
whatever our ego-deluded heart tells us, we fail to find our con-
gruence with the Great Purpose. Our hearts need cleansing; the
veils need lifting. That is the purpose of spiritual practice.

The concept of human rights expresses our concern for the
well-being of other people. The expression of human rights,
however, has been diverted by our self-centeredness into a demand for our own self-assumed rights. We claim the right to
drive a gas-guzzling vehicle, even if we don't really need one.
We claim the right to habitually eat more than we need to eat,
to consume more than we need of the world's goods, to have

more than two children and contribute to overpopulation. We dream of owning our own mini-mansion, and many fulfill that dream. As a direct result of all these "rights," we cause the mass extinction of 25,000 species each year, the increasing threat of global warming, the failure to alleviate the grinding poverty and malnutrition of untold millions, the alienation from society, from each other, from our own deeper nature. Our focus on our "rights" deflects our attention from our responsibilities.

We even claim the right to mistreat people. This takes innumerable forms. We feel justified in acting rudely when crossed in any way. We market superfluous goods, creating false needs, preying on desires and fears, leading people to lose themselves in the great consumerist endeavor, in a market economy based more on greed than on need. We demand special treatment, special recognition, fast service. We leave courtesy behind when we start our engines, in our "right" not to be delayed. All these layers of our self-assumed "rights" obscure our personal responsibilities.

To hear the promptings of our conscience, to notice the intuitive twinges of our true heart, requires clarity and presence, requires an ability to look beyond our personal desires, a willingness to pursue responsibilities rather than rights. We cannot demand to be comfortable and also be responsible. The truly spiritual path does not offer a way of escape from responsibilities, indeed it offers a way toward becoming more fully, skillfully, and creatively responsible. Through responsible action, based on conscience, we create a place in ourselves to host our small particle of the Divine Purpose, to spiritualize our corner of the universe.

Awareness of Intention

If our free will is a gift, or perhaps an investment, entrusted to us by God, then we are under a serious obligation to use our freedom well, not to squander it in a solely self-serving lifestyle, and not to abuse it through harmful actions. This is why all the religions and every serious spiritual path put such emphasis on morality as a baseline requirement. Wrong acts and egoistic acts diminish our possibilities for an open, direct relationship with the higher worlds. Conversely, acts of service and kindness, of presence and prayer increase our possibilities for connection with the higher.

But the difference between these classes of right and wrong action cannot always be seen from the outside. A knife can serve good or ill. The discriminating factor is intention. We look into ourselves and notice our intention in whatever we are doing. And by seeing our intention, we usually and immediately know which class it falls into.

Sometimes, though, we are caught in a moral dilemma, unable to easily judge the right action. Then at least we can be quite clear that our intention is to do the right thing whatever it may be, even as we contemplate the murky waters of our predicament. At other times our intentions are mixed. Then we can look to discover and do the right thing despite our tangled motives. Another set of situations occurs when negligence leads to harmful consequences, unintentionally. To prevent that, we can form the intention to be at least as conscientious as the circumstances call for.

Because the core reality of life and the higher worlds is action, will, we need to pay careful attention to how we participate in that reality. One fundamental way into the great stream of responsibility and will is to be wholly aware of our intention in everything we do. Only with this awareness do we have any possibility of choice.

Do the Right Thing

Presence is not enough: we are given these bodies to act in this world. While the Eastern spiritual traditions emphasize presence and being, Western traditions spotlight action and purity of will. Complete inner work requires both: presence in the ground of being and action informed by wisdom and kindness.

The difficulty comes in choosing what to do, what actions to take. When we wake up in the midst of our life and start to question what we are doing and why, we see that our life has a great momentum built up over years. Our routines and patterns have us. Indeed, other people define us by our habitual modes of interaction, our personality. This is not necessarily a bad thing. Perhaps we live in just the way that optimizes what we can give, spiritually and otherwise. Contemplation of our life may, however, reveal gaps into which new and creative actions could fruitfully enter. Or we might see that we could create gaps, making room for new possibilities in our life. Again, though, we face the pesky question of what changes to make, what to do differently, if anything.

Perhaps we are waiting for the call, waiting for crystal clarity, waiting to be chosen. But in reality those who choose are chosen; we choose ourselves. But what to choose? Doing the right thing calls us to choose wisely the course of our lives, our profession, our spouse, our hobbies, our friends, and our leisure pursuits. The simple and immediate knowing in our heart of hearts, and in our mind of minds, can guide us in assessing rightness intuitively. The heart may know when reason fails. The mind may know when the heart waffles confused. But the intuitive wisdom of conscience lies deeper than both, though often shrouded in the fog of our habitual modes of thought and feeling.

Nevertheless, we choose; we choose because we must choose. Rather than wobble in paralysis, we choose, we act, ready to accept the consequences should we make a mistake. Sometimes only hindsight can tell us whether we made the right choice. It can even take a perspective of years to assess our choices objectively. And, yes, some mistakes prove costly and leave us with deep remorse. A certain courage, though, emboldens us to take the prudent risk. Later, we at least have the satisfaction of having chosen, of having acted, of having loved.

Another side of doing the right thing arises in the more immediate and situational opportunities we face day to day. The Golden Rule of doing unto others as you would have them do unto you and the injunction to love your neighbor as yourself, both point toward the need to develop a heartful wisdom in how we live. Often, however, we sink toward the opposite, toward the lure of irresponsibility, avoiding what we know to be right, shirking our duties and obligations toward ourselves, our family, our community, our nation, all of humanity, all living creatures, and God. Doing the right thing certainly must include being responsible, living up to our duties and obligations. The hard and exacting discipline of always doing the thing we know to be right, despite the sometimes acute desire to take the easy way out, to shirk our duty, demands that we be awake and ready to heed our higher nature. This transformative, perpetual discipline purifies our heart, strengthens our will, and keeps our feet on the path when all else fails.

Wisdom, which grows through our inner work, through

our understanding of ourselves, and through our mistakes, guides us in the muddled situations and the difficult choices. In its essence, wisdom derives from conscience. And conscience is the voice of God within us. The degree to which we act in accordance with wisdom and conscience defines the degree to which the Unconditioned Will of the World acts through us. Thus we discover our role: to participate in that Greatness that moves and spiritualizes the universe. The unfolding of history, from the story of our personal life to the story of the evolution of all life, is the manifestation of that spiritualizing action.

The master does nothing of her own, but acts in accord with the Great Tao. The actions of the saint spring from the love that emanates from the Unconditioned Will. As for us — we accept responsibility for doing the right thing in our own limited domain, for perpetually working to deepen our wisdom so that our actions may more closely align with the Great Will. This is our task, our joy, and our hope.

Justice: As We Sow, We Reap

Does it matter what we do? The ancient idea of personalized, hidden cause-and-effect states that our actions determine the events of our life, even those that seem completely unrelated. We find this notion of universal justice enshrined in the Hindu and Buddhist concept of karma, in the Old Testament and Koranic God rewarding goodness and punishing misdeeds, in Christ's parables of sowing and reaping. But not until we see this principle actually operating within our own life, do we notice how truly remarkable and strange it is. When some unwanted occurrence overtakes us, and our mind intuitively connects it with some long past action of our own, an action which does not appear to have caused the new occurrence, at least not in the ordinary causal chain of events kind of way — only then do we begin to look in awe and wonder at the law of karma working behind the scenes. Morality abruptly takes a new, imperative hue as we see that doing the right thing eliminates one source, perhaps the major source of ill fortune in our lives. Acts of kindness toward others suddenly transform into ways of creating good karma for ourselves. This attitude of acting responsibly and with honorable intention so as not to create bad karma serves as a legitimate motivation for right action — a motivation that eventually may transform into unselfish love.

But questions abound. Is this karma business true? Do our actions have both an obvious and a hidden impact on our lives? Is karma merely our imagination that sees connections between events, connections that are not actually causal in a physical sense? Is the law of karma the power behind the Golden Rule of doing unto others as you would have them do unto you? Is karma one of the governing principles of the spiritual ecosystem? If we bear guilt for our past actions, and who among us has led a completely innocent life from day one, then does that guilt color our perception of the connection between our prior misdeeds and current events? Does our guilt create expectations of punishments to come, expectations inevitably fulfilled? Are these "punishments" just random acts of nature, which we interpret as karmic events? And once we have paid the price, voluntarily or not, are we indeed less burdened by the wrongs we have committed and for which universal justice has now exacted payment? As yet, science has not risen to the stage of proving or even giving a theoretical basis for the law of karma. So we each rely on our own experience and judgment in assessing these crucial questions. The questions themselves guide our investigations into how this world really works.

The flip side of the karmic coin implies that those who give receive. Through kindness and generosity we can pay in advance, though best without expectation of any return. Advance payment to clear away the dregs of karma can also take the form of extra prayers and meditations, penance, austerities like fasting, or forgoing indulgences. A sacred vow to carry out such a self-imposed program can help ensure its actual implementation and efficacy. We leave it to universal justice to determine whether, when, and how to repay us. Sometimes, what seems like misfortune turns out to be the best possible thing that could have happened to us. Conversely, what seems like good fortune can turn to ashes in our mouths.

The more we see it all at work, the more faith we have in an inexorable and universal principle of justice. Like Newton's third law of physics, we realize that for every action there is an equal reaction, that the wrongs we intentionally commit eventually rebound on us in kind. Insofar as we hew to the spiritual path, our perception of the hidden workings of the universe establishes our faith that the events that enter our lives are not accidental, but are "meant" for us: to heal us, help us grow, or present us with opportunities to serve. We see that the invisible scales of justice weigh our karmic accounts of good deeds and bad, of actions in accord with conscience and those opposed to it and motivated instead by grasping, attachment, and egoism. We begin to live with great care and attention to doing the right thing with wholesome intention in all circumstances. We may even undertake right action intending that its results redound to the merit of others.

We should not forget, however, that justice and karma do not represent the ultimate authority over our lives. In India, for example, the popular understanding of karma has led many to a fatalistic approach to life, that everything is foreordained by our actions in previous lives. However, the law of karma does not erase free will and does not prevent us from rising above past mistakes. We can change our behavior and change our karma. With enough inner work, we may even arrive at being able to act unselfishly, without ego, without attachment, and without regard to reaping the fruits of our actions, and thereby cut the knot of karma. To the degree that we are empty and free, karmic consequences, though painful, do not cause us to suffer. And at any time, the Divine compassion may grant forgiveness to the remorseful and forgiving.

Excellence

"Be ye therefore perfect, even as your Father which is in heaven is perfect."[26]

Try to recall a time when you performed some action perfectly, when you brought your very best to the situation, when you gave a 100% effort completely appropriate in every respect, when afterwards you discovered profound satisfaction in what you had done. If you cannot remember such an event, then imagine one, based on your experiences that approximate true excellence.

Our lives flow imperfectly, and part of spirituality entails accepting the limitations of our life circumstances, as well as our personal limitations. But another part of spirituality calls us not be passive in front of our possibilities for improvement. How much of our lives do we spend in half-hearted efforts, doing the bare minimum required of us? Sometimes the minimum may be best, but more often we just take the lazy way out. Too much of the time, we shut our eyes to the possibilities and live a half-way life.

The practice of excellence invites us to embrace the very highest standards in our personal manifestations. We pursue excellence not only in our ethical or moral standards, such as integrity, steadfastness, courage, commitment, kindness, and tolerance, but also in our standards of perfection in action. The shining examples of people who exhibit uncompromising dimensions of excellence can help us set new benchmarks for ourselves. Stretching our own standards to aim higher than we currently reach draws us toward our possibilities, our evolution.

The potential field of excellence spans our entire life, from our most hidden thoughts and emotions, to our interactions with other people, to the practice of our profession. Those engaged in creative endeavors, like musicians, artists, and scientists, know when the creative energy has entered and brought excellence to their creations. Every moment of our lives offers a legitimate opportunity to ask ourselves "What does excellence demand of me in this situation?"

How does the pursuit of excellence relate to our spiritual life? It relates in two important ways. First, the practice of excellence requires complete attention, wholeness of presence, and total engagement: ongoing attention to be aware of opportunities for excellence, and focused attention during the manifestation to which we wish to bring excellence. And attention is one of the primary muscles we must strengthen to deepen our inner life.

Secondly, the source of true excellence is no less than the Divine Perfection itself. Conscience, our channel to the Divine Will, connects us with excellence. The practice of excellence opens our perceptions to recognizing, to intuiting what excellence requires in any situation, giving us an effective means for hearing our conscience. Self-centeredness beckons us to the subjective, easy way out and must be left behind. Objective excellence calls us to empty ourselves so that we can hear the voice of conscience and act in accord with the Tao. We can even say that when a person goes beyond herself in an act of real perfection, then God, the Divine Will acts through her. Not unlike the creations of the great masters such as Bach and Michelangelo, our smaller moments of perfection also endure. But great or small, perfection is perfection. Through its inherent relationship to the Divine, any act of perfection, empty of egoism and full of excellence, transcends time to enter the world's eternal storehouse of the sacred. The pursuit of excellence calls us to a life of quality and offers us a way of direct service to the Great Perfection.

Dharma: The Evolving Pattern of the Spirit

The writers of the ancient Vedas used the term dharma to describe the law that governs and sustains the universe. In Buddhism dharma means the truth as embodied in the teachings of the Buddha. We take dharma in a broad sense referring to the inner working of the universe, at all scales. To live in accord with the dharma means to live responsibly and to pursue the path of spiritual practice. The governing and sustaining principle of the universe has two aspects: changeless and dynamic. The changeless, eternal aspect of dharma creates the framework of the cosmos, including time, space, and the fundamental laws of physics. The dynamic aspect of dharma concerns the fulfillment of the purpose of the universe through an evolving pattern of spirit, through the spiritualization of the universe. In both senses dharma is the manifestation of God's

Will.

The evolution of life works through interacting layers of patterns: the patterns of species, the patterns of individuals, and the pattern of the environment. The inner evolution of the Earth, the solar system, and the universe also operates through interacting layers of patterns: patterns of energies and patterns of will encompassing scales varying from our own individual life all the way up to the great life cycle of the universe. These patterns operate on the whole range of time scales from the moment, to the day, to our lifetime, to the life of the Earth, to the life of the Sun, to the lifetime of the universe. The greater the scale the deeper the energies involved. While the patterns do manifest in time and space, their substance resides in a timeless domain. To the extent that we open ourselves to the timeless, we can have access to the patterns of dharma.

The working of these great patterns concerns us directly and intimately. Conscience, our inner perception of truth, reveals the evolving patterns and attunes us to how our own actions can best align with the larger patterns of spiritualization. Our personal destiny centers on fulfilling our individual role in serving the dharma. The wonder and the inspiration come in realizing how our own small life connects with the vastness of the heavens.

What Is My Calling?

What we do matters. We can ask ourselves what we would do with our time if we did not need to earn a living. The pursuit of pleasures in a self-indulgent lifestyle would soon leave us empty and dissatisfied. We would start looking for a productive way to be of service to others, to society. We would seek a way of serving that corresponds to our own unique talents and propensities, a way that engages the whole of ourselves, a way that calls to us. We would look for work that we love.

The first difficulty confronting us lies in not understanding ourselves well enough to know our calling. To help in this we can contemplate our past to see what themes recur, what we hold to be important, how we act and respond, what we dream of doing, what education, training, skills, and hobbies we have. We might engage a career counselor. From all this, a direction may emerge.

The second difficulty arises from the obvious and mundane fact that most of us must work for the necessities of life, to support ourselves and our family. This constraint apparently limits us in reaching toward our calling. We have a job or career, with little time or energy left to discover or pursue our calling. But it need not be that way.

One approach is to transform our attitude toward our job to make it into a calling. Every job has some aspect of service. Someone pays us to do this job. What we do somehow benefits those who pay: the organization we work for and its customers. If we can focus on this service goal and bring our wholehearted best to it, this job can be our calling. Then not just money, but also the heart-fulfillment of providing the useful can flow from our labor.

If we cannot transform our attitude toward our job, then perhaps clarity about our calling will suggest another job or career to us. To be able to earn our living doing something we love that provides real service to others is a formula for a meaningful life. So we resolutely and responsibly take the steps necessary to create that situation, to create our calling in our life.

Whether or not we can transform our job, we can look to bring more meaning into the rest of our time. If we have a family, then being a conscientious and loving parent can be our calling. We can pursue our calling in our spare time: the weekend musician, the part-time feeder of the homeless, the summer evening gardener.

You might ask why this section on career counseling should appear in a work about soul and spirit. Some jobs can be so draining and deadening that they sap our spiritual possibilities. Finding your calling can bring a renewed energy to your life, an energy that spills over into your inner work. And to reiterate the first sentence: what we do matters. The spiritual path is not only about inner work. Your calling can harmonize your outer life with your inner life, fusing them in a life of spirit, service, meaning, and fulfillment, bringing you toward your true purpose, toward a right relationship with the Divine Purpose.

Tikkun Olam: Perfecting the World

Isaac Luria, the renowned sixteenth century Kabbalist, used the phrase "tikkun olam," usually translated as repairing the world, to encapsulate the true role of humanity in the ongoing evolution and spiritualization of the cosmos. Luria taught that God created the world by forming vessels of light to hold the Divine Light. But as God poured the Light into the vessels, they catastrophically shattered, tumbling down toward the realm of matter. Thus, our world consists of countless shards of the original vessels entrapping sparks of the Divine Light. Humanity's great task involves helping God by freeing and reuniting the scattered Light, raising the sparks back to Divinity and restoring the broken world.

We meet related concepts in other religions. Christ promised to return with the coming of the Kingdom of Heaven and exhorted people to prepare through love, wakefulness, and charity. In Buddhism, the Bodhisattva vows to forgo final liberation until all beings have been freed from suffering. The Gnostics held that a spark of Divinity resides entrapped within the soul of humans.

Tikkun olam encompasses both the outer and the inner, both service to society by helping those in need and service to the Divine by liberating the spark within. As we are, the Divine spark lies hidden beneath our layers of egoistic self-centeredness. That spark is our conscience, through which the promptings of the Divine Will flow toward us. By pursuing spiritual inner work to strengthen our soul and purify our heart, we grow more able to bear that spark without shattering, more willing to act on what we know to be right, less willing to act in harmful or grasping ways, and more able to notice the quiet presence of conscience beneath the din of our chattering minds and reactive emotions. The work of transformation, of building a soul creates a proper vessel for the Divine spark, for our unique share of the Divine Will, returning that spark to the service of the One Who sent it. By working to perfect ourselves, perfect our soul, and serve society, we each contribute in our own unique way to the perfecting of the world. This is our duty and our calling as human beings.

To contemplate and enter the process of tikkun olam, repairing or perfecting the world, we need to understand the concept of world. All the major religious traditions present a hierarchy of worlds or levels of being, from the one we ordinarily inhabit to the ultimate world of Divinity.

In Kabbalah, for example, the worlds include Asiyah or Action, Yetzirah or Formation, Beriyah or Creation, and Atzilut or Emanation. Beyond and permeating all these is the Ein Sof, the One God, the Boundless and Unconditioned. Each of these worlds corresponds to a progressively higher level of spiritual energy and its related level of soul. The world of Action utilizes the sensitive energy, from which the nefesh soul forms. The world of Formation is built on the conscious energy, the basis of awareness, from which the ruach forms. The world of Creation and Light works with the creative energy, from which the neshama forms. The world of Emanation brings the high energy of love, from which the chaya forms. And corresponding to the ultimate Ein Sof, touching the yechida soul, we have the transcendent energy.

The basic principle of Kabbalah is that the seeker pursues spiritual practice to transform his or her being and rise through the levels of worlds, to bring his or her own will back to the Divine will, while opening a way for the higher energies to flow down to this world, and thereby advancing the great process of tikkun olam. For millennia Kabbalists have sought to serve this process, for example by meditating on and opening to the higher energy, the Divine light above the head. They allow the light to spread through them as if sitting in its midst and draw the light down for the Earth, for life, for their own soul. The possibility of opening to the Divine light stands within reach of us all, if we are prepared to do the necessary inner work.

Tikkun olam places our spiritual practice at the heart of the epic, unfolding history of the universe: the evolution and spiritualization of the whole of creation. With each small act of kindness, with each moment of presence and practice, with each effort to see, cleanse, and integrate our inner life, with each heartfelt prayer opening to the higher energies and the higher will, we build the new world and serve the Divine Architect of meaning. Rather than view tikkun olam as a return to the perfection that existed before God created the universe, we consider the spiritualizing action as reaching toward a new and greater perfection than existed before, toward perfecting this flawed world by imbuing the whole of it with the Divine spirit. Because of the freedom God necessarily placed into the world, we can surmise that the outcome of the whole process truly remains uncertain, that our free choice to serve the Divine and our planet through fulfilling our highest destiny really matters, that despite our insignificant size with respect to the universe our personal inner work makes a difference. If we can raise ourselves to the station where the Divine can see and act through us, then we complete the momentous work of restoring at least one part to the Whole. And so, with the great Kabbalist, Isaac Luria, we discover a vision of unbounded meaning: perfecting ourselves, perfecting the world, and helping God.

Why Are We Here?

In our quieter moments, or in times of personal crisis or loss, we may wonder about the purpose of our existence. The question has a network of interrelated layers and extensions, from the personal to the universal, expanding from ourselves outward. If one person fulfills his or her own true destiny, then the whole of humanity is helped to move toward its destiny.

But how do we know what our personal destiny is? No formula exists for this, but we can recognize a few universal characteristics of destiny. First, it is unique. If God is unique and if every one of us is, in our core, a particle of God, then we are each unique. So to imitate another will not work. A time will come when it just does not fit. Of course, we may receive hints of the range of possibilities of life by looking at the examples of other people who seem to have achieved their own destiny. But we are called to become ourselves, unabashedly and wholeheartedly. If humanity as a whole is to achieve its greatness, it can only come through each of us fulfilling our unique role, our individual, infinite singularity in the fabric of life.

Second, we can create our destiny. It is not laid out for us to discover. It is not hidden in the recesses of our personal psychology, nor in our personal history. It is not a function of the sum of our abilities and propensities. It is not demanded of us. Rather, destiny is an invitation to fulfill the potential of our personal pattern, in the context of our family, society, and culture, and is brought forth by our own flair. Destiny cannot be pinned down, but is easy to recognize in those who achieve theirs.

Third, destiny has both inner and outer aspects. Outwardly, we may find, create and fulfill our destiny as a good parent, a carpenter, a nurse, a physicist, a poet, an artist, a salesman, a stock broker, or any of the myriad possible roles a human being can play. Inwardly, destiny concerns how far we may go in approaching the Divine. This depends on how assiduously we pursue the inner path of purification and integration.

Lastly, the seed of our destiny is planted in us at birth, and comes not from our parents, but rather from God. As a particle of God (which means the whole of God, since God is indivisible) we have free will. God is free and so are we. Within the constraints of our material circumstances and possibilities, we can choose how we shall live, how to respond to the events of our life, what to create through the vehicle of our life, what to contribute to the collective good. This gift of a Divine spark comes with a responsibility to serve. Through discovering/creating and fulfilling our destiny, we may each repay the promise of our birth.

A Meditation: Why Am I?

Some paths teach us to meditate on the question: Who Am I? We may ask a different, perhaps deeper question: Why Am I? This question inevitably leads us both into and beyond ourselves. That our life has a purpose implies a relationship to something greater than our self.

For this meditation, prepare by sitting quietly and relaxing. Then turn your attention to question: Why Am I? Just hold the question. Answers will come. See and acknowledge every thought that comes in answer. Then allow each answer to pass and return to the question. Let the question take you deeper into yourself and deeper beyond yourself. Let the question connect you to that Greatness which embodies the answer.

Sanctuary

"But thou, when thou prayest, enter into thy closet, and when thou hast shut thy door, pray to thy Father which is in secret;"[27]

Amid the ever-changing flux of life, we need a place of rest and recuperation, a safe zone of no fear and no concern, a place to regenerate body, mind, emotion, and spirit. The first candidate is our nightly period of sleep. For most, bodily sleep serves as a refuge and does regenerate us. Our home also can be a refuge, a place we can relax and just be our unguarded self.

A sanctuary, though, is different; it breathes the air of the sacred, as the place where the higher and the lower, the Creator and the created, meet. In this sense, the house of worship serves as the paradigm of sanctuary. Effective ones produce in us a state of awe and reverence, by their architecture, by the tenor of their worship community, or by both. Those with access to such a place count themselves among the fortunate.

Many of us, however, do not have such a suitable, readily accessible, and awe-inspiring sanctuary for our worship. And even those who do find their sojourns there limited. We need an inner sanctuary, one that stays with us. The sacredness of our purpose creates the pillars of our inner temple of meditation and prayer. Crossing its cleansing threshold, we begin our truest work. Outside our sanctuary, life draws us to be other than ourselves. Within, we can only be our truest self. The sanctuary enables us to orient our whole being and will toward what matters most.

Entering that inward sacred space, we relax and let go. Drawn by our purpose, we leave behind all our worries and obligations, our grudges and material ambitions. Patiently, we let our very patterns of thought, emotion, and action subside. This leaves us in empty awareness, pure consciousness. Waiting there, we establish our true inner sanctuary, our base camp for the ascent. In this place we find a sweetness and a simple freedom. Then gazing toward the higher, we reach beyond consciousness itself, toward the sacred light and, finally, toward the awesome, benevolent will of the Divine.

This inner abode serves not only as a sanctuary for us, but also as a sanctuary for the higher. Through our inner sanctuary the sacred finds a place in this world and can live in us. Not that we share the space with the sacred, for ultimately we are one with it. To provide that sanctuary is an essential part of our role and our opportunity. Through our spiritual practice we become a sanctuary for the higher, as it is a sanctuary for us.

And each time we leave our sanctuary and return to life, we may find our life slightly more transformed. Until the day when the walls of our inner sanctuary fall away and the whole of life becomes a sacred space.

To practice this, enter your own sanctuary, shore up its pillars by turning your face toward why you are there, and accept that you are worthy of that place. Established there, do your work of inviting the sacred to enter.

Approaching the Divine

Where is God? Where should we look for God? Where can we look? To approach the Divine or invite God to touch us, what direction shall we address? If we only look outward, we limit our search to the material world of space-time. God in the material world takes forms such as scripture, houses of worship, the beauty of nature, great art, and the kindness of strangers. As wonderful as these are, they leave us hungry, not fully satisfied with this outer experience of God. Indeed, their primary value lies in the very hunger they elicit.

If we look inward, will we find God in the jungle of thoughts, emotions, and impulses that populate our inner psychological world? God enters our inner world as creativity, faith and love, though all too rarely, and as our need for meaning, completion, and freedom. Our kaleidoscopic inner world, even at its best and highest, leaves us with the same question: where is God?

Delving into the pure stillness, the pure consciousness beneath our inner tumult we find peace. Yet God continues to elude us, for God resides beyond consciousness itself. But by repeatedly entering this profound inner stillness, our veils of separation grow thin.

From that quiet place inside, we summon our disparate parts, our heart and mind, our entire being in an unspoken prayer, calling out into the stillness, beyond the silence, reaching toward, opening and surrendering to that Greatness that resides at the core of all. In this forecourt of the Divine, in the foothills of the Sacred, we may encounter a sudden influx of a potent energy that we allow to work on us, to create our being and feed our soul. This Primordial Sacred Sun comes as an infinite whirlwind of light and energy.

Beyond that lies the formless Divine Mountain: the Will of the Universal Purpose, the ultimate Creative Force and Compassionate Heart of the World, in a realm of radical freedom. Again and again we return to seek being, to drink at the fountain of life, to serve the Earth by asking and receiving these gifts from above.

At other times, in that quiet place inside, we do nothing, we just allow, allow, and allow all to be as is. And in that becalmed allowing our will renders itself open to the grace of contact with the Divine Will, at Its initiative. Our role remains purely one of openness and non-doing.

But who among us can approach God? Though entering full unity with the Divine may require complete purity of heart, the crucial point for us is that the attempt to move closer also purifies our heart. Our soul-blight of self-centered egoism, of seeking more for ourselves, gradually gives way to our need for the Real, for Love, for service, meaning, and understanding. Certainly we overreach in calling upon God, but the very act brings us closer. As we look more toward the Ultimate, we look less toward our imagined self. We leave behind our self-referential immaturity and aspire toward the heights of inner and outer kindness, toward that Unknowable that we know awaits us.

Surrendering to the Divine

We hear this notion of surrendering to the Divine and it even sounds nice — in theory. But do we take this possibility seriously enough to work toward it? If we do, then we are immediately faced with our lack of understanding of what it really means. To begin to comprehend what surrendering to the Divine means, we need to explore, try out various approaches, make our mistakes, find our dead ends, and keep at it until that sacred grace responds. And even then, it only gives us a better notion of the direction, while leaving the actual how-to-surrender somewhat unclear. So we continue to experiment, placing the whole of ourselves into this most central issue, this peak of spiritual practice.

To whom do we surrender? Though It remains unknown to us, we rely on our faith in that Loving Greatness, within and behind every level of our reality. The Divine is there and here, and though we neither see It nor touch It, by considering the next question, we discover where to look.

What do I surrender? Well ... what can I surrender? Giving all my worldly possessions away would only impoverish me materially. My body inevitably will die, so I cannot really give that away. Give up my anger and fear? That might be a good start, if I could do it. But all those unbecoming manifestations are only peripheral to the root of the problem: my egoism, my self-centeredness.

Where is this egoism? If egoism is a usurper of my will, then I must look to my will. Though I cannot see my will, I can, with some care and practice, look toward where my attention and intention come from. That direction points toward the source of my will, indeed the Source of all will. But that direction is usually blocked, or at least polluted by ego. So I have identified the problem, egoism, and I know where to look: toward my innermost core, toward the one in me who chooses and decides and adopts attitudes.

How do I surrender? First, I need to move into that place of who I am, or at least who I think I am. From there I can explore the practice of surrender. I must gather the whole of myself, body, heart, and mind, into the one-pointed intention to elevate my will toward the Divine, perhaps silently crying out to God, with my heart fervently and solely wishing to cleave to that ineffable, loving Source. I must relinquish my very self to That, from my most fundamental core. I must open my own inherent sense of who I am, to abdicate my interior throne, the place where I reside within myself. I empty myself utterly. I pour out all that I think and feel that I am. All that belongs to me, all my inwardness, even myself, I send away into the stillness.

By all of this or perhaps by just giving up, I create a gap in my center. And into that gap, I wordlessly beg the Divine to enter, to live in me, as me. Even as my egoism keeps popping up in the middle of this process, I keep at it. I keep exploring and practicing this obscure and undervalued art of surrendering to the higher.

This does not necessarily mean that we enter a high world of light and bliss. While that may be wonderful and important in many ways, it is not the ultimate and it does not require us to change fundamentally. The truest transformation comes in purifying ourselves of our egoism and leaving that empty gap open to our Loving Creator, Who may enter us. Not that we enter the Creator, but that the Creator enters us. As a thirteenth century Kabbalist put it: the seeker rises to the point that *"the higher will is clothed in his will, and not only so that his will is clothed in the higher will."*[28] Surrender is the precondition for

261

entering the realm of Unity. Any vestige of separateness cannot find a place There.

Understanding of this question of surrender can only come by facing it directly and in practice, by actually making attempts at it during the deepest part of our prayer or meditation. The culmination of spirituality lies through that gate. This is not about an encounter with something high. It is about abandoning our inner seat of honor so that the source of Love becomes us. This is not something we can try once and be done with it. It entails a lengthy process of purification, increasing our need, and the actual practice of surrendering to the Divine.

SEVEN PILLARS OF SPIRITUAL PRACTICE

Like life itself, the spiritual path begins and ends with letting go. And in between we have much to do and discover. In ending this book, we summarize the path by looking at the seven basic pillars of spiritual practice:

1. Relaxation, letting go, and equanimity
2. Building the energy reservoir
3. Developing the energy body
4. Opening to consciousness
5. Presence and I am
6. Conscience, right action, and kindness
7. Prayer and meditation

Each of these seven represents a cluster of types of practice, which can be considered as a graduated series. In this linear view, we can see that healing and letting go of destructive habits of body, heart, and mind protects the energy we acquire though practices like conscious breathing, sensing, attention exercises, and opening to the spiritual depths. Without the letting go, our energies waste themselves fruitlessly. With the energy leakage curtailed, our energy body gradually builds up. Then our body of sensation can awaken us and provide a platform in the present from which to pursue our inner work. From this base of sensation, we can more readily open to the stillness of the conscious energy underlying all awareness, all experience. Into this conscious realm, our will can enter to establish real presence, our place in the inner and outer worlds. In presence, we can discern the promptings of conscience and love. In presence, we can have the inner freedom to do the right thing even in difficult situations and to act in kindness toward others. Finally, with a clear conscience and a yearning heart, we can work toward a full relationship with the Creator through prayer, gratitude, joy, love, and opening to that Boundless Heart of the World.

As an alternative to this linear-progression view of the path, we can see that the seven pillars of practice intertwine to form a nonlinear whole, balancing and complementing each other, serving and developing different sides of our being. If we have more energy, we can have more presence, and find ourselves able to face difficulties with equanimity. While we may engage in right action both inwardly and outwardly, by turning to prayer we recall the source and purpose of that action. The interlinked practices of letting go and the I Am of presence also balance each other. If I only work at letting go and relaxing, I might become weak and spineless. If I only work at active presence, I might become rigid. With both, I may find my way. Lastly, the practice of developing the sensitive energy body grounds us in the here and now, while consciousness, prayer and meditation give us wings.

A cyclical view also illumines the path. Over the years of inner work, we return to the same practices repeatedly, but each time with deepened understanding and being, with greater appreciation for the context, purpose, and effects of the practice, and with enhanced ability to engage in it. We return to a practice as to an old friend, with joy and renewed vigor. And because we are different, the practice itself is different, and through it we ascend to unexpected and previously unknown heights. So the cycle of the path becomes a spiral or helix: we repeatedly return but, if we have worked diligently in the meantime, not to the same place. To inspire us to persevere, we may even be given an occasional glimpse of what lies ahead on the next turn of the spiral.

Ultimately, the whole of spiritual practice is about service and the path becomes our life. The production of finer energies, the strength of presence, the clarity of conscience, the openhearted kindness, the depth of prayer and meditation — all contribute to the spiritual evolution of the world. Our inner work serves our own welfare in building our soul, our neighbor's welfare in creating an atmosphere of peace and joy, and God in fulfilling our true destiny. To become conscious participants in that Divine Greatness, that is our hope and our quest. The one priceless gift that we can offer is our willingness and determination to travel to its end the path that purifies our heart and establishes our soul, that we may bear the seeds of Love into this world.

May the One, to Whom we owe our existence and Whom we all serve, find us worthy, accept our work, bless our efforts, and grant us entry to that sacred realm in this very life.

NOTES

1. Bennett, J.G., *The Dramatic Universe Vol. 2* (London: Hodder and Stoughton, 1961), 74-76

2. Bennett, J.G., *Deeper Man* (Santa Fe: Bennett Books, 1978), 177

3. Ferguson, E., Ed., *Encyclopedia of Early Christianity, Second Edition, Vol. 2* (New York: Garland Publishing, 1997), 1081

4. Halevi, Zen ben Shimon, *The Way of Kabbalah* (New York: Samuel Weiser, 1976), 168

5. Bennett op. cit. 56-68

6. Bennett, J.G., *Energies* (Santa Fe: Bennett Books, 1964), 90

7. Bandura, A. "Self-Efficacy." in Ramachaudran, V.S. ed. *Encyclopedia of Human Behavior Vol. 4* (New York: Academic Press, 1994), 71-81

8. Holland, Muhtar, trans., *Beads of Dew from the Source of Life: Histories of the Khwajagan, The Masters of Wisdom* (Ft. Lauderdale: Al-Baz, 2001), 9

9. Matthew 6:12

10. Matthew 20:16

11. Matthew 5:5

12. Genesis 24:63

13. Buber, Martin, *I and Thou* (New York: Scribner, 2000)

14. Tracol, Henri, *The Taste for Things That Are True.* (Rockport: Element Books, 1994), 115

15. Mark 13:35-36

16. Luke 21:36

17. First Thessalonians 5:17

18. Palmer, G.E.H. et al, trans., *The Philokalia: The Complete Text Volumes I-IV* (London: Faber and Faber, 1979)

19. French, R.M., trans., *The Way of Pilgrim: and the Pilgrim Continues His Way* (San Francisco: Harper, 1991)

20. Matthew 5:5

21. Bennett, J.G., *The Dramatic Universe Vol. 4* (London: Hodder and Stoughton, 1966), 426

22. Eckhart, Meister, *Selected Writings*, trans. Oliver Davies (New York: Penguin Books USA, 1994), 237

23. Luke 22:42

24. Buswell, Jr., R.E., translator, *Tracing Back the Radiance: Chinul's Korean Way of Zen* (Honolulu: University of Hawaii Press, 1991)

25. Exodus 3:14

26. Matthew 5:48

27. Matthew 6:6

28. Translation from Scholem, Gershom, *Origins of the Kabbalah* (Philadelphia: Jewish Publication Society, 1987), 418

ABOUT THE AUTHOR

The son of Holocaust survivors, Joseph Naft was born in a Displaced Persons' camp in northern Italy in the aftermath of World War II. Recovering from wartime devastation, the family soon immigrated to the United States. That legacy of unspeakable evil engendered Naft's abiding interest in how the seemingly intractable problem of human violence can be resolved.

While childhood experiences of the spiritual depths set the stage for Naft's lifelong pursuit of the sacred, he first learned formal meditation practice in 1970. In 1974, he studied Buddhist, Sufi and Christian practices during a year in residence at J. G. Bennett's school of spirituality in England. Subsequently he pursued a range of spiritual practices in Turkey under the guidance of Sufis from the Mevlevi, Helveti, Rifa'i, and Naqshbandi orders. He has also undertaken extensive training in Buddhist meditation. Finally, his Jewish roots remain close to his heart, both the traditional form of Jewish worship as well as meditation methods from Kabbalah.

Joseph Naft has taught meditation and spiritual practices since 1976. His other books include *Weekly Inner Work for The Sacred Art of Soul Making* and two novels: *Agents of Peace* and *Restoring Our Soul*.

INDEX

A

acceptance 58, 60, 79, 80, 81, 96, 115, 121, 131, 148, 184, 199, 201
anatta 39
anger 24, 47, 55, 57, 58, 79, 80, 81, 83, 84, 91, 95, 101, 116, 161, 162, 190, 192, 193, 205, 260
anicca 38
appreciation 31, 76, 112, 129, 173, 265
arrogance 42, 43, 81, 96, 147, 148, 149, 183, 215
art 13, 30, 103, 104, 232, 258, 261
assimilation 7
atman 67
attachment 32, 33, 36, 42, 48, 100, 101, 134, 190–192, 198, 201, 206, 214, 216, 245, 246
attention 7, 22, 24, 27, 28, 51, 52, 53, 55, 56, 62, 66, 67, 68, 71, 72, 84, 86, 112, 119, 126, 136, 137, 140, 141, 142, 143, 145, 153–155, 162, 164, 166, 168, 170, 172, 181, 188, 201, 213, 214, 216, 217, 218, 222, 223, 224, 227, 239, 240, 245, 247, 256, 260, 264
automatic energy 5, 8, 23, 24, 25, 26, 35, 36, 154, 220
autopilot 8, 36, 137, 138, 165, 169, 172, 174, 176, 200
awakening 32, 37, 47, 54, 109, 115, 118, 162, 163, 167, 201, 232
awareness 5, 6, 12, 18, 25, 26, 27, 28, 29, 44, 51, 52, 53, 54, 56, 58, 64, 65, 66, 67, 69, 70, 71, 72, 73, 76, 82, 87, 96, 108, 110, 112, 114, 123, 125, 127, 131, 138, 141, 143, 145, 146, 153, 158, 164, 165, 167, 169, 170, 171, 173, 174, 175, 176, 177, 179, 180, 181, 192, 193, 195, 196, 197, 199, 200, 201, 202, 208, 209, 212, 213, 214, 218, 219, 223, 224, 227, 231, 233, 241, 253, 257, 264

B

balance 14, 15, 17, 19, 38, 143, 201, 264
being 1, 5, 6, 7, 15, 18, 19, 20, 25, 29, 31, 33, 35, 36, 37, 40, 48, 49, 50, 55, 58, 59, 60, 65, 67, 73, 80, 81, 85, 89, 92, 93, 98, 104, 109, 112, 115, 127, 138, 142, 144, 156, 163, 167, 168, 169, 170, 172, 173, 176, 177, 178, 192, 194, 195, 196, 199, 200, 202, 205, 207, 208, 209, 211, 213, 215, 217, 218, 219–221, 222, 230, 233, 234, 235, 241, 252, 253, 257, 258, 259, 264, 265
Bennett 21, 27
Bhagavad Gita 77
Bible 186
biblical 108, 134
bodily excesses 61
bodily sensation 18, 54, 174, 175

273